Ten Days That Shook Scotland

Fort Publishing Ltd

First published in 2010 by Fort Publishing Ltd, Old Belmont House,
12 Robsland Avenue, Ayr, KA7 2RW

Front-cover photographs: *Top* – Eric Caldow, on the left, leads the Scotland
team out at Wembley in 1961; goalkeeper Frank Haffey is behind him.
Bottom – Scotland captain Jimmy McMullen is congratulated by fans after
his team, the 'Wembley Wizards', had beaten England 5–1 at Wembley in
1928. (both photographs courtesy of Getty Images)

Graphics by Mark Blackadder

Typeset by 3btype.com

Printed by Bell and Bain Ltd, Glasgow

ISBN: 978-1-905769-21-6

Contents

Preface

Scotland does not have to look too hard for days of drama. The history of the game in this country is full of them and selecting ten days that shook Scottish football would be a nigh-impossible task for even the omniscient among us. The difficulty stems from the rich history of the game. Scotland's footballers invented the modern passing game, the first ever international match was played in Glasgow and, as the statisticians will confirm, Scotland holds just about every European attendance record. It is also the case that no other country of a comparable size has produced four clubs that have reached European finals, a wonderful achievement that puts the disappointments of recent years in their proper perspective. And let us not forget our passion for the game; despite the current malaise, which we can only hope is a temporary phenomenon, Scotland is a football cauldron that rivals even Brazil in its feelings for the beautiful game.

Not surprisingly, this little country of ours has produced a multitude of legendary players, many of whom feature in the pages of this book. Gallacher, James, Meiklejohn, McGrory, Morton, Young, Steel, Bauld, Reilly, Law, MacKay, Baxter, Johnstone, McNeill, McGrain, Jardine, Dalglish, Souness, Miller. A full list of such notables would be almost endless. Scotland is almost as well known for its managers, men whose steely characters were forged in the often harsh environment of the industrial central belt. The names of Struth, Busby, Shankly, Stein and Ferguson will be remembered for as long as this great game is played.

All of this shows just how deeply ingrained football is in Scottish life and in the Scottish psyche. If the apparently never-ending conveyor belt of talent has broken down in the past decade we can but hope that it is up and running again before too long. There is probably no single reason for the fault, and conversely no magic bullet that will put it right. But put it right we must, and quickly. Scotland needs football and, dare I say it, football needs Scotland.

Given the ease of travel in the twenty-first century one can only speculate on the numbers who would travel to watch Scotland in European or World Cup finals. In 2003 Celtic took upwards of sixty thousand to Seville, while in 2008 approaching two hundred thousand either followed Rangers to Manchester or watched on the big screens at Ibrox. A tournament with its denouement in Europe would surely attract tens, perhaps hundreds, of thousands of Tartan Army foot-soldiers. That would work wonders for the atmosphere and the spectacle.

Thanks to everyone who agreed to be interviewed for this book. Their time and their insights are greatly appreciated.

Terence Murray, October 2010

John Cairney

1

From the Spiders' Web: the Historic First Defeat of Queen's Park

John Cairney

It was 7 February 2009, a slushy, snowy Saturday afternoon, and a Scottish cup tie was being played at Parkhead. It was almost a sensation. Celtic, champions of Scotland's premier league, were struggling to hold back the second-division amateurs of Queen's Park. Substitute Adam Oakley had scored for the Spiders in the sixty-fifth minute and it put them only one goal behind the hoops with just twenty-five minutes to go. Rather harshly, the scorer was booked by the referee for his wild celebration of this feat, and when he was later booked for a foul, he was inevitably sent off. Yet, even with ten men, the amateurs maintained their pressure. Celtic were plainly shocked, as their nervous defence showed, and there was no doubt which team was more relieved to hear the final whistle. 'It was our cup final,' said their forward Steven Nicholas, who had a near-miss himself. 'We never let our heads drop. . . . We just went for them.' And they nearly got them too. Had Queen's Park equalised they might even have gone on to win and that would certainly have shaken the football world.

The last time Queen's Park beat Celtic was in a Glasgow Cup semi-final, also at Parkhead, in 1985, when only a thousand or so had turned up to watch. Before that, one has to go back to 1957, and the old first division, for a victory by the gentleman from Hampden over the east-end artisans. So it couldn't be said that the black-and-white hoops went into the latest match between them as favourites. 'We did really well in the last twenty minutes,' continued Nicholas, 'but any match is about what happens on the day. I think we've done ourselves proud.' That was certainly true, but then Queen's Park is a proud club. Even today, while still true to its original amateur philosophy, it is totally professional in its approach to the modern game.

There are no less than eight teams playing under its aegis on the brand-new 3G synthetic surface of Lesser Hampden, which was laid thanks to the benevolence of Glasgow's east-end tycoon, Willie Haughey. Running costs at the club are around £130,000 annually and this is met by the committed fundraising efforts of Queen's Park supporters, a lucky run in the Scottish Cup now and then and grants from the Scottish Football Partnership. Occasional gestures of financial help have also come from bigger clubs, like Celtic themselves, who, in the Seventies, donated £10,000 to assist the Hampden Park renovations. These gestures apart, the amateur club's continued survival is a tribute to the stamina and resourcefulness of a steady stream of dedicated men, young and old, from its very beginnings.

As a result, Queen's Park Foot Ball Club, as it was originally called, still stands like a lighthouse on the rock of its own probity despite the battering waves of professionalism that have pounded it for almost one-hundred-and-fifty years. They have resigned themselves to losing their best players to the professional game season after season and to trawling the shallow waters of school, church and juvenile clubs for new talent that will gradually make its way through the system up the team ladder to the Strollers on Lesser Hampden and then on to the Spiders and the shrine-like enclosure of Greater Hampden itself. Many of them, in fact, will go on to play for Scotland, and one who did, James Crawford, a Glasgow east-ender with a blistering turn of speed, also went on to play for Great Britain in the 1936 Berlin Olympics. However, the most remarkable fact of all is that the first Scotland team was composed entirely of Queen's Park players. Yet it all started so innocently, almost accidentally.

Around the middle of the century some Highland immigrants had infiltrated to Glasgow as far south as Crosshill and Pollokshaws from their first redoubt around Anderston Cross, bringing with them the leisure pursuits of shinty, curling, throwing the hammer, tossing the caber and other such Highland sports. They practised these on the bare wastes of Queen's Park recreation ground on the south side of Glasgow, much to the annoyance of the local Irish keelies who favoured the latest novelty sport, football. This was a rough amalgam of ancient football and rugby rules, set down on a single sheet of paper pinned to a tree at the side of the Cambridge University playing field.

James Lillywhite, an English county cricketer turned sports retailer in London, saw a way of marketing his product by propagating this new leisure pastime, which needed a round ball, football boots and various 'uniforms' as they called the playing jerseys. It was he who advised the new Queen's Park on the rules. Glasgow newspapers printed them. Local youths soon picked them up and started playing the upstart game on the local Queen's Park recreation ground.

This did not go down well with the Highlanders of the south side, who needed space for their hammers and cabers. The new footballers hardly enjoyed playing under a hail of hammers, so a compromise was reached. The ball players decided to show the putters and throwers how to play the foot game and so association football, stolen from the English public schools by the scruffy proletariat, came to Glasgow. Thus simply was a rudimentary Queen's Park Football Club begun as a football entity that was to outlast the British Empire.

The first formal meeting of the club took place in a private house in Eglinton Terrace on 9 July 1867 with the team captain, Mr Black, in the chair. Mr Ritchie was elected president and Mr Klinger (of German extraction) appointed secretary. After flirting with some Highland names, the club eventually settled on Queen's Park Foot Ball Club as their official title. The first committee was formed and an entry fee for members was fixed at one shilling with an annual subscription of sixpence. At first the gentlemen played amongst themselves, making up contesting sides as they went along: marrieds versus the singles, smokers against the non-smokers and so on until they refined their football skills. This was not so easy among the welter of conflicting and confusing rules that existed at the time, the game being an uneasy mix of old football and rugby with some all-in wrestling thrown in, but gradually they found a collective style that suited them. They were among the first to realise that football was a team sport, so almost from the start they developed a passing game. Having found their tactics, they now looked for other teams to practise them on. This was a further difficulty. There were very few other teams.

This lack highlights the missionary role the early Queen's Park sides played in bringing the beautiful game to Scotland. They played anywhere and everywhere, wherever they could find eleven opponents. On occasions, they even played by moonlight. Soon they were not so much a part of Scottish football, they *were* Scottish football. From the beginning they were adamant about playing according to the Association rules rather than accepting the remnants of the rugby code that some clubs still adhered to, like touchdowns and rucking, which later were permanently to divide the two types of football. Queen's Park held that football was a game played with the feet, not the hands, and they would play it as such whenever they could find someone to play.

They won their first 'challenge' in 1868 against Thistle FC from the Glasgow Green, winning 2–0 'within the hour' and before long were thrashing Alexandra Athletic by twenty-one goals no less, thus setting a victory pattern against all-comers that was to give them an unbeaten record for almost a decade. Over this period they took the game from the rather hit-and-miss playground brawl with everyone chasing the ball to the dribbling-and-passing game that became their hallmark.

The first photograph taken of the team soon after their foundation shows them as exactly what they were, the Caledonian Corinthians of their day. Eleven young men, uniform in their second, but longer-lasting, strip of horizontal, black-and-white stripes of jersey and striped long stockings. These young men are already winners and exude confidence. It was a Glasgow Victorian trait. They could not be more individual. Seated or standing, no two poses are the same; arms are folded defiantly across the chest, the foot poised in proprietorial fashion over the round ball. Other arms rest negligently on the arm of respective chairs and are even crossed loosely on its back. It is noticed that one gentleman, with no attempt at false modesty, sits at the right, with his left leg raised high on his right knee, held firmly there by his right hand while the left is placed under his exposed left thigh. I did say they were individual.

This was their studio image when the camera was still a novelty. What was significant, however, was that these same young men made a blend on the field of play; they merged as a football unit, not before a camera but before the eyes of spectators on a fixed date at a fixed place. That was their innovation. At this time, there were no more than ten football teams in Scotland and nearly a hundred in England so the balance was always in favour of the Southrons, as the Scots players called them. If football was in its infancy, then international football was still in the womb. It is true, however, that there were so-called 'international' matches between England and Scotland in London but they were not serious affairs. Known as the 'Alcock Internationals' (after C. W. Alcock, secretary of the Wanderers Football Club, who arranged them) there were five such challenges for which Alcock not only chose the venue, but also selected both teams, mostly made up of Englishmen and those Anglo-Scottish residents, or those with Scottish names like Lord Kinnaird (born in Kensington), who were available to him. In 1870, Alcock wrote a letter to the *Glasgow Herald*.

> In Scotland, once essentially the land of football, there should still be a spark left of the old fire, and I confidently appeal to all Scotsmen to aid to their utmost the efforts of the committee to confer success on what London hopes to found, an annual trial of skill between the champions of England and Scotland.

The members of the Queen's Park's committee resented this sham Scottish representation and resolved to do something about it. With no precedent to guide them, they determined that if things were to be done, they should be done properly. The first Scotland versus England rugby match had taken place the year before in Edinburgh, but this committee did not feel the need to look to the east for advice. This Queen's Park committee was a formidable group, as can be seen in their official photograph. In contrast to the team, the formally posed committee is anything but casual. This was the Glasgow man 'of the better sort' seen at his best. Their collective stance makes one feel that the picture must have been taken on a Sunday. Bowler hats are perched on trousered knees or on the end of canes, hands are in pockets or slid, like Napoleon's, into the buttoned jacket. Spruce moustaches abound and hair is meticulously pomaded. The seated figures do so with circumspection, and those who stand, are verticals of quiet authority. These are men to be reckoned with, and it was their collective energy that pitched the club forward during its first decade. Charles Alcock, in his London remove, didn't know what he'd taken on.

Not that the Scots were unknown in England. The club had joined the new FA in 1870 in order to have a greater range of opponents available and the slight differences between the Scottish and English playing rules often led to confusion and argument in these invitational encounters, which often were little more than 'bounce-ball' with the extra hazard of dialect differences. The Scots quickly made their mark in the initial FA Cup, drawing 0–0 with the Wanderers in the sixth round, having had the benefit of byes in the earlier rounds, but they were forced to scratch from the return game because not all of their players could get the time off work to travel south. There was also the cost of train fares and accommodation in London to consider. This economic consideration was to cost Queen's Park further chances of FA Cup glory. The following season they had to scratch to Oxford University at the same late stage in the competition for the same reasons.

The club's exasperation was further exacerbated by Alcock's high-handedness in deciding all matters relating to the previous so-called England–Scotland encounters. Queen's Park insisted that an international match could only be played by genuine nationals, that is between Scottish-born Scots and English-born Englishmen and that such fixtures deserved wider public attention. The game needed to go public. Football at the top level needed top-class application, and it was this that the Queen's Park committee provided.

They started in the time-honoured way by passing round the hat. This was followed by smoking concerts, raffles, begging letters, any legitimate way they could think of to raise funds that would bring Alcock's team north and put them up for a few days in Glasgow. The Englishmen, as ever, had to be lured north. The final gesture made by Queen's Park was that the game would be played according to the English FA rules. Agreement having been reached, a date was fixed for the first representative game, Saturday, 30 November 1872, St Andrew's Day. The problem now was where to play the game? Having no ground of their own, they couldn't ask the English team to play on a public park. Besides, the committee needed a paying crowd in order to recoup the English team's expenses. No Englishman would pay to come to Glasgow.

The Glasgow Academicals rugby club offered their ground free of charge but the Queen's men chose to go with the West of Scotland cricket club, whose enclosed ground at Hamilton Crescent was available at a cost of £10 with a further £10 available if takings exceeded £50. For the first time ever, a game of football was advertised beforehand in the press. The committee considered this rare expense a worthwhile gamble. When 2,500 tickets (the ground's usual capacity) were put on sale in town at Miller's, the hatters, and Keay's, the hosiers, in Argyle Street they went almost at once. They could have sold the whole printing again, and more besides. The match was the talk of the town. If the committee was surprised at this they were astonished at what happened on match-day.

Glasgow shops and offices at that time worked on Saturday afternoons but no work was done that day. The kick-off was timed for two o'clock but long before then the hordes were descending on Partick. The Whiteinch tram car was bulging at the seams as it made its way from Jamaica Street with would-be spectators and every form of wheels – from taxi-cabs to open carts, motorcycles to lorries and push-bikes – was trying to push its way through the mass of cloth caps and bowlers marching towards the little cricket ground. This was the bowler-hatted ancestor of the Tartan Army, drawn as one by the prospect of a clash with the Auld Enemy and gathering in support of the first-ever Scotland team as if summoned by fiery torch. These men were more than would-be spectators; they were enthusiastic patriots rallying to the cause. It was partisan, unexpected, uncalled for, even unseemly in some aspects, but it was very Scottish and it was football. Such scenes had never been witnessed before in the city, at least not for a football match.

The surrounding streets were choked with an overwhelming, predominately male presence. It was hardly a place for ladies. There was no room. Had there been, they would needed to have averted their eyes from the sight of many suited backs facing the walls doing what men do when they have to. Other men, unable to get in at the turnstiles, were standing on top of lorries and carts trying to get a glimpse of the playing area. Others bribed their way up to the first-floor windows of nearby tenements for a bird's-eye view. This was the first outbreak of football fever in Glasgow, and it was a disease that was to prove long-lasting.

The occasion had taken everyone by surprise. After all, the game itself was still very young, and yet it must have entrenched itself sufficiently to whip a goodly number of Glaswegians into a frenzy of anticipation that had nothing to do with its being St Andrew's Day. Of course there was an element of nationalism in such a spontaneous exhibition of support, but, after all, this was an international event. Police reinforcements had to be called to maintain order, not because the crowds were disorderly, far from it, but because they were so many. This was the face of football to come, and no one in authority was in the least ready for it; least of all, a future Queen's Parker and Scotland international full back, Walter Arnott, who was ten years old at the time. He remembers:

> We started off in the forenoon to walk to the ground – a distance of nearly five miles; but after reaching our destination found that there was no chance of getting inside the ground. How disappointed we felt after such a weary walk, at the poor prospect of our getting a view of the game. We earnestly begged a cabman to accommodate us on the top of his cab, and it was from that perch, I witnessed the first encounter between the two nations.

The kick-off was delayed until quarter past two in order to get everyone in and settled behind the ropes, by which time it was estimated that around four thousand spectators were in place, with as many outside as in, and all straining to get a better view. This was a manifestation of people power. Football had made its mark, and its first imprint was a Queen's Park boot. For an afternoon, it was more than a club, it was a nation. The team from the Glasgow south side ran out of the pavilion as Scotland, proudly wearing their dark-blue uniform with a red lion displayed on their hearts. It is still Scotland's main football strip to this day. England wore their traditional white with black knickerbockers, which made for a good contrast.

The home team wasn't picked by the committee but by the Queen's Park captain and goalkeeper, the bearded Robert W. Gardner. The full backs were William Ker and J. Taylor; the half backs, J. J. Thomson and James Smith and the forwards, Robert Smith, Robert Leckie, Alex Rhind, W. M. MacKinnon, J. B. Weir and D. Wotherspoon. The Smith brothers, James and Robert, played their football for South Norwood in London, but had been and still remained members of the Queen's Park club. Billy MacKinnon, a centre forward who was to play in the next six Scotland teams, was the forerunner of the typical Scottish forward, slightly built but tenacious, more brainy than brawny, and an artful dodger, as the term of the time had it. It meant he could beat a man with the ball at his feet by jinking past him. It was said of MacKinnon, 'He cannot be surpassed as a forward. One of the most brilliant dodgers on the field, and has great endurance.' He must have had, he lived to be ninety.

The England team was noted for the number of university men in its ranks and their positioning owed more to the old rugby practice than to football usage. Some of their team wore caps, a throwback to their public-school beginnings but also a marker during play. Teams had caps of different colours for this very purpose. They replaced the cowls which had been a part of the first football uniforms, but which were found to be uncomfortable in the heat of the game. Caps then became the fashion and when they ceased to be worn on the pitch, they became symbolic of representative honour won by the individual player, but that was to come later.

For this first real international encounter, the England captain was C. J. Otway of Oxford at left half-back. In goal was R. Barker of Herefordshire Rangers; E. H. Greenhalgh of Notts was three-quarter back; R. C. Welch of Harrow Chequers was at right half back; F. Chappell was fly kick; J. C. Clegg (Sheffield), C. Chenery (Crystal Palace) and A. S. Kirke-Smith were middles; J. Brockbank of Oxford was right-side forward, W. J. Maynard of 1st Surrey Rifles was centre and J. F. Morice of Barnes Club was left side. There was no referee but two umpires; one from each side, W. C. Alcock himself, and Mr William Keay, the hosier, of Queen's Park, each patrolling half of the playing area.

The England team was by far the stronger and taller and more experienced and it was expected that 'individual skill was generally on England's side but the Southrons did not play to each other as well as their opponents who seemed adept at passing the ball'. This is said by Richard Robertson, in his account of this match in his official *History of Queen's Park (1867–17)*, published in 1920, to which I am indebted for the excerpts from contemporary press reports. It would seem that the English, according to the *Glasgow Herald*, had all the advantages of weight and pace, but the strong point for the home club was that they played excellently well together. Play was generally acknowledged to be 'excellently good' from both teams, although the crowd was convinced Scotland had scored through Leckie, as the *North British Daily Mail* reports:

> . . . a good kick by Leckie caused tremendous cheering from all parts of the ground, so satisfied were the majority that a good goal had been scored for Scotland. To the great chagrin of the Scotch it was given no goal, the ball having passed hardly an inch over the tape.

The match finished goalless and it would not be the first time that Scotland was disadvantaged by a controversial decision. A firm cross-bar between the posts was the direct result of this particular incident. Another innovation introduced by the fledgling Queen's Park was the throw-in to be taken by both hands, and also a fixed half-time where teams would change ends in the interval. These points were to enter the FA rule book in due course.

Meantime, the huge crowd enjoyed this inaugural venture, little realising they were in at the start of something very big. Afterwards, the two teams gave three cheers to each other on the pitch and the crowd dispersed in good humour leaving the Queen's Park Football Club to go back to being a club again pleased that the committee's real objective had been attained, which was to assert a proper international status to these fixtures. Like the Glasgow gentlemen they were, they politely entertained their visitors to dinner and songs around the piano at the Carrick's Royal Hotel afterwards. Both teams realised they were celebrating something more than a challenge match. It was, in retrospect, a pivotal football occasion. West of Scotland cricket club were left wondering just what had happened on their prim little ground that day. They did not know it but a seed had been sown between the wickets that was to flower in the great Hampden and Wembley contests to come.

Interest in the sport now spread like wildfire and directly resulted in the formation of the Scottish Football Association by eight of the clubs then extant. Queen's Park, as the senior club, called a meeting at Dewar's Hotel, in Bridge Street, Glasgow, on 3 March 1873, to discuss the setting up of a Scottish Cup on the lines of the FA Cup in England. The clubs attending were Vale of Leven, 3rd Lanarkshire Volunteer Reserves, Clydesdale, Dumbreck, Glasgow Eastern and Granville. Kilmarnock sent a note of support. This move to better organise Scottish football was begun on the initiative of Queen's Park, and it was strictly on their terms. As the *North British Daily Mail* had put it ten days before:

> Thus, football in Scotland was begun by the Queen's Park Football Club, whose true sporting spirit aimed right in elevating the game to a higher platform than pounds, shillings and pence, to purify and ennoble, to rear and produce, not procure and pay. Always, and at all times, even till our own day, to play the game, and play it for the game's sake.

New clubs sprang up everywhere. Forsyth's, the city outfitters, were soon calling themselves, 'Football Costumiers' and were hard put to meet the demand for 'jerseys, caps, cowls, belts and knickers'. The latter item was certainly a gentleman's novelty. Forsyth's boasted that it stocked the colours of every club in Scotland, which made no great demands on its warehouse but it was sufficient of a hint that merchandise already mattered in the growing game.

This business acumen was further illustrated when later, in 1882, Scotland again played England at the first Hampden Park, now Queen's Park's ground. Forsyth's provided each Scottish player with a black velvet cap with the date of the game and the name of the opponents stitched on it as a memento. So began the tradition of 'capping' all international players. To be thus 'capped' for one's country is still the ambition of every young footballer, even when the game is now ruled as it is by the bottomless purses of the few.

The original Hampden Park was rather forced on the Spiders. The club was becoming too big to operate from a public playing field. They needed to stretch. Glasgow Corporation owned a piece of ground on the other side of Cathcart Road and after some haggling the Queen's men got it at a rent of £20 per annum providing they kept the fencing in good order. It was only a move across the road but they had come a long way as a football club. 1 October 1873 was a landmark day for Queen's Park. They were now the possessors of the first private football ground in Scotland.

New properties were already springing up all around the ground and to the south, on a ridge called Prospecthill, a local builder had erected a row of houses that he named Hampden Terrace. It took the club a little time to go with the name, but, with the completion of a lean-to shanty as a pavilion, the first Hampden Park came into being. It was hardly a level playing field but the committee and friends got to work and five days later it was ready to receive Dumbreck in a cup tie.

For the first time, Queen's Park wore their famous black-and-white hooped jerseys, which was to give them their Spider cognomen, and in that inaugural Hampden game the jerseys inspired the wearers to a 7–0 victory. Other fixtures followed by invitation, match secretaries being kept busy exchanging letters although some games were hardly more than scratch encounters, but even so the Spiders were all-conquering. Not only did they not lose a game, but they had never even lost a goal, even though more and more Scottish teams were springing up as readily as the houses around them. Some were even beginning to threaten the Queen's Park invincibility. One of these was Vale of Leven.

Queen's Park were always to have rather a tense relationship with this Dunbartonshire side. They were chalk and cheese in style as well as support and this did not make for smooth relations as each match showed. This particular encounter was played on 15 January 1875 before a crowd of no less than ten thousand, described by a local newspaper as 'a mixed mob of gentlemen and roughs'. The latter were accused of pulling up palings around the ground and using them to vault on to the terracing. On the field, things were just as challenging. Fair shoulder charging was allowed then and this game 'became famous for its charging'. It was a case of the boxer fighting the puncher, or the foil being used against the broadsword. In either event, the finesse of Queen's Park with their practised combination game was put severely to the test in a rowdy tussle.

The teams:

Queen's Park: J. Dickson; J. Taylor and R. Neil; C. Campbell and J. Philips; T. Lawrie, J. B. Weir, D. McGill, W. MacKinnon, T. C. 'Herriot' (Highet) and H. McNeil.

Vale of Leven: Wood; Jamieson and A. McIntyre; J. McIntyre and McLintock; Paton, Ferguson, McGregor, Lamont, Baird and McDougall.

Umpires: Mr Mitchell (Queen's Park) and Mr Wright Vale of Leven.

A special train had brought the Vale of Leven supporters from Alexandria. They were vociferous from the start but it was Queen's who scored first. Herriot made a clever throw-in, received the return and crossed for McGill to shoot through. Just on half-time, the Vale forced a corner and McLintock placed to the head of Paton, who forced it through a scrimmage and under the tape just on the stroke of half-time. This stunned Queen's Park. It was the first goal ever scored against them in eight years of playing but the players were undaunted and, in the second half, they laid siege to the Vale goal.

McNeil did great work even though he was much knocked about by repeated charges, but latterly made some splendid runs. Lawrie also played well but his forward man, Weir, was too well watched to be of much service . . . from the outset he seemed to be 'spotted' as a dangerous man and had to stand furious charges from McLintock. The styles of play of the two clubs were wildly different, Queen's Park being more scientific, relying on their skill in dribbling and their ability to place the ball in the best position to make use of it. Vale of Leven seemed to devote themselves to heavy charging with a view to the temporary disablement of the opponent . . . Then McNeil got a place kick [a free-kick today] for hands and passed it neatly to Philips who passed it on to Weir who served it back to McNeil to shoot through for the winning goal.

Victory for the just – but only just. It was described in the press, rather archly, as 'the storming of the maiden fortress'. The fortress hadn't quite succumbed, invincibility had been maintained, but with a slight dent in the Hampden shield. Other dents appeared as Queen's lost goals to Clydesdale in the Scottish Cup and to Notts County at Nottingham in a friendly. Their winning ways continued, but for how long? These lost goals were a further indication that the gap between Queen's Park and the other Scottish clubs was narrowing. Even so, defeat was unthinkable.

Despite great strides, there were still not enough teams of quality to give Queen's Park a real game and, after beating Renton to win the Scottish Cup for the second time, they were forced to look beyond their own borders and try England. No border raid was ever more thorough than that perpetrated across the Tweed by these young men with the educated feet. Apart from creditable advances in the FA Cup already mentioned, they also defeated teams in the north of England and the Midlands but it was their earlier no-scoring draw with Alcock's famous Wanderers at the Oval in London in 1872 that had been their greatest triumph to date.

They had not met since then, so Queen's Park made a challenge to meet them at the second Hampden Park at Mount Florida on 9 October 1875 and the result was a triumph. The Queen's men won 5–0 before a large crowd, which enjoyed the goals and the forward play of J. B. Weir in particular, who was given great freedom this time – there was no McLintock. A contemporary writer notes, 'It is a well-known fact that Weir, the Prince of Dribblers, can keep possession of the ball for a time against the best player in Scotland.' He was a star, without doubt, but he was just one good player in a good team. The forwards were by now three, Weir, on the right, Billy MacKinnon, the Dodger, at centre, and the popular Henry McNeil out on the left. Behind them were three back-up players, T. Lawrie, C. Herriot and Moses McNeil. And behind them, two half backs, Charles Campbell and James Philips with Joseph Taylor and R. W. Neil at full back and John Dickson in goal. Only Dickson, Lawrie and Herriot had not been capped for Scotland and the tall Charlie Campbell was noted for being the finest header of a ball in football.

The Wanderers played an experimental formation with the novel central player, no less than Alcock himself, surrounded by four wing half-backs, Turner, Greig, Kendrick and Heron. Chambers was in goal with one full back, Stratford, in front of him and two half backs, Kinnaird and Rawson. The former was to become an eminent figure in football both as a player for Scotland and as an administrator for the FA. So there was plenty of talent on show. This is what had attracted the huge crowd to Mount Florida. So much so that the spectators were asked on the posters, 'Please do not strain on the ropes,' which then surrounded the pitch.

The English team that day wore variously coloured identifying caps but the Scots confined themselves to different stockings for their full backs, half backs and forwards. They had never taken to the new centre-half-back position as adopted by Wanderer's Alcock. He was arguably their best player and had total responsibility in the middle of the field. He drew the other four half backs around him defensively as required and used them as a shield when he moved forward. Alcock may not have had the stamina that such a role demanded and, as a result, the totally attacking game favoured by the Queen's Park forwards came into its own. Weir and MacKinnon revelled in the freedom, and given Harry McNeil's speed on the left wing and the crosses which the others, including Campbell, converted, goals were inevitable. To concentrate on power in defence instead of attack meant, for Queen's, to play in order to prevent a defeat instead of attempting to win, and such a strategy was totally negative in their eyes.

Yet the attacking centre-half-back had worked for some teams. James Kelly was to show this in the new Celtic team of 1888, where he was the unashamed pivot of the team, as he had been at Renton, and inspired his side both as an extra defender and extra attacker. Alcock tried to do the same but without the same success and the Scots took every advantage to score a handful of goals. The English became rattled and over-anxious and finally succumbed to a Queen's Park team at its best. They had become a *team*. As the *Umpire* of 21 August 1884 had previously noted: 'Take any club that has come to the front and the onward strides will be found to date from the hour when the rough and tumble gave place to swift accurate passing and attending to the leather rather than the degrading desire merely to coup an opponent.' The same publication later printed another comment which, in our own day of coach control and managerial majesty, is worth mentioning here: 'Tell it not in Gath. Publish it not in Askelon. Strategy can never take the place of eleven good pairs of nimble legs.'

Well, twenty-two south-side legs had mastered the Wanderers on the day and they looked forward to the return in London.

This took place at the Oval, four months later, on 5 February 1876, a never-to-be-forgotten day in the annals of the Spiders. It was typical February weather, snowy and slushy underfoot, and the teams came out onto an iron-hard, ridged pitch with a freezing gale blowing and not a blade of grass showing. The shivering players lined up as follows:

Wanderers: W. D. Greig; W. S. Rawson and A. H. Stafford; F. H. Birley (capt) and F. M. Maddison; C. H. Wolliston, H. Heron, H. S. Otter, C. H. T. Metcalfe, F. Heron and J. Kendrick.

Queen's Park: J. Dickson: J. Taylor (capt) and R. W. Neill; C. Campbell and J. Philips; H. McNeil, J. B. Weir, D. McGill, W. MacKinnon, T. C. Herriot and M. McNeil.

Umpires: C. W. Alcock (Wanderers) and W. C. Mitchell (Queen's Park)

Referee: R. A. Ogilvie (Note that Wanderers had reverted to their old formation.)

Further discomfort to the Scots was the narrow width of the pitch in comparison to the wide spaces of their own Hampden. This resulted in the ball going out of play much of the time (it went over the pavilion at one stage) and the Queen's Park players found it difficult to find their rhythm or get their game going. The stronger, more robust Wanderers sensed this unease and pressed hard. It was seen early that Weir was struggling. He had sustained a knee injury some weeks earlier but insisted on playing. The thinking was that a Weir with a 'game leg' was better than no Weir at all, but this was a mistake. He was hardly half the player he normally was and the Queen's attack frequently misfired. Consequently, the team could not do itself justice.

Nevertheless, the game was gallantly contested by the plucky Scots until Wanderers got a corner after half-an-hour. Maddison placed it well and the ball was headed through by Wolliston. The visitors were one down. Notwithstanding, they picked up after the interval but after only five minutes, the Wanderers scored again. Heron passed on to Wolliston who found Kendrick on the left who then ran in to put through for a second goal. Queen's Park had never been in this position before in any game, but they rallied their forces, including the limping Weir, and pummelled the Wanderer's goalmouth, 'showing an extraordinary agility, but to no avail. No one individual stood out in the game but a good kick at goal by MacKinnon just failed in the dying minutes.' The whistle blew for time and the dispirited North had to cede the day to the South.

It was a disaster, and the news was immediately telegraphed to the *Daily Mail* in Scotland. It genuinely shook the country and led to what amounted to national mourning – Queen's Park, the Scottish Invincibles, had been beaten for the first time in nine years. It was hard to believe. It was another Flodden when a Bannockburn had been expected. The worst had happened, a proud flag had been lowered in defeat for the first time in its history and heads were bowed. It was a calamity hardly to be borne. There was some genuine excuse for the club in that J. B. Weir, their best forward, had been 'disabled', as the match report puts it. His contribution was much missed and the key player's absence obviously 'put the team out of joint'.

Yet they had not played badly. The London press states this clearly, 'The crack Glasgow club is a little ahead of all other Association clubs' and another agrees that, 'Their great weakness was the partial disablement of Weir', but said he should not have played at all adding, 'a game leg is not a thing to be carried on to the football field. It is no mere complimentary phrase to say [that] the Scots played well enough to win nine times out of ten.' But they didn't. The magnificent, all-conquering image so skilfully fashioned over those first years had been shattered. The delicate Spider's web had been cruelly ripped apart. And by Englishmen. It was hard for Scotland to take. The citadel had been breached. Nothing would ever be the same again.

They returned home to be beaten again – by their nemesis, Vale of Leven, 2–0, in another towsy match played in driving rain on the last Saturday of December. Even the ball burst during the game, deflated in a pile of wet leather, lying helplessly on a pitch that resembled the Queen's Park duck pond. The Queen's Park players knew how it felt. Although they went on to win ten Scottish Cups by 1892, beating Celtic 5–1 in their last final, it was that watershed year of 1876 that marked, alas, the end of the Mount Florida ascendancy. It was hard to believe that such a confident reign should ever end.

Queen's Park never changed their ethos but times changed around them and with the new professionalism the ideals of the Victorian gentleman inevitably gave way to the material demands of the twentieth-century pragmatists and a whole new league of changes. Never mind, their example had not been lost, and the amateur Corinthians were founded in England to uphold the same principles. As Queen's Park had for Scotland, Corinthians provided the England team against Wales in 1884.

Even as it faded as a football power, Queen's Park provided not only for Glasgow, but also for Scotland, a lasting souvenir of its status as the founding club, a third Hampden Park in October 1903. This signalled the last, grand gesture of the first club in the land, and the beginning of Hampden as a football Mecca, the repository of memories of great moments for players and spectators alike. One of the honours of Scotland, a jewel in its football crown, the Mount Florida ground, known today simply as the national stadium, is iconic, the unquestioned temple of Scottish football, the home of the SFA and the Scottish football hall of fame and museum.

But it is no museum piece, it is a living experience, a vibrant fact of modern football life, a continuing expression of what football means to Scotland. As long as Hampden stands, it will remain a tribute to the Queen's Park Football Club and the farsightedness of a group of ordinary Glasgow men and what they created out of a recreation ground. It not only survives, but also thrives, still clinging to the real values, still despising the money principle in sport, still living up to its cherished motto, *Ludere causa ludendi* – 'the game for the game's sake'.

Where's yer London Wanderers noo?

Hugh MacDonald

2

There Were No Winners: the Scottish Cup Final of 1909

Hugh MacDonald

The televisions flicker silently. They produce the newsreels of a life. Sitting in the Scottish Football Museum in Hampden is akin to seeing one's life flash in front of oneself in the form of Joe Jordan's toothy grin, the cocky celebration of Denis Law and a succession of captains lifting the Scottish Cup.

The pictures remind one of jubilation and despair. The video loop of Scottish Cup victories is sprinkled with that routine feature of the cup being brandished towards an unseen horde of roaring fans. It is the inevitable end to a final even though it sometimes takes a replay. It has occurred every year since 1874. Except once. The cup was not won in 1909. No captain lifted it in a mixture of elation and exhaustion. No set of supporters crowed about victory in the pub afterwards.

The cup was whisked away from a Hampden that was burning. The crackles of flame were interspersed with the roars of rioters and the wails of the injured. The Scottish Cup final of 1909 ended in ignominy, chaos and blood. The replay did not go into extra time in a playing sense. Instead, police battled for more than two hours as the crowd rioted, setting Hampden ablaze and intent on razing the stadium.

The facts are simple. It was 17 April 1909. Rangers and Celtic had drawn 1–1 in a replay after being locked at 2–2 the previous week. Fans rioted. Hundreds of supporters and police were injured. The cup was withheld. There is no name of a 1909 winner inscribed on the venerable trophy. But beyond these details lies a swampland where certainty sinks in a mire of conflicting stories.

The eyewitness evidence of what happened on that fateful Saturday is carried towards me in the football museum. I take my eyes from the television screens and accept a small box. It is crammed with yellowing press reports and the testimony given at a Scottish Football Association inquiry. They are carefully removed and examined. More than a century on, they have not lost their capacity to excite. The sober tones of the *Glasgow Herald* serve to put the violence into a stark relief. The inches, feet, even yards of newsprint tell the story of what happened.

But there is no context. There is little background. The journalists have viewed the fights, ducked the stones and escaped with their lives. There is little appetite for rational analysis just a day on from the riot. The 1909 debacle still defies certainty, however. Nor can it be explained away by arguments that have become routine in the decades since. This was not a sectarian riot. The Rangers versus Celtic match had not yet been draped in the dreadful garb of pseudo-religious warfare. David Potter, a Celtic historian, points out in his biography of Willie Maley, Celtic's manager at the time: 'Although Celtic were definitely the Catholic and Irish team of Scotland (and proud of it) Rangers had not yet involved themselves with the extreme Protestant cause.'

It was also not prompted by injustice on the field of play. The first match produced a moment of refereeing controversy but the replay drifted to a 1–1 draw. So what happened to produce mayhem on the south side of Glasgow?

Most contemporary sources are less than illuminating. John Allan in his *The Story of the Rangers*, written after consultation with participants on the day, observes wryly: 'Everybody concerned thought someone else was to blame.'

The accepted version of events is that many of the supporters expected extra time to be played. They were outraged that after paying at least another shilling to watch a cup final they would be forced to reach into their pockets again before seeing their favoured captain lifting the cup. Some may have believed the teams were playing for a draw, conspiring to arrange another pay day when sixty thousand fans would help fill the clubs' coffers. After all, that is how Rangers and Celtic achieved their 'Old Firm' monicker. On 16 April 1904 a well-known periodical of the time, the *Scottish Referee*, carried a cartoon of a man with a sandwich board. The caption on the board reads: 'Patronise the Old Firm, Rangers Celtic Ltd.' It is the first recorded mention of the term. But many fans on that April day merely thought they had been bilked out of extra time.

They had rushed to Hampden to witness two clubs who were growing quickly. Rangers and Celtic were becoming the dominant forces in Scottish football. More than 120,000 fans watched the final and the replay. Willie Maley of Celtic was often heard to say that there was money in football. There was no dissent from the Rangers side.

Ironically, though, the riot was almost certainly sparked by a misunderstanding. Maley undoubtedly wanted extra time to be played. He had asked both Rangers and the SFA to accede to his request that the match be played to the finish. He was not inspired by a selfless regard for the budgets of the supporters. Celtic had a fixture backlog as they pressed to win the Scottish championship in a run that would encompass six consecutive title-winning years. This move was reported in some newspapers. The fact that Rangers and the SFA chose to reject Maley's suggestion does not seem to have been recorded as prominently.

The final whistle at the replay was greeted by indecision on and off the field. Celtic and Rangers players lingered. Did they expect extra time? The crowd murmured. The corner flags were removed as the SFA announced another replay. The crowd roared. A riot began. But who were the troublemakers? And what led to them to such an unbridled anger? The build-up to the final offers some clues.

*

The crowds queuing up outside Hampden for the Scottish Cup-final replay of 1909 were in cheerful mood. It was a bright, sunny day and the collision between the emerging giants of the Scottish game was met with an anticipation laced with something a bit stronger among many of the supporters. There may have been expectation in the air but there was also the unmistakable whiff of consumed alcohol. Football had grown quickly as a spectator sport in Scotland. More than sixty thousand had watched the first playing of the final on the tenth of April. The same number queued eagerly to pay their shilling for the replay a week later. Both clubs had strong supports originating in the brake clubs of the late 1880s and early 1900s. A brake was a horse-drawn vehicle that could carry about thirty supporters. They had their own banners and sang their distinctive songs. Many supporters drank and some could be rowdy.

Football was not exclusively a working-class sport. There were many members of the middle class shuffling their way forward to the Hampden pay boxes. But all appreciated that an afternoon at the football could include both mischief and something even worse. The Ibrox disaster of 1902, when twenty-six people died in an awful accident with no links to hooliganism, was still fresh in the memory. But most supporters had witnessed the odd 'break-in' when fans surged on to the pitch in protest or in untamed jubilation. There was a quiet menace about football that may have thrilled some of the middle-class attendees and certainly infected others.

Hampden was wonderfully resplendent in the sun. Named after a seventeenth-century English parliamentarian who had fought in the Civil War, it was taking its first steps towards becoming an icon of the Scottish game. It had been refurbished with great enthusiasm. It was a highly modern stadium with a two-storey brick pavilion, expansive changing rooms, baths, committee rooms and a gymnasium. Opened only six years earlier, its slopes were already gaining a reputation for being a perfect spot to create football memories.

Four men travelled to the ground that day with differing emotions. Willie Maley, William Wilton, Jimmy Quinn and Harry Rennie looked on the match from their own distinctive perspectives.

Rennie, the Rangers goalkeeper, was a tortured soul. With Rangers leading 2–1 in the first match, he had played a leading role in ensuring a replay would be needed. He was adjudged to have fielded a cross but then to have taken the ball over the line as he swivelled to avoid the onrushing Quinn. The Celtic centre forward was a rampaging figure and was allowed by the laws of the game to charge the goal-keeper. Rennie was correct to take evasive action, but did he misjudge his position and, in effect, score an own goal? The referee, J. B. Stark, formed that opinion immediately, indicating a goal had been scored despite protests from Rangers players.

John Allan, in the *Story of the Rangers*, reveals the devastating effect on the Rangers goalkeeper.

> Rennie was not in the habit of shedding tears over football; he was a philosopher in his way; but in the pavilion at the finish of this match he cried like a boy from sheer vexation that such a mistaken decision, as he thought it, should have robbed his club of the cup.

Rennie's post-match comments carry an elegance and delicacy that are never replicated in the media scrums of the modern day. 'At the time it happened I regarded it, and continue to regard it, as one of the most artistic saves in my merry football career,' he said. Speaking of the atmosphere created by 'a huge concourse of 60–80,000 intelligent Britishers throbbing with the intensest of intense expectancy,' he added: 'I knew that . . . if I saved the ball in the way it ought to be saved, the cup was ours.'

So what was going through his mind as the long, loping cross came in on his goal?

> It did occur to me simply to palm the ball out, but in a flash I dismissed that idea as panic and unworthy of the standard of play usually associated with the Glasgow Rangers Football Club, unworthy of the importance of that particular match, unworthy of the many distinguished and talented people who honoured the match by their presence and who expected, and had every right to expect, an exhibition of the finer points of the game; unworthy, even of my own reputation. I seized the opportunity to give a demonstration of the real art of goal-keeping.

And how was this effected, Mr Rennie?

> I stretched my long and vigorous arms upwards, sensed the speed and spin of the ball with ten powerful and sensitive fingertips, and

with the profoundest concentration of mind, that entirely obliterated everything but the task in hand, I sighted the ball against cross bar and goalpost and bringing hands and ball down together, I simply nursed it into subjection.

But how did the referee believe the ball had been carried over the line?

I half bent and half twisted my extremely lithe body from the waist, throwing back my hips, for the double purpose of adjusting my body relative to my arms and to get into the best position to evade the charging Jimmy Quinn. I side-stepped to the left, and with a leap, punted the ball away to midfield thus accomplishing what I thought to be a high class and effective bit of goalkeeping.

The referee begged to differ.

Quinn and Celtic would be given another chance to lift the cup. The legendary centre forward from Croy had no reason to fear another match. He had, in truth, no reason to fear anything. His great physical power saw many opponents cower before him. His technique was sure in front of goal. He had already scored a hat trick in a cup final against Rangers. He saw the replay as another chance to repay the faith shown in him by Maley.

Maley was already a Celtic legend. Born in Newry on 25 April 1868, he had emigrated to Glasgow as a boy with his soldier father and his mother and brothers. He was a Celtic player at the inception of the club and went on to become secretary and manager. He believed simply, according to David Potter, that 'God had chosen him for the job'. He had produced a formidable Celtic side. The team won everything it entered in 1907. Maley – a first-class athlete who had won the Scottish 100-yard championships at Hampden in 1896 – had developed a fit, skilful team.

Quinn, signed by Maley from Smithston Albion, was central to its success. He was also involved in another Scottish Cup controversy between the two sides. In the 1905 semi-final, Quinn was sent off after a clash with an opponent. Some say he struck a Rangers defender and then kicked him. Others claim he merely bumped into his opponent. The accounts tend to be divided on lines of blue or green partisanship. But the incident sparked a crowd invasion. Players rushed to the dressing room as the fans could not be controlled. Celtic conceded the match. Quinn was also sent off in the New Year's Day game between Rangers and Celtic in 1907.

Brilliant, strong and dangerous, Quinn epitomised the notion that Rangers–Celtic games could be rowdy and controversial. Spectators knew, too, that a crowd invasion could be engineered with some ease. He had scored in the first game and was looking forward to doing the same in the replay. A man who was no stranger to an alcoholic libation, he looked forward to toasting a cup success.

Maley had other worries. He looked at the fixture backlog with some trepidation. Driven and highly successful, he believed he had a duty to guide the club to success. He was in the midst of an era of achievement that would bring the club six consecutive titles. But he was never satisfied. He had no argument with Mr Wilton of the Rangers. There was mutual respect and they even travelled on scouting trips together, though Maley gave his Rangers counterpart the slip by leaving a Falkirk game at half-time to travel to Stenhousemuir to sign Quinn.

Wilton was also accustomed to success, though it had deserted him lately in the championship. He was the first manager of Rangers, taking up the position in May 1899. He had tasted an almost instantaneous triumph. Rangers had achieved the first 100 per cent record in the league, winning all eighteen games and scoring seventy-nine goals in 1898/99. He led his side to four consecutive titles. He would go on to win ten titles as manager. But his last, in 1920, was tragically followed by his death, aged fifty-four, in a boating accident.

He approached the Hampden of 1909 with a keen desire to snatch dominance away from Maley's Celtic. The sectarian element that would poison the atmosphere of the Old Firm lay some years in the future. Celtic undeniably had links with Roman Catholicism, having been founded by a Marist brother in Brother Walfrid. But the club was keen to stress that it was all-inclusive. 'It is not his creed nor his nationality which counts – it's the man himself,' said Maley. Rangers were far from being an exclusively Protestant club. The influx of shipyard workers from Belfast just before the First World War and the intensity of the Home Rule question in Ireland are both seen to have polarised the debate, taking the

Old Firm from a football cartel to a bitter rivalry that extended far beyond the football stadium.

But on that sunny day in April 1909 the rivalry was sporting. Wilton wanted Rangers to flex their muscles once again. He had agreed with the SFA stance that the rules should not be changed to allow the final to be played to a finish. Maley was tense, worried about the final and its effects on the tiring legs of his players.

Fatefully, though, he was part of two interventions that lit a fuse that ran up Somerville Drive to Hampden. Maley had been quoted saying that Celtic did not want a third match. His approach to Rangers and the SFA to allow extra time had been recorded in newspapers. The refusal to accede to the request had not been as widely publicised. There was a significant element of supporters of both sides who believed that whatever happened the cup would be lifted in triumph that afternoon.

Maley, perhaps unwittingly, had also contributed to the scepticism about the motives of the Old Firm. After two successive draws between the Old Firm in the Glasgow Cup final of 1907, he was heard to boast about how much money the clubs were making from replays. The fans muttered as they delved in their pockets for another shilling. There was a growing unrest that they were being taken for mugs. They flowed into Hampden, filling its vast terracing, in the mood for a great cup final. There was no appetite for a third course.

*

The game was in stark contrast to what followed. It was a drab affair. Jimmy Quinn, for Celtic, and Jimmy Gordon, for Rangers, scored. The replay drifted towards a close with both teams playing with a distinct lack of adventure. Some fans later insisted that this was a sign of the clubs' desire to play for a third time. But Maley did not want a third match. Any collusion would necessarily have involved the Celtic manager and he was keen to finish with the Scottish Cup so as to tie up the league. More likely, the timidity of both teams could be ascribed to being aware that they could be caught on the break. The ninety minutes limped, rather than raced, to an end.

If the match was a damp squib, there was soon to be a spectacular explosion. As the final whistle blew, some players stayed on the pitch. *The Scotsman* reported that all the Rangers players quickly made for the dressing room but John Allan tells a different tale in the *The Story of the Rangers*. 'It was a terribly unfortunate thing that, at the finish of the second game, several of the players lingered on the field after the whistle had sounded,' he writes. 'A photograph of this incident, reproduced on the Monday following the match, showed six or seven Celtic players and two Rangers men on the field when they should have been in the pavilion.'

Did some players believe that extra time was to be played? They were soon disabused of that notion. The referee was clear that the match was ended. A linesman raced to the corner and pulled out a flag with a flourish, indicating that no more play would be witnessed.

Mayhem then broke out. The match was being watched by a group of sports journalists. The representatives of the *Evening Times*, *Scotsman* and *Glasgow Herald* quickly assumed the style of war correspondents.

There was just the briefest of simmering. 'Large numbers of the vast crowd could hardly realise that the play was finished for the day and they stood awaiting the turn of events,' notes the *Glasgow Herald* correspondent. He adds: 'Presently a few individuals invaded the playing pitch, apparently more in a spirit of curiosity and mischief.'

The riot then exploded. But how had a desultory pitch invasion suddenly been transformed into a violent mob? A middle-class reader of the *Glasgow Herald*, revealing his roots by the elegance and undisguised snobbery of his observations, wrote a letter to the newspaper on the Monday. It states simply that a 'half intoxicated' young man had come on to the pitch and performed a dance in front of an unamused policeman, who knocked him to the ground and assaulted him. The reader claimed that this attack enraged spectators.

Others sources assert that the mob was already angry and was proceeding to the pavilion to vent its spleen about the lack of extra time. The riot then took on proportions that were to be measured in blood and casualties.

There were moments of black humour. Sensing trouble was brewing,

Tom Maley, brother of Willie, grabbed the Scottish Cup and the receipts of £1,400 and took them to safety. Inside the pavilion, a sedate Scottish Football Association committee was arranging the replay for the Wednesday. This announcement was made to the disgruntled crowd. It had the effect of a bugle sounding the charge.

From then, Hampden was bereft of light moments, banter or any goodwill. The stadium was, instead, polluted by violence and shouts of anger as the whiff of burning wood drifted on the south-side air. The violence started just after five o' clock. It took more than two hours for the authorities to bring it under control. 'The scene is described as resembling that of a battlefield,' says *The Scotsman* correspondent in his Monday report.

The first flashpoint was outside the pavilion where the fans had just heard that a second replay was to take place. Angered by the announcement, a portion of the crowd made their way to the passage leading to the dressing rooms. The *Glasgow Herald* reports that several hundred spectators were involved in this invasion and that the passage was guarded by only two policemen. It was rushed by the mob but its tight dimensions allowed the policemen to hold the line. Bottles and stones were launched as the disgruntled spectators expressed their frustration. Foiled in their attempt to reach the dressing rooms, thousands of supporters moved to the rear of the covered stand. They began dismantling it while raining missiles down on police. Out on the pitch, the nets were pulled down and goalposts uprooted. Supporters began breaking up the posts. But soon there was a significant development in the violence.

A group of supporters tore down barriers, threw them on to the running track and set fire to them. Others retreated to the north terracing where they bombarded the police with missiles. Mounted police charges were ineffective on the high-banked terracing. Policemen on foot, too, were easy targets. They were hit by missiles but could not form a cohesive charge as the barriers prevented a straightforward route to the rioters.

The fires proliferated. 'An infuriated crowd surrounded the blazing pile and danced and cheered wildly, while willing hands seized more wood to feed the flames,' reports the *Glasgow Herald*. 'Quite a number of the crowd were in possession of bottles containing whisky, and they were actually seen to pour the fluid on the broken timber in order to aid its quicker ignition. Soon a huge bonfire was in progress, fed by fuel brought from every possible quarter,' *The Scotsman* correspondent observes.

Police regrouped for another mounted charge. They could make no impression as the fans sprinted for the safety of the terracing. Those supporters who stood their ground extracted terrible casualties. An *Evening Times* correspondent expressed his horror at seeing two policemen dragged from their horses and badly beaten.

A baton charge by forty policemen seemed to make some sort of impact. But, again, the crowd resorted to an earlier tactic. 'The mob retreated to the high terracing where they were comparatively safe from pursuit, the labyrinth of barriers and cross stays making it quite impossible for the police to act together,' the *Glasgow Herald* notes.

The police, at least, believed the conflict was contained to the pitch and terracing. 'But suddenly an enormous crackling was heard. The daring malcontents had done further damage,' observes the *Glasgow Herald*. The stadium entrances on Somerville Drive were set on fire. As police reinforcements rushed to the ground they were joined by firemen. Both faced a violent response to their arrival. Members of Queen's Park fire brigade were astonished to be embroiled in scenes they simply had never witnessed, never envisioned. As they rolled out their hoses, the rioters cut them up and set the vandalised equipment on fire.

Southern, Central and other city brigades arrived but met the same fate. According to the *Glasgow Herald*, 'Tired of harassing the police, the rioters turned their attention to the firemen and amid showers of stones these brave fellows contrived to work.'

Indeed the police and firemen resorted to desperate measures to contain the fires. They picked up the missiles thrown at them and promptly let fly at the crowd. One newspaper man reports the 'astonishing sight' of policemen and firemen forming lines to throw stones at rioters so that lines of hoses could be laid.

Out on the pitch, the crowd continued to resist the baton charges and drew blood from the police. 'Any policeman unfortunate enough to lose touch with his comrades was set upon and unmercifully beaten,' said one observer.

There were bizarre scenes. One police inspector was badly cut on the temple by a bottle and almost immediately had his baton split in two by a stone. In another incident a fan dragged a policeman from a baton charge and, as the officer retreated, the supporter beat him savagely and without mercy, leaving the helpless constable in a crumpled, bloody heap. His attacker then produced a handkerchief and beckoned for ambulancemen to come to the aid of his victim.

In other parts of the ground there were no such moments of truce. The *Glasgow Herald* correspondent saw one policeman 'struck on the head and rendered unconscious while attending to a comrade who had been injured'. Ambulancemen ducked for cover or grabbed the pitch as stones hailed down on them as they were tending to the injured.

Firemaster Waddel arrived about an hour after the riot began. He was immediately left in no doubt as to its severity. He was greeted with a cry from one rioter: 'Here's the heid yin: let's go for him.' Police were told: 'There are two policemen lying dead over yonder and you will be next.' Mercifully, both observation and prediction proved untrue.

But the fighting was brutal and there were casualties, as *The Scotsman* verifies.

> When all the reserves had been hurried up from the district police offices, there would be about 200 constables on the field, including about 16 horsemen. The difficulty was to drive the crowds up the slopes surrounding the pitch, and the method adopted was to force them out of the grounds in batches. But long before comparative order had been restored, the casualty list had reached appalling proportions.
>
> A number of medical men who happened to be present, set themselves devotedly to the work of attending to the injured. These gentlemen included two doctors, Jamieson, father and son, and Dr D. McArdle, of Stobhill Hospital. Later they were reinforced by assistance from the Victoria Infirmary, which is situated in the neighbourhood. Ambulance wagons were summoned, and, after being temporarily attended to, the sufferers were conveyed to the Victoria Infirmary. One of the injured was attended at the Royal Infirmary, which is several

miles distant. The spectacle presented in the football pavilion and neighbourhood, where the medical work was proceeding, resembled nothing so much as what one would picture occurring in the rear of a battle. Numbers of men were being brought in in an unconscious condition, suffering from wounds in the fight, and, in some instances, from the crushing which occasionally took place.

Most of the injuries seemed to be the result of being hit with stones or by batons. But some surgeons later reported knife wounds among the police casualties.

The battle began to abate about seven, two hours after it had exploded. It left a scene of destruction and blood, as *The Scotsman* explains.

It would be about ten minutes past five o'clock when the football match finished, and an idea of the prolonged character of the riot will be gained when it is stated that order was not restored till half-past seven. Gradually the police effected a clearance of the pitch and its environs, but not before the field had been reduced to a wreck. At one time a section of the crowd tore up and down the field with a road roller, cutting the ground badly, and committing every damage in their power. With the exception of the pavilion and the press box, all the other erections were damaged or wrecked by fire or assault. The police stationed outside the barricading had their hands as full as those inside. When the unruly roughs were ultimately ejected from the field, they remained in great crowds outside, and continued the fusillade of brickbats. Not a piece of glass escaped which could be reached by stones, and the crowd exhibited a delight in wreaking their revenge on the persons of the police and firemen, and in the destruction of the property of the club.

Fortunately they were unaware that the football association officials were occupants at the moment of rooms in Somerville Place, on the opposite side of the street from the main entrance to the park. These gentleman had in their possession, drawings to the amount of £1,400, and were also guarding the Scottish Cup, which would have been awarded to the victor of the game.

Both these, of course, had been saved by Tom Maley.

As the crowd drifted off into the night and the casualties were taken by wagon to the Victoria infirmary, a more innocuous activity took place. As *The Scotsman* reports, the craze for souvenirs began.

> The crossbar of one of the goal posts was carried from the field into Somerville Road in front of the burning pay boxes and a crowd of men and boys hacked at it with pocket knives and pocketed the chips. Among the debris littering the ground were a number of policemen's helmets, which had been lost in the day's struggle. These were also the objective of the souvenir-hunter, being cut into strips and carried away.

As it approached eight o' clock, an uneasy calm prevailed at Hampden. The houses in Somerville Drive had been packed with people watching the mayhem unfold. Slowly, those windows closed and the inhabitants returned to their lives. *The Scotsman* was puzzled by one aspect of the affair, as its report on the Monday makes clear.

> Curious to relate only one man was arrested in the course of the out-break. He has been lodged in the Queen's Park Police Office and will be brought up to-day on a charge of assaulting a policeman and a soldier. It is stated that a plain clothes constable obtained the assist-ance of the soldier to effect the arrest. The police were, of course, practically powerless in the matter of apprehensions. Instances are recorded of rioters being taken into custody, but so savagely were the police handled that they were forced to let go their quarry.

There were, in fact, other arrests. The charges against two men accused of cutting up firemen's hoses were found not proven. In addition, the alleged attacker walked free. There was no retribution in court for the police.

It is impossible to record just how many were injured. More than one hundred were thought to have been treated at the Victoria infirmary but the records are sketchy. Medical staff placed the taking of notes sec-ondary to staunching wounds. Similarly, many of those treated at the ground staggered home without being officially recorded as hurt.

As darkness settled on the battlefield, firemen were content that no fires were left burning. The scene, though, was extraordinary, as the *Glasgow Herald* notes. 'All over the pitch lay portions of the goalposts, netting and barriers, while at the exits and entrances the charred woodwork and twisted turnstiles showed that the fire brigade had not come too soon.'

Police were stationed overnight at the ground to prevent any return by the rioters. But the appetite for battle had been sated. The anger of the fans had been fully spent.

The thirty constables guarding Hampden were merely sentries guarding a scene of destruction. The evening papers on Saturday had, of course, reported the riot in florid terms and on the Sunday the great stadium became a place of pilgrimage for the insatiably curious, as *The Scotsman* points out.

> All day yesterday crowds of people flocked to Mount Florida to view the scene. A force of police still guarded the ground yesterday, and the public were rigidly excluded from it. Early in the morning the services of a number of joiners had been requisitioned, and the barricading and shattered gates set to rights as much as possible.
>
> Notwithstanding their exertions, however, the place presented a sorry sight. All the woodwork at the Somerville Drive entrances had been burned away or remains charred, and what is left is a mass of torn, twisted, or bent galvanised iron, The enclosure itself is a litter of stones and broken bottles, and scarred patches where fire has been at work. All the public lamps in the vicinity have been smashed. Only the roughest estimate can be obtained of the amount which will be required to set the place to rights, but £800 is considered a moderate figure. Interesting questions as to liability must arise. It may be confidently expected that many different claims will be lodged.

The riot was over. Its effects, though, had still to be fully realised. Hampden faced another spell of renovation and improvement and would not host a Scottish Cup final until after the First World War. The Sunday after the final was a time of reflection for all parties concerned. Celtic and Rangers had to meditate on their next move. The SFA had to make a judgment on whether a cup final could be played after such dreadful events. Decisions had to be made.

And soon.

*

The mood was suitably sombre when members of the Scottish Football Association strode into the offices at 6 Carlton Place, Glasgow, on the Monday night after the final. The general committee had moved quickly to arrange an emergency meeting. Just a few miles up the road, the damage at Hampden was being assessed with joiners and other workmen making emergency repairs. Council staff were also busy in restoring street lighting as the streets surrounding the stadium were strewn with broken glass from lamps. The SFA were in no doubt about the severity of the riot. The committee had visited the wrecked ground while members had talked to police and were told fatal injuries had only been avoided through some sort of miracle.

That day's newspapers had expressed outrage. The *Glasgow Herald* opines: 'Saturday was a black day in the history of football in Glasgow. The riot pales into insignificance every other happening, here and elsewhere on the football field. To equal it one must go back to the days of the Bread Riots in 1848.' *The Scotsman*, with just a hint of Edinburgh sniffiness, states: 'Glasgow, which holds the record for football disasters, was on Saturday afternoon and evening the scene of a riot which will rank as one of the most disgraceful blots disfiguring the annals of the game.'

The committee was in the midst of a storm. It summoned representatives from Celtic and Rangers to solve a great dilemma: what was to be done? The Scottish Cup lay safe but unclaimed. Should there be another replay? If so, where and when? And who was to blame for the riot?

The inquiry made little progress as to the cause. Both James Hay, the Celtic captain, and James Stark, his Rangers counterpart, testified that they had no instructions from their officials as to the playing of extra time. Hay said that when he was leaving the field he met two or three Rangers players, who asked the referee if there was any word of playing an extra half-hour. The referee replied that he had no word and marched straight to the pavilion. In answer to a further question, the referee admitted some of the Rangers players were on the field as well as Celtic players after the whistle was blown.

Willie Maley, the Celtic manager, told the inquiry there had been no arrangement either between the teams, or the committees of the teams, before the match to stay on and play an extra half-hour in the event of a draw. He could not explain why it was that some of the Celtic players remained on the field after the referee blew the whistle. Asked if there was any representation made by his club to Rangers to have the game played to a finish Mr Maley replied that he had asked one of the Rangers committee on Tuesday whether they would play extra time but no agreement had been reached. Mr McKenzie, a representative of Rangers, corroborated that statement.

There was a further twist when Mr Campbell, a linesman, said he thought a good deal was being made of the fact that players remained on the field for some time after the finish of the game. As a matter of fact, the time the players remained on the field was not longer than they would remain in any game, he said. The referee asked him if there was any arrangement for extra play, and he replied that there was not, and before he went in he would say that 'at least three-fourths of the players were in front of him, and there was really very little time wasted in getting off the field'.

Mr John Liddell of Queen's Park, chairman of the committee, said it might be true that there was some hesitancy about the players leaving the field, but he was perfectly satisfied they did not remain on field with the instructions of the directors.

So players and clubs seemed to be in the clear. All that remained was a decision on the destiny of the cup. The position of the Old Firm was firm. A joint statement for the clubs reads:

> Although it was mooted during the week that extra time might be played in the event of a draw, it was found that the cup competition rules prevented this. On account of the regrettable occurrences of Saturday, both clubs agree to petition the association that the final tie be abandoned.

There was a proposal made to replay the tie outside Glasgow but both clubs were adamant. One side would scratch rather than play another game.

Liddell then formed a motion that was carried by fifteen votes to eleven. It states: 'That to mark the association's disapproval of the riotous conduct of a section of the supporters at Hampden Park, and to avoid a repetition, the cup competition for this season be finished and the cup and medals withheld.'

The association gave Queen's Park £500 towards repairs to the stadium and ordered the two clubs to pay £150 as a penalty.

In the space of a few hours, the riot had been consigned to history. Scottish football moved on. But there were lingering questions that the inquiry would not address. Did the clubs collude to produce another game? This is highly unlikely. Celtic's much publicised move for extra time was a strategy specifically designed to avoid a replay.

But there were sceptics who continued to believe that the Old Firm were involved in a suspiciously high number of draws. This was addressed by Milo, a columnist in the *Glasgow Herald*. Answering readers' complaints about an 'excessive' and 'suspicious' number of draws, Milo researched all of the Old Firm matches in the twenty-one years since the inception of Celtic. In the Scottish Cup there were 14 matches with 3 draws; the Glasgow Cup had 23 matches with 9 draws; the Charity Cup had 13 matches with 1 draw; and the league had 41 matches with 15 draws. He argues:

> It may appear abnormal and even sinister [to readers] that 28 games out of 91 should end in draws; but when the equal merits of the teams during the 21 years over which the matches range is taken into account I should say there is really nothing very wonderful or certainly nothing suspicious in the disclosures.

He is sceptical, too, about any outrage over alleged collusion to force an extra game. 'Aversion in a free country does not usually take the form of crowding in tens of thousands to support a match.' In short, he concludes that the twenty-eight draws can be explained by the two sides being matched in skill and that, for him, there were no suspicious circumstances. He attributes the riot to the mistaken belief that extra time would be played.

History records this as the verdict, too. But there may have been mitigating factors. Meetings of Glasgow city council and the trades council had been disrupted by violent outbursts that very week. There was disquiet in the air. There was also a growing sense that life could not stay as it was. The working class, who were thought to have made up much of the rioting crowd, were no longer content to suffer in silence. The First World War, only five years distant, would change almost everything.

One moment, however, has remained intact. The final of 1909 stands alone as the Scottish Cup competition in which there were no winners.

Frank Gilfeather

telling reporters. 'I am very pleased with our display. It was even better than I expected. With a little luck we should have been two up at half-time.' The watching Stanley Matthews agreed, insisting that 'The Scots played very well. I thought they were unlucky.' Even the Austrians acknowledged that they had been lucky to win, with the president of their association taking the view that his team would be unlikely to have a harder game in the tournament. It meant that everyone connected with Scotland now looked forward to the encounter with the world champions with a degree of optimism.

Until, forty-eight hours later, the roof fell in.

On 18 June, the day before the game against Uruguay, Andy Beattie told the world he had resigned. There is a little confusion about what he meant by the word *resigned*. It certainly did not mean that he would walk out before the Uruguay clash. The only question was what would happen if Scotland qualified for the next phase. According to the *Daily Record*, Beattie would leave Switzerland immediately after the game with Uruguay, whether or not the team got through to the quarter-final, which was still mathematically possible. However, by contrast, the *Evening Times*, published on the same day, reports Beattie as saying that 'I will see the team through the World Cup,' which implies that he would relinquish his position only after Scotland were knocked out. No matter his precise day of departure, it is evident that Beattie was deeply dismayed by his lack of power and the hostility he faced from many in the game. Beattie told the *Times* that his appointment had not gone down well 'in certain quarters', and the paper agrees, pointing out that the appointment of a team manager had not been generally approved in Scottish football.

While the Scottish public may have been shocked by Beattie's decision those in the know were not. Waverley of the *Daily Record* had known for months that things were not as they should be and he also felt that Beattie would be a big loss to the team because 'he is a real straight shooter . . . who from a collection of units has welded together a team'. As George Reid, the chairman of selectors, had been behind Beattie's appointment we can only assume that it was George Graham, the autocratic secretary of the SFA, who, perhaps resenting a diminution

3

Better than Bannockburn: the Wembley Wizards

Frank Gilfeather

In sporting terms Scotland had come through the 1920s, the Roaring Twenties as they were known, with much to be proud of. It started at the beginning of the decade when George Duncan – who was born in the Aberdeenshire village of Methlick, and had turned down the chance to become a professional footballer with Aberdeen – won the first Open championship after the Great War at Royal Cinque Ports in Kent. Two years later, he failed to regain the claret jug by a single stroke, losing out to Walter Hagen, who, along with fellow American Bobby Jones, dominated world golf in the 1920s. Duncan represented Great Britain in the Ryder Cup in 1927, 1929 and 1931 and later became a course designer.

There were other Scottish heroes. Eric Liddell looked destined to be a star of rugby, winning seven Scotland caps between 1921 and 1923, before turning to athletics and taking gold in the 400 metres at the Paris Olympics of 1924 after he had withdrawn from the 100 metres, his forte, because the heats were held on a Sunday and it would have been against his strong religious beliefs to compete. Liddell was a true sporting hero, on whom the film *Chariots of Fire* was based.

Boxing was a very popular sport and Scotland produced a long list of top competitors and champions. Edinburgh's Johnny Hill, who was Scotland's first world champion, took the flyweight title in August 1928 by outpointing the American, Newsboy Brown, before fifty thousand fans at Clapton Orient's football ground. Tommy Milligan, the Wishaw middleweight, was another star of the fight game, winning British, Empire and European championships. In June 1927 he faced Mickey Walker, the American world champion. At London's Olympia, Milligan lost in the tenth round, halfway through the contest, in what was a brutal battle.

Proud though Scotland was of Liddell and Hill it was football that fired the imagination, with games against the three home countries – England, Wales and Northern Ireland – occupying a special place in the hearts of supporters. The national team had not let the fans down. Between 1920 and 1927 Scotland's record against England was won four, lost two and drawn two. Against Northern Ireland, Scotland won all eight games over the same period, while in matches with Wales the record was won five, lost two and drawn one.

These were exceptional statistics by any standards but in the home internationals of 1927/28 the first two games were something of a let-down. Scotland had been beaten 1–0 by Northern Ireland in Glasgow and had drawn 2–2 with Wales in Wrexham. These results had made supporters apprehensive about what might happen at Wembley, where, on 31 March 1928 Scotland were due to face the Auld Enemy in the final match of that year's championship. All the fans could do was hope that the disappointing results against Wales and Northern Ireland were a blip and that normal service would be resumed for the England game.

The big priority of course was to pick a team that could do the business at Wembley. In those days the national side was selected by a committee. There was no team manager, no independent figure to make choices, something that made many Scots feel distinctly uneasy. There was even more disquiet, not to say concern, when the team was announced in front of a large crowd outside the SFA's offices in Glasgow, a gathering eager to hear the names of the eleven men who would face England. As each name was read out, there were gasps of disbelief. No Davie Meiklejohn, of Rangers, nor Jimmy McGrory, the free-scoring Celtic centre forward. And why was the name of Celtic's Willie McStay missing? These were men of some stature in Scottish football, stars of the Old Firm with its massive following throughout the land.

It's not a great side,' the *Daily Record* observes. 'Hardly a ringing endorsement for the team.' Another newspaper, *The Bulletin*, offers a similar line: 'We're on our knees and we know it. We have no native players who can be expected to hold their own with England's Association team at Wembley.'

Quite what the Scottish fans made of such comments we do not know. Suffice it to say that the pundits' analysis of the team would not have filled them with confidence.

There was also the not insignificant matter of the England side enjoying a physical advantage over the Scots. The fact that Alex Jackson, at five foot seven, was Scotland's tallest player underlined the feeling north and south of the border that the visitors would be no match for their hosts. It was no surprise, then, that the fans had plenty to discuss in pubs and workplaces up and down the land. It was the kind of controversy that would have kept the radio phone-ins of today very busy.

Why did the selectors opt for what seemed to many people such a risky, almost experimental, eleven for the biggest game in the domestic calendar? There is no doubt that another representative fixture earlier that month had a big influence on their thinking. Just a matter of days before the selectors met, on the tenth of March, the Scottish League were on the receiving end of a 6–2 hammering from their English counterparts in front of a sixty thousand crowd at Ibrox. That was a terrible result and they would also have had in mind the defeat to Northern Ireland, a country that Scotland invariably saw off without too much trouble.

The other factor was the outcome of a trial game – such trials were common at the time – three days after the Ibrox debacle. The game, which had home-based players on one side and Anglos on the other, took place at Firhill and many of those with English clubs performed well. When the outcome of the trial game was considered alongside the poor displays of the home Scots in the inter-league match there was only going to be one outcome: the Anglos would be back in favour. So it was that eight men who earned their living in England and three home-based players were named in the side.

This was a bitter pill for many in Scotland to swallow. The Anglos were considered mercenaries by many of their fellow Scots; they were men who had gone down south for English gold. In a titanic encounter – as the game with England undoubtedly was – the fans and the press reasoned it would be so much better to have volunteers rather than pressed men. It was a case, however, of needs must or as the *Evening Times* puts it, 'It goes against the grain to find oneself preferring so many Anglo Scots, but necessity is a hard mistress.' And so it came to pass that just three men who plied their trade in the Scottish league got on the London train. A well-known cartoon of the time depicts the scene; the caption rather forlornly notes that the trio would be one short for a cards foursome on the long journey south.

Scotland:

Goalkeeper: Jack Harkness (Queen's Park), who later became the chief football writer on the *Sunday Post*, was still an amateur in his earlier games for Scotland, one of the few to be capped before embarking on a professional career. It wasn't long after his appearance at Wembley that he joined Heart of Midlothian. He was just twenty-one and became the club's highest earner.

Right back: Jimmy Nelson (Cardiff City), Greenock-born and described as a fast, dour full back, was actually raised in Belfast after his family moved there when he was a child. Nelson joined Newcastle United later in his career before ending his football days at Southend United.

Left back: Tommy Law (Chelsea) reached the big time at a young age and, according to *The Times*, was 'the most brilliant player produced by Chelsea for a long time'. Only twenty, he was brought in to replace Willie McStay of Celtic.

Right half: Jimmy Gibson (Aston Villa), who was from Larkhall, started out with Partick Thistle before joining Villa. He was, according to *The Bulletin*, 'the greatest natural footballer of modern days' and had tremendous energy, an ingredient required in the engine room of the team.

Centre half: Tom 'Tiny' Bradshaw (Bury) was a straightforward, no-nonsense defender who looked the part at six foot two and fourteen stone. He was instrumental in guiding Bury through their best-ever spell in the first division and was later signed by Liverpool before finishing his football with Third Lanark.

Left half: Jimmy McMullan (Manchester City) was Scotland's captain. A motivator with tactical nous, McMullan was the player who made his side tick. His tactical awareness took him into management – the only one of the Wizards to do so – when he was appointed boss at Aston Villa.

Outside right: Alex Jackson (Huddersfield) was a major star in English football with Huddersfield Town, having moved south from Aberdeen where he had spent just a single season.

Inside right: Jimmy Dunn (Hibernian) was effervescent and enthusiastic. It was after his display at Wembley that Everton recognised his worth and stepped-in to sign him from the Edinburgh club. He enjoyed seven seasons on Merseyside.

Centre forward: Hughie Gallacher (Newcastle United) was a massively talented goal-scorer on both sides of the border. He was also the archetypal flawed genius who couldn't manage his chaotic private life which, through alcoholism, sank into a world of debt, bankruptcy and despair.

Inside left: Alex James (Preston North End) was, like Gallacher, born in Bellshill and they were good friends at school. Turned down by Hearts for being too small, James joined Raith Rovers before signing for Preston and later Arsenal, where he became a club legend.

Outside left: Alan Morton (Rangers) became one of the greats of Scottish football and tormented full backs at club and international level throughout his illustrious career. Starting out at Queen's Park, he joined Rangers in 1920 and stayed with them for thirteen years.

The biggest controversy centred on the selection of Hughie Gallacher, who displaced Jimmy McGrory. Apart from anything else Gallacher had not played in earnest for a couple of months because of a suspension and was hardly likely either to be match fit or at his sharpest. For all his goals on the domestic front, however, McGrory, a hero at Parkhead, was not seen as suitable for the Scotland cause. He was looked upon as an out-and-out goalscorer but lacking in technique.

Gallacher was an intriguing character. Born in Bellshill in 1903, he became a professional footballer at seventeen with Queen of the South, having honed his skills with Tannockside Athletic and Hattonrigg

Thistle, two local sides. It was around the time of joining Queen of the South that he married and fathered two children. Three years later he and his wife separated, by which time he had joined Airdrieonians where he established himself as a leading goalscorer with a staggering 91 strikes in 111 games over four years. Few Airdrie fans of the day would disagree that his efforts were largely responsible for the club being runners-up three times in the league championship and winning the Scottish Cup. This was a special footballer.

By then, he had been capped for Scotland and had hit home five goals in his first four international games and it was no surprise when, in 1925, Newcastle United, one of the giants of English football, came calling and paid Airdrie a record fee for the Geordies of £6,500 to take him to St James' Park. The transfer fee was money well spent. In his first season in the north-east of England he scored twenty-three goals in nineteen games. The following term, and now as captain, his thirty-six goals in thirty-eight league games did much to help his team win the first-division championship and he was hailed a hero on Tyneside.

Interestingly, in the following three years at the club, he was regarded as less successful. Despite that, he was never under the twenty-goals-a-season mark and his overall record qualifies him as a leading contender for the title of the greatest centre forward of all time, with 463 goals in 624 games during his career and an 82 per cent strike rate for Newcastle, equating to 133 goals in 160 league appearances.

Life was never as rosy for Gallacher as it appeared. There were frequent disagreements with his bosses at St James' Park while there were countless referees with whom he didn't see eye to eye. It was after one verbal skirmish with a man in black that he was suspended for the two months prior to the 1928 Scotland–England game.

Off the pitch, Gallacher developed a taste for alcohol. There was also the damaging incident in which he was involved with the 17-year-old daughter of a pub landlord, a liaison that resulted in him assaulting her brother, who had objected to the affair. Gallacher ended up in court. As his personal life spiralled out of control, his career slid and he was transferred from club to club, eventually ending up at Gateshead, by which time he had succumbed to alcoholism. In the summer of

1957 – on the day before he was scheduled to appear before magistrates at Gateshead, accused of assaulting and maltreating his 14-year-old daughter – he took his own life by stepping in front of an express train, a horrific incident that saw him decapitated. Hughie Gallacher could take no more pain but, even today, he is revered on Tyneside as one of football's all-time greats.

The Scotland team was far from being a one-man band. There were others whose abilities were almost on a par with those of Gallacher. Among them was Alex Jackson, who was born in the West Dunbartonshire village of Renton, and was something of a pioneer in football terms. He had joined Dumbarton from Renton Victoria in 1922 and a year later, at the age of seventeen, he and his brother, Wattie, headed for the United States to play in the American Soccer League with a team called Bethlehem Steel in the Lehigh Valley, Pennsylvania.

After a short time in the States, Jackson came home to Scotland, where he joined Aberdeen. His outstanding performances at Pittodrie attracted Huddersfield Town, then the English champions, and the Yorkshire club secured his signature for £5,000. From that point, Jackson, a highly confident and outgoing character, blossomed. He helped Huddersfield retain the title in 1925/26 and the runners-up place in the following two seasons.

Jackson was known as the Flying Scotsman because of his incredible pace and he was reckoned by most good judges to be the most complete winger of his generation. Chelsea certainly had no doubts about his ability and paid £10,000 for his signature in 1930, which was a massive sum for the time. In 1928, and still at Huddersfield, however, this enigmatic character was at his peak, though even he could not have foreseen his contribution at Wembley on 31 March.

The other Alex in the Scotland forward line – James – had bet Jackson ten shillings he would score the first goal at Wembley and was as extrovert as his colleague.

'You're on,' Jackson told him, 'but to make it more interesting, we'll make it a treble stake for a hat-trick.'

It was indicative of the chutzpah of those two small men with big personalities.

Alex James, twenty-five at the time of the Wembley match, started his professional career with Raith Rovers before moving to Preston North End in 1925 for £3,000. He did exceptionally well at Deepdale and, with fourteen goals, was the team's leading scorer in his debut season. The great Tom Finney, a Preston and England legend, was a big fan of James. Finney was a schoolboy when he watched in admiration as the Scot starred for the Lancashire club, and in this passage he vividly conveys his impressions.

> He was the top star of the day, a genius. There wasn't much about him physically, but he had sublime skills and the knack of letting the ball do the work. He wore the baggiest of baggy shorts and his heavily gelled hair was parted down the centre. On the odd occasion when I was able to watch a game at Deepdale, sometimes sneaking under the turnstiles when the chap on duty was distracted, I was in awe of James. Preston were in the second division and the general standard of football was not the best, but there was a magic and a mystery about James that mesmerised me.

There was however, despite the brilliant displays, considerable tension between Preston and their star player. There were a number of reasons for this: they weren't prepared to pay him higher wages; they didn't always release him for international duty; they were in division two, where his undoubted skills did not have as wide an audience as the bold Alex would have liked.

And so, a year after he tantalised the England defence in 1928, the desire of Alex James to compete at a higher level was consummated when Herbert Chapman, the legendary Arsenal manager, signed him for £8,750. To satisfy the Scot's wish for more money, the Gunners arranged for him to take a £250-a-year job as a 'sports demonstrator' in Selfridge's department store in Oxford Street. In addition, he was paid handsomely for a weekly newspaper article in a London evening newspaper, which was ghosted for him by a sports journalist.

Alex James was the beating heart of the great Arsenal team of the 1930s. He inspired the Gunners to the FA Cup in 1930 and then helped them to another cup triumph and four championships before he hung up his boots in 1937. The team revolved around James, a playmaker without peer in the English game, and Arsenal would not have been the same force without him. But it wasn't just his ability to dominate the midfield that the fans loved. Alex James was a showman, the biggest draw in football. Dubbed the Clown Prince of Soccer he started a fashion for baggy shorts, which, combined with a short, stocky build, made him look almost comical. He loved to win but he loved to entertain even more, delighting the Highbury crowds with his feints, flicks and back heels. Herbert Chapman understood his importance not only to the team but also to the box office, although there is a story, which may or may not be apocryphal, that he ordered James to cut out the circus tricks until Arsenal were three goals up.

Hughie Gallacher, Alex Jackson and Alex James. Three outrageous talents. Three outrageous characters. But there was another member of the Scotland eleven who could match any of that trio for football ability, although his personality could not have been more different. His name was Alan Morton.

Nicknamed the Wee Blue Devil, Morton is quite simply one of the greatest Rangers and Scotland players of all time. A sober, sensible, well-educated man he was devoted to football and to his other occupation of mining engineer. A stickler for discipline Morton turned up every day for training in his perfectly cut three-piece suit, stiff-collared shirt and tie. He played nearly five hundred times for Rangers, scoring 115 goals in the process, an outstanding return for a winger. His teammates thought the world of him; many indeed considered him a better player than even the great Stanley Matthews. Such was the esteem in which Morton was held at Ibrox that on his retirement from football in 1932 he was invited onto the Rangers board, where he remained until 1971.

Scotland would need not only the golden quartet of Gallacher, Jackson, James and Morton to play out of their skins but would also have to hope that the other seven members of the team, who were not without ability, could rise to the occasion. The reason was quite simple: the England team they were to face was, as England teams always are, a formidable outfit and packed with players from the leading clubs of the time.

England:

Goalkeeper: Ted Hufton (West Ham) was considered by many as the best goalkeeper in the world.

Right back: Roy Goodall (Huddersfield Town), a Yorkshire-man, was the England captain. He was sixteen years at Huddersfield, the most powerful side in the land, and the only team to have won the first division three times in a row.

Left back: Herbert Jones (Blackburn Rovers) had been a soldier in France during the First World War and took part in the famous kick-about between British and German troops in France on Christmas Day 1915. 'It was really sad to play football with them, then a few hours later have to start shooting and killing them,' he once said.

Right half: Willis Edwards (Leeds United) was with his club for eighteen years before joining the backroom team and ending up as manager.

Centre half: Tom Wilson (Huddersfield Town) was from mining stock in County Durham and was remembered as the 'gentleman of football' among his peers.

Left half: Henry Healless (Blackburn Rovers) was a utility player and not overly blessed with technical ability but one who gave his all for the whole ninety minutes.

Outside right: Joe Hulme (Arsenal) had been at Blackburn before his move to Highbury. He had searing pace and excellent ball control.

Inside right: Bob Kelly (Huddersfield Town) had broken the English transfer record three years earlier when he moved from Burnley to Sunderland, before joining Huddersfield in 1927.

Centre forward: Dixie Dean (Everton) was one of the greatest goal scorers of all time, hitting 349 goals in 399 appearances during his twelve years at Goodison Park. His international record was equally impressive: he notched eighteen goals in just sixteen appearances for his country.

Inside left: Joe Bradford (Birmingham City) was another prolific goal-grabber and is Birmingham's all-time leading goal-scorer, racking up 267 goals in 450 games for the Midlands side.

Outside left: Billy Smith (Huddersfield Town) was the fourth

Huddersfield player in the England side that day and another prolific goal-scorer for his club, for which he made 574 appearances.

*

As always the England–Scotland encounter of 1928 was a fixture that gripped Britain. Eleven specially commissioned trains left Glasgow on the eve of the big game, transporting countless fans to the heart of London. RS McColl – fabulously rich as the owner of a well-known chain of newsagent shops and captain of the Scotland side in 1900 – paid for nine of his erstwhile teammates to join him for the occasion.

Those Scots without a wealthy benefactor dug deep to find the rail fare. For twenty-five shillings and sixpence – around £34 in today's values – a one-day excursion was available with the LNER and the LMS railway companies travelling third class from St Enoch station in Glasgow to London and leaving at half-past ten the previous night. Strangely, in those days there was only first- and third-class travel on the trains. Fans set off from every corner of Scotland, though few, if any, were expected to attend the Oxford–Cambridge boat race on the Saturday.

Because travelling by rail was the only way to reach London – an ordinary supporter owning a car would have been out of the question – it presented the railways with a major logistical problem. However, where there is a will there is a way and more than ten thousand Scotsmen were mobilised with thirty-three trains leaving the west of Scotland, eleven of them from Glasgow. It was decided by railway chiefs to have them filter through Carlisle at agreed intervals. Some were sent south from there through Crewe, others through Leeds, and the railway-company shareholders rubbed their hands at how a game of football could help generate such income.

The *Weekly News* – then one of Scotland's biggest-selling newspapers and one with a huge football content – gives a flavour of the Scottish invasion of the capital.

> Now it is rather startling to find such douce buddies as Kirk elders and bank tellers flaunting garish tartan tummies and flying Scottish favours in the Strand on a Saturday morning and possibly going gyte in the afternoon if [Hughie] Gallacher scores a goal at Wembley. In the

minds of the public there seems to be some association between putting a tammy over one's head and straw in it.

Meanwhile, the official Scottish travelling party, boosted by a plethora of SFA officials but with only four players – Jack Harkness, Alan Morton, Jimmy Dunn and the reserve player, Tully Craig, of Rangers – journeyed south on the Royal Scot, which left at ten in the morning.

Two hours later the SFA party lunched in the dining car where later, at four, they took afternoon tea. They arrived in London Euston at quarter past six in the evening and headed for the Regent Palace hotel to meet up with their England-based teammates. By then, the tension had begun to build and, by way of relieving that tension, the Scottish players were taken to see the boat race the following morning, the kind of pre-match preparation that today might be regarded as unusual.

However, it helped them relax and, as normally happens in any team, there was banter, not to say the odd bet between players on which of them would score. Alex Jackson would have been able to give his teammates an insight into many of the England players. He had not only played against them, but also four of them – Roy Goodall, the captain, Tom Wilson, Bob Kelly and Billy Smith – were colleagues at Huddersfield Town.

Later that night the busy lounge of the Regent Palace, which is off Piccadilly Circus, rang to the sounds of Scottish accents. There was excitement and laughter in the air as dozens of football supporters melted into the swish surroundings to meet and chat with their heroes, the men who were to represent Scotland against the Auld Enemy at Wembley the following day.

How were the players feeling? Were they confident of causing an upset? Could they possibly keep Dixie Dean, the prolific England centre forward, in check? The questions came thick and fast until, almost on the stroke of ten, Robert Campbell, chairman of St Johnstone and president of the SFA, interrupted proceedings. He looked at Jimmy McMullan, the team captain, sitting amongst the throng of well-wishers.

'Jimmy,' he said, 'I think you should take the players upstairs for a pep talk.'

At that, the players rose from their seats, pulled down the jackets of their two- and three-piece suits, straightened their ties and bade their disciples goodnight. There wasn't much to say, and when McMullan gathered his teammates together in privacy, his speech was short and to the point.

'The president wants us to discuss football,' he pronounced, 'but you all know what's expected of you tomorrow. All I have to say is, go to your bed, put your head on your pillow and pray for rain.'

The gods were clearly listening. For, when the Scotland party awoke the following morning, driving rain swept across the capital, bringing with it a heavy pitch to suit Scotland's tanner ba' experts. The incessant rainfall was manna from heaven for the Scots and, on the morning of 31 March, despite a forecast that had promised dry weather, cloudbursts provided them with the type of conditions they longed for. A wet, slippery surface would suit the small men with low centres of gravity and the ability to twist and turn with the ball against more cumbersome opponents.

The miserable weather, however, did not affect the mood of the fans, 80,682 of them. It was the biggest ever crowd for an international in London and the Empire stadium, Wembley's official name, was atmospheric and exciting, especially when the teams emerged from the dressing-room area and on to the famous turf.

The size of Scotland's task was hammered home as they walked alongside their English counterparts. Could they really be expected to overcome the strength, power, height and athleticism of these giants in white jerseys? It was also a question on the minds of the scattering of Scotland supporters who breached security and ran onto the pitch to wish their heroes good luck before being chased back on to the exposed terracing by a clutch of London bobbies.

The teams were presented to the Duke of York – later King George VI and father to Queen Elizabeth II – and to King Amanullah of Afghanistan. It is a ceremony footballers find little more than a distraction and by the time the national anthem had concluded and the band of the Irish Guards had departed, the nerves of both sides were on edge. Then referee Willie Bell, a Hamilton man, brought the captains,

Goodall and McMullan, together for some words of wisdom and the toss of the coin.

There were no moments of feeling each other out, no early sparring. The match burst into action as soon as Mr Bell signalled the kick-off and it was abundantly clear that the home side intended to inflict as much damage as possible, and as quickly as possible. Within moments, England had the Scots reeling as winger Billy Smith left Jimmy Nelson for dead and bulleted in a left-foot shot from the edge of the area that cracked off Jack Harkness's post before being cleared. If alarm bells weren't ringing with McMullan and Co, they should have been.

Perhaps, though, the sheer cockiness of the visitors overcame any apprehension. For, in double-quick time, it was the Scots who launched an attack. McMullan's clever pass to pick out Jimmy Gibson suddenly opened up the England defence and when the Aston Villa player fed Alex James, the pint-sized Preston man found Gallacher. Quickly, the ball was moved to Morton and, once he had slipped past Goodall, he delivered a perfect cross for Jackson, racing in from the opposite wing, to head past Ted Hufton. Only three minutes had been played.

Stunned by losing such an early goal, England tried to regroup. It was, of course, essential for the men in white shirts to hit back as quickly as possible and not allow the visitors time to settle on their lead. Harkness was kept busy in goal with a display of acrobatics and agility, not to say more than a modicum of courage when diving at the feet of an English forward to prevent an equaliser. Then there was the breathtaking double stop from a powerful, long-range Dixie Dean shot and the follow-up from Joe Bradford, who was desperate to capitalise on the goalkeeper's parry.

In time, though, Scotland's half backs – McMullan and Gibson – took a grip on proceedings, protecting their defenders and looking for opportunities to instigate attacks. In contrast, Willis Edwards, of Leeds United, and Henry Healless, the Blackburn Rovers left half, proved ineffectual, surrendering that crucial part of the pitch to the Scots.

Still, being one goal down was far from an insurmountable deficit for England's stars, though quite what they thought of the wing play of Scotland's Morton and James was anybody's guess as the little men on the flanks revelled in the space afforded them, allowing them to provide Gallacher with the kind of ammunition that had Hufton working overtime. The pressure began to tell and with a minute remaining of the opening forty-five minutes the West Ham United goalkeeper was once more picking the ball out of the back of his net. A wayward pass from his winger, Smith, ended up at the feet of James and he and Gibson set in motion a manoeuvre that was to be extremely profitable. James and Jackson exchanged passes and the former swivelled on the edge of the penalty box and beat Hufton with a low shot, leaving the keeper thumping the ground in frustration. With a two-nil lead, and their fans singing lustily and completely oblivious to the rain, the Scotland side were rightly walking on air all the way to the changing room when the referee blew his whistle for the interval.

Did the supporters imagine that when their heroes emerged for the second half they were taller and their chests were puffed out a few inches more? Or had the team peaked too early? Could they sustain such exuberance and flair?

The secret, as the physically challenged men from north of the border recognised, was to keep the ball on the ground and out of the air, where the taller Englishmen had a distinct advantage. Another key factor would be how the Scots operated off the ball, finding space for teammates to send them telling passes. Oozing confidence, the team in the dark-blue jerseys restarted the game with panache as their opponents failed to restrain them. James rattled a shot against Hufton's crossbar moments before the keeper was forced to save a good effort from the same player.

There were two penalty claims by Scotland as first Gibson, then Gallacher, were brought down in the area. Perhaps Mr Bell, the Scottish referee, shrugged them off for fear of being accused of bias. As the game evolved and James and Morton toyed with Goodall and his full-back colleague, Bert Jones, Scotland's dominance was palpable. Another goal was inevitable. In the sixty-fifth minute, Morton, on the by-line, again made a fool of Goodall before crossing for the unmarked Jackson, who replicated the opening goal by beating the hapless Hufton.

Wembley went crazy as thousands of deliriously happy men wearing tartan tammies and scarves sang their hearts out. Could this really be happening? That must have been the question in the minds of many among the visiting support. But their cheers had hardly subsided when the Scots struck for a fourth time. With English spirits deflated, and the heads of FA officials in the stand shaking in disbelief, there was another shock in store. No sooner had the game restarted than Gallacher took possession and ran at the English defence, evading a series of tackles and showing great skill and tenacity. Eventually, the boot of Jones brought him down in the box. The loose ball fell for James, whose quick-fire shot went into the England goal via the body of the prostrate Jones. The Scotland dream was a reality.

If the England side were not demoralised before that fourth goal, they were now. Unable to cope with the vigour and zest of the Scots, they could not lift themselves from their gloom. It was a day on which every player wearing Scotland colours hit his best form against opposition that failed to move from the starting blocks and that bore a progressively heavier psychological load the longer the game went.

Surely there wouldn't be a fifth goal? Wouldn't the Scots be content to play the passing game and settle for what they had? That thought never entered their heads.

Morton took McMullan's pass on the left and, as he had done so often during this tantalising match, the Rangers winger crossed perfectly from the line and there, yet again, was Jackson with an unstoppable volley from close range. It was the winger's third goal, and he became the first player to score a hat-trick at Wembley, a hat-trick that would prove to be his passport to bigger things in football.

He was not a man to accept the plaudits easily, however, choosing instead to hand the kudos to Morton for his precision crosses. 'I only had to hit them,' he said.

Bob Kelly's late consolation goal for England was meaningless. A great victory had been achieved by Scotland, the Wee Blue Devils were transformed into the Wembley Wizards and the headline writers shouted 'hallelujah'. Unbridled joy filled the air above every Scottish supporter, player and official as Jack Harkness rescued the ball on the final whistle. He later presented it to his SFA bosses and today this symbol of a magnificent occasion for Scottish football has pride of place in the museum housed within Hampden Park.

Newspapers north and south of the border heaped praise on Jimmy McMullan and his brave side and their breezy approach to the beautiful game. The *Daily Mirror* uses words like 'routed and thrashed' in describing the England team. The *Sunday Chronicle* writes of a country being 'humiliated on its own soil before its own partisans' while *The Times* calls England's defeat a 'humiliation'.

North of Hadrian's Wall, the post-match analysis centred on the positive attitude displayed by Scotland. The *Glasgow Herald*'s report suggests the success of the Scots was 'primarily another demonstration that Scottish skill, science and trickery will still prevail'. Nothing like rubbing salt into English wounds.

Football matches, as any player or manager would agree, can turn on one incident and Hughie Gallacher pointed to Billy Smith's miss as a key moment. Had the winger scored in those early stages rather than hit the post, he opined, the home side might have gone on to win handsomely. As it was, they were dismantled by a team with a cavalier approach to the job in hand. The wing play of Jackson and Morton was instrumental in breaching England's rearguard. It forced England's midfield players, Edwards – a Leeds United half back for a total of fourteen years and neither booked nor ordered off in an illustrious four hundred-game career – and Healless, into more defensive roles in order to try and stem the attacks coming their way. This, in turn, afforded Gibson and McMullan time and space to dictate play and allowed Scotland to control the game.

Jackson's first goal, in the third minute, had sprinkled a semblance of belief on the Scots on the pitch and on the terracing while the second, from James, just before the interval, cemented that faith. Two stunning goals from those players, in the sixty-fifth and sixty-sixth minutes, crippled the Sassenachs and Jackson's third, five minutes from the end, simply emphasised Scotland's vast superiority on the day.

England 1, Scotland 5.

Could it have been better or more emphatic? Would there ever be another occasion on which the international side would perform so admirably? The Scotland team and its fans had to wait another four decades for such a demolition job. It was on 15 April 1967 that performances from the likes of Jim Baxter and Denis Law emphasised how good the Scots could be as they toyed with their opponents, who were of course the current world champions. The 3–2 score line in Scotland's favour did not reflect dark-blue dominance in the course of a display that was characterised by wonderful technique and sheer joie de vivre.

But, as long as the history of Scottish football continues to be written and rewritten, no match will have greater importance than when David trounced Goliath on his own patch on 31 March 1928. The Scots who travelled such a long way to cheer their side would never forgot the occasion. They sang, they danced, they drank, and they wallowed in pride. They had witnessed football as it should be played and felt privileged when they uttered the boast: 'I was there'.

The pubs of London embraced the tartan-wearing fans that night. It was almost as if the people of the capital felt genuinely pleased for them and they were cheered and applauded everywhere they went. Indeed, according to a report in the *Glasgow Herald*, even the bands in the city's hotels and restaurants played Scottish songs to mark the event.

We do not know how many of the travelling support failed to make it into work on the Monday morning, although it is reasonable to assume there was some absenteeism. No doubt, too, that production in the Scottish factories, coal mines and shipyards would have increased in the following weeks, if not months, because of the inevitable feel-good factor brought about by the result and the way it was achieved.

For football fans north of the border, this was better than Bannockburn because, unlike Robert the Bruce's great victory over the English in 1314, this was a battle won on foreign soil. Alex Jackson's three goals may have seen him crowned King of Scotland, but it was the teamwork, resilience, pride and, above all, the sheer brilliance of eleven heroic Scots that won the day.

They will be forever known as the Wembley Wizards.

Matt Vallance

4

Motherwell: Champions of Scotland

Matt Vallance

When Motherwell took the league title to Fir Park in 1932, it sent shock waves through Scottish football. From its inception in 1890 the Scottish league had been dominated by the Old Firm of Rangers and Celtic. The Steelmen had been the main rivals to the Glasgow giants over the previous five seasons, but challenging for the championship was one thing, winning it quite another. However, against all the odds, not only did Motherwell win the championship but also they won it by five clear points, scoring no less than 119 goals in the thirty-eight game programme. By any standards, it was a phenomenal achievement.

Rangers shared the first title with Dumbarton, with the Sons winning the second in 1892. But that success, the triumph of Heart of Midlothian in 1895 and that of Edinburgh neighbours Hibs in 1897 – when Hearts finished runners-up – were the only times the league flag wasn't flying over either Ibrox or Celtic Park in the first ten years of league football. During that period, Celtic won four titles, Rangers three, including the shared crown with Dumbarton. In four of the first ten seasons the Old Firm finished first and second and only in that Edinburgh-dominated 1896/97 season were both sides out of the top two.

The Glasgow monopoly on the league tightened in the decade from 1900 to 1910. Celtic completed their record-breaking run of six straight titles between 1905 and 1910, Rangers captured the league flag in 1901 and 1902 and Hibernian's win in 1903 and Third Lanark's surprising success in 1904 were the only times in which the rest were given a look-in. Again in this decade there were four Old Firm one-twos, while the blips in 1903 and 1904 marked the only occasions in the decade that neither Glasgow club was in the top two.

The stranglehold exerted by the Old Firm was almost irresistible. The first of Celtic's six-in-a-row of successive league titles, in 1905, began a sequence of twenty-seven years in which the title went back and forth across Glasgow. Fourteen of these seasons saw a familiar look to the final league table, with the Old Firm claiming the top two places.

Rangers and Celtic were not just behemoths in the Scottish game. They were as formidable and as wealthy as any club in Britain. In the days when clubs relied almost entirely on gate receipts the Old Firm generated huge revenues, enabling them to keep their players out of the clutches of southern predators. It meant that men like Davie Meiklejohn, Alan Morton and Bob McPhail of Rangers and Jimmy McGrory, Patsy Gallagher and Jimmy McStay – superstars by any standards – did not have to be sold to balance the books. Results against top English opposition show just how good Rangers and Celtic were. In 1932/33 Rangers won the league and agreed to play Arsenal, then the English title holders, for the unofficial British championship. Rangers beat the Gunners 2–0 at Ibrox and then won 3–1 at Highbury in front of a crowd of 46,000. Arsenal were by some distance the most powerful team in England during the Thirties and to record an aggregate victory by five goals to one was a considerable coup for the men in light blue.

Celtic too could more than hold their own against the top sides from south of the border. In 1938 the club famously lifted the Empire Exhibition trophy, which was contested by the top eight clubs in Britain, four from Scotland and four from England. Celtic beat Sunderland – who had been champions of their own country two years previously – in an early round and then defeated Everton – who would win the English title the following year – in the final.

But, as the Twenties roared, a challenge to the Glasgow duopoly emerged from neighbouring Lanarkshire. Airdrie split the Old Firm in four straight seasons from 1923 to 1926, but a Scottish Cup win in 1924 was to be their only concrete reward for this championing of the underdog. However, the departures of players such as Hughie Gallacher and Bob McPhail saw the Diamonds lose their lustre. Was there another club in Scotland capable of picking up the baton?

Airdrie's Lanarkshire neighbours Motherwell certainly showed promise. Their results in the mid-to-late 1920s marked them out as a team that could end the near three-decade domination of the Scottish league by the Old Firm. But who were the players who had achieved such a high level of consistency? And who was the man at the helm, the manager who had taken a provincial club to such heights?

*

Back in 1932, football was all about the players. The days of the celebrity manager were still some three decades in the future. However, had managers been as celebrated then as they are today, Motherwell boss John 'Sailor' Hunter would surely have been as famous as Busby, Shankly, Docherty, Revie, Clough, Stein, Ferguson and the rest. (There are two rival explanations for the Sailor nickname: his rolling gait or the fact that he wore a sailor suit as a boy.)

Born in Johnstone in 1879, Hunter, a centre forward in his playing days, began his career with Westmarch XI, then moved on to Abercorn. These were Paisley's two other senior clubs, the third and more famous of course being St Mirren. He signed for Liverpool in 1898, helping the Merseysiders to the club's first league championship in 1901. In 1903 he returned to Scotland, with Hearts, for a £300 fee, and played for the Tynecastle club in that season's losing Scottish Cup final.

Hunter next joined Woolwich Arsenal, as the Gunners were then known, before moving on to Portsmouth and then, in 1907, he signed for Dundee, with whom he won his only Scotland cap in a 3–2 loss to Wales in Wrexham in 1909. Happier days at Dens saw him become a Scottish Cup winner in 1910, as Dundee won the national trophy for the only time, beating Clyde 2–1 after two earlier matches had finished 2–2 and 0–0.

John Hunter hung up his boots at the end of the 1910/11 season and became Motherwell manager. The club had hardly set the heather on fire prior to his appointment. They had been elected to the first division in 1903 and in that first season must have been grateful that promotion and relegation were not automatically determined by performances in the league, since they finished second last. Bottom in 1905, they improved to ninth place in an expanded league in 1906, finishing tenth, tenth, twelfth, tenth and fifteenth in the seasons up to Hunter's appointment at the end of the 1910/11 season.

Hunter's first season saw an improvement to fourteenth, before, in 1913, they finally got into the top half of the table, finishing sixth. The club slumped to eighteenth in the expanded twenty-strong league of season 1913/14, repeated that performance in the season that followed, before climbing to fourteenth in 1916, then eighth in 1917.

By now, John Hunter was growing into management and in 1918 he guided Motherwell to fifth place, replicating this feat in 1919 before seeing his club rise to third, behind Rangers and Celtic, in 1920. Motherwell roared during the Twenties. Fifth in 1921, was followed by a slump in 1922, Motherwell ending the campaign in thirteenth in a twenty-two-club first division. They were thirteenth again in the twenty-club first division of 1923, tenth in 1924 before sliding to eighteenth, avoiding relegation only on goal average after they and the relegated teams, Ayr United and Third Lanark, each finished on the thirty-point mark.

Hunter rebuilt his side during the 1925 close season; the result was a climb to fifth spot in 1926, by which time Motherwell were primed for lift-off. Season 1926/27 saw the club finish second to Rangers, splitting the Old Firm, before losing second spot to Celtic only on goal average in 1928 and by a single point in 1929 as the top three were again Rangers, Celtic and Motherwell. In 1930, with Celtic dropping to fourth, Motherwell finished second, scoring over one hundred league goals in a season for the first time. Celtic hit back to reclaim second spot from Motherwell in 1931, adding insult to injury by beating the Lanarkshire side 4–2 in a Scottish Cup-final replay, after the first tie had finished 2–2, but, once again, more than one hundred goals were scored.

Over the years, Hunter had assiduously built-up a settled squad, and of the sixteen players used in the 1932 title-winning season, ten were or would become full internationalists. Hunter knew a player when he saw one. He also wanted his sides to play attractive, attacking football. Motherwell scored more than a century of goals in every season from 1929/30 to 1932/33, followed by a mere ninety-seven in 1933/34. He also encouraged players to express themselves. Stevenson, McMenemy and Ferrier were regarded as amongst the most skilful players during a golden age for Scottish football, while centre half Allan Craig was much more than a mere stopper, as was the fashion for centre halves then.

That single title in 1932 stands out, but Hunter's record from 1926 to the outbreak of the Second World War in 1939 stands comparison with any provincial manager in any era: fifth, second, third, third, second, third, first, second, second, seventh, fourth, fourth, fifth and twelfth; those are outstanding statistics for a club like Motherwell. He managed the club throughout the war years, finally stepping down, in favour of George Stevenson, in 1946. However, he stayed on at Fir Park, as club secretary, acting as the administrative link between the club and the football authorities, until finally retiring in 1959, aged eighty. Motherwell granted their greatest servant a pension and he lived on in retirement for a further seven years.

That keen eye for a player was obvious from the start of his managerial career. During the early years scrambling around at the foot of the table, he recruited young players and allowed them to mature in a successful reserve side. Then, when he judged them ready, they were put into the first team. He nurtured the early career of Hugh Ferguson, a prolific goal scorer whose goal for Cardiff City carried the FA Cup out of England for the only time in 1927. The Motherwell fans weren't too happy when Hunter sold Ferguson, who had scored a record 284 goals for Motherwell, to the Welsh club for £4,000, but this unhappiness soon passed, as successor Willie Macfadyen began to hit the net regularly. Much the same thing happened with Allan Craig, whom he sold to Chelsea in 1934, only to immediately replace him with John Blair, a fringe player during the championship-winning season, but destined to be another international centre half, being capped in a 3–2 away defeat to Wales in October 1933. Blair was one of six players who won their only cap that day; club-mate McMenemy was another, as was a young Manchester City player named Matt Busby, so the Motherwell pair were in good company.

In today's game, players are ready to cash-in on their talent and agents are happy to help move them around. While managers are like groceries, with a sell-by date, after which the players, bored with hearing the same voice all the time, stop reacting. For these reasons one-club careers such as Hunter's are a relic of times past. But, it is only through longevity with a single club that managers are able to influence matters. Willie Maley and Bill Struth had real power across the Old Firm divide; Jim McLean in more recent times had that power with Dundee United. These three, plus Hunter, stand out as probably the most influential club managers in the history of Scottish football. They had genuine clout in both the dressing and board rooms. Hunter ought to be lauded as a true giant of the Scottish game.

The manager's personal qualities and management style are also very important and in an interview given to the *Daily Mail* in the wake of that league triumph Hunter gave the world an insight into his working methods. What he told his interviewer, with its emphasis on good man-management, would not look out of place in a business textbook.

> Give the players a square deal. Make them happy. Have harmony in the dressing room. As an old player I am conversant with the ups and downs of the players. Make your ambition theirs and get their confidence, exercise discipline reasonably and the best that is in them will emerge spontaneously.

It is also clear that Hunter had the backing of his board. English clubs, inevitably, came calling, desperate to sign the men who had taken Motherwell to such heights. It is recorded in *Motherwell: A Football Club. A History of the Steelmen* (by John Swinburne, published in 1985) that the great Herbert Chapman, manager of the all-conquering Arsenal, put a cheque on Hunter's desk, with the words: 'I want Stevenson and Ferrier. Just fill in the amount yourself, John.' It is to the great credit of the Motherwell chairman and directors that Chapman was sent away with a flea in his ear.

Praise for Hunter's managerial skills there has to be. However, football is all about players and even across the eight decades since that title win, the names of the Motherwell team reverberate in Fir Park folklore. Half-a-dozen: McClory, Ellis, Craig, Macfadyen, Stevenson and Ferrier would be on the short list for any all-time Motherwell team, even though there will be few, if any, Motherwell fans still alive who saw them. That squad were indeed a special bunch.

Allan McClory (goalkeeper): A former miner, Hunter signed Armadale-born McClory from Shotts United in 1924. He was thrust into the first team almost immediately and gave amazing service to the club over the next thirteen seasons. He was an ever-present in six seasons, four of these, including the championship-winning one, being consecutive. At six foot and twelve stones, McClory was a big man for the time, winning three Scotland caps: a 3–0 Ibrox win over Wales in October 1926; the 1–0 loss to Ireland at Firhill in February, 1928; a 3–2 Pittodrie win over Wales in November 1935. After Motherwell he played in the Irish League for Brideville, before a short spell with Albion Rovers in 1938, then, aged forty-seven, after the war, he hung up his bunnet after a short spell in the service of Montrose.

John Johnman (right back): Johnman was Motherwell's established right back at the start of season 1931/32, with over two hundred appearances since making his debut in 1924. But, after losing his place through injury, he was unable to regain it as Willie Dowall made the place his own.

Ben Ellis (left back): Welshman Ellis was signed from Irish League club Bangor in October 1930 and within a month won the first of his six Wales caps. In his history of the club, former MSP and lifelong Motherwell fan John Swinburne rates Ellis as one of the three best left backs in the club's history, alongside Archie 'Baldie' Shaw and Joe Wark, high praise indeed.

Hugh Wales (right half): The consistent Wales missed very few games during his nine seasons with Motherwell, who signed him from home-town team Kilwinning Rangers in 1929. From then until the outbreak of the Second World War in 1939 he averaged thirty-three games a season and his thoughtful promptings from midfield provided a lot of ammunition for the forwards. He was capped once by Scotland, against, ironically enough, Wales, at Tynecastle, in October, 1933; Wales won 5–2 and nine of the team, including Hugh Wales, were never picked again. These nine discards included the great Alex James.

Allan Craig (centre half): But for his career running parallel to Davie Meiklejohn of Rangers, Craig would surely have won more than a paltry three caps. A Paisley Buddie, he joined Motherwell from local Paisley side Celtic Victoria in December, 1924. He broke through the following season and between then and the 1931/32 championship season, he missed a mere six matches. He won his Scotland caps in 1929, when he made his debut in Scotland's first overseas match, a 7–3 Bergen win over Norway, before playing in the final match of a three-game, end-of-season tour, a 1–1 draw with Germany in Berlin. His final international was the 3–0 Wembley loss to England in April 1932. In January 1933, he was sold to Chelsea for £4,000, going on to captain the London club before retiring in 1939.

Willie Telfer (left half): Like McClory, a Shotts miner, Telfer was signed from Blantyre Celtic in 1929, and spent ten years with the club, before winding down his career with Airdrie during the Second World War. Like Wales on the other side of the half-back line, he was a cultured player with a nice weight of pass. He won two caps, both against Ireland: a 4–0 Belfast win in September 1932 and a 2–1 loss at Celtic Park a year later.

John Murdoch (outside right): A local boy, from New Stevenston, Murdoch first broke through with the great Airdrie side of the 1920s. He crossed the Lanarkshire divide in 1928 and went on to play over 350 games for the two Lanarkshire sides, Dundee and Dunfermline in a fourteen-year career, which saw him score nearly one hundred goals. Motherwell undoubtedly had the best of him and he won his only Scotland cap with the club, in a 0–0 Belfast draw with Ireland, in February 1931.

John McMenemy (inside right): McMenemy perhaps suffered from the old Scottish curse of: 'Ach him, a kent his faither'. His father of course was Celtic legend James 'Napoleon' McMenemy. The son inherited much of his father's subtlety and was a superb passer of the ball. But perhaps the inevitable comparisons with his father contributed to his failure properly to establish himself at Celtic, whom he joined as an 18-year-old in 1926, before winning a Scottish Cup-winner's medal the following year. Motherwell's move to snap him up for £1,100 in 1928 represented a good bit of business. Like John Blair, he won his solitary Scotland cap in the 3–2 Cardiff loss to Wales in October 1934, when he was a late call-up to replace his injured brother Harry, of Newcastle United. He rang down his career with Partick Thistle and then St Mirren.

Willie Macfadyen (centre forward): Teammate McMenemy said of Macfadyen's goal-scoring feats in the championship season: 'He scored 52, but managed to miss another 152.' Unfortunate in the timing of his career, he was competing for the Scotland centre-forward's jersey with legends such as Celtic's Jimmy McGrory – whose Scottish goal-scoring record for a single season he annexed in 1932 – and that man-of-many-clubs Hughie Gallacher. Macfadyen did, however, score in both his internationals: the 3–2 loss to Wales in October, 1933 and the 2–2 Hampden draw with Austria's *wunderteam* in November of that year. He succeeded a great goal scorer in Hugh Ferguson and these two, plus Ian St John and Willie Pettigrew, have to be considered Motherwell's greatest strikers.

George Stevenson (inside left): When it comes to choosing Motherwell's greatest-ever player, Stevenson and his left-wing partner Ferrier surely have to be on the short leet. From Kilbirnie in Ayrshire, Stevenson was a first-choice for Motherwell from signing in 1923 right up to the outbreak of the war in 1939, before returning to manage the club in succession to Hunter, in 1946. Dubbed 'the prince of inside forwards' he had all the attributes: his close control was exceptional, he was a superb finisher and his understanding with Ferrier was said to be almost telepathic. He is still Motherwell's most-capped player. While he was manager, Motherwell won the Scottish Cup for the first time, beating Dundee in the 1952 final. His son-in-law, Jim Forrest, was a Motherwell stalwart of the 1950s and early 1960s and won one Scotland cap, against England in 1958.

Bob Ferrier (outside left): Born in Sheffield to Scottish parents and therefore, under the rules of the time, ineligible to play for Scotland, he had to be content with several appearances for the Scottish League. The former Petershill winger was arguably the equal of his contemporary, the great Alan Morton of Rangers, and he is without question one of Motherwell's three greatest outside lefts, along with Andy Weir and Davie Cooper. He had all the qualities that a winger requires: great skill, peerless dribbling and pinpoint crossing. He made innumerable opportunities for others but was also a prolific scorer in his own right, notching close to three hundred career goals, an astonishing return for a winger.

Tom McKenzie (wing half): The former Cambuslang Rangers and Kilwinning Rangers player made just one appearance in the championship season, but, by the time the war broke out, he was a fixture in the Motherwell team as captain. The war effectively ended his career.

John Blair (centre half): Stood in for Allan Craig in four games during the championship season, before succeeding him on Craig's transfer to Chelsea. Glasgow-born, he was signed from Yoker Athletic and Motherwell was his only senior club, as the war curtailed his career. Blair won his only Scotland cap in the 3–2 loss to Wales in Cardiff in October 1934. His nephew, Charlie Cox, was a member of the Motherwell cup-winning team of 1952.

Willie Dowall (utility player): The former Kilbirnie Ladeside player made his first appearance of the season against Rangers early-on in the title-winning season, as a winger, but displaced Johnman from the right-back role as the season progressed. He made over one hundred appearances for the club after signing in 1929.

Willie Moffat (inside forward): Moffat was a utility forward, able to slot into several positions. Signed from Hamilton Accies, he scored several times during the campaign, after marking his debut against St Mirren with a goal.

Willie Wylie (centre forward): The former Benburb man had the unenviable task of understudying Macfadyen, but, when called into the side, he kept the points accumulating with some well-taken goals, scoring four in five games. He was never a regular starter during his five seasons with the club, but nineteen goals from thirty starts is a good return.

*

The 1931/32 league campaign was one of the most memorable of all time. That was not only due to the dramatic nature of the race for the title but also because of the most high-profile death in the history of the Scottish game. It is a season that will never be forgotten so long as the game is played in this country.

After losing a Scottish Cup-final replay to Celtic in April 1931, Motherwell headed off for a tour of South Africa. This proved in no way taxing, a lot of goals were scored and on the eve of the 1931/32 season, which kicked off on 8 August, the *Glasgow Herald* hailed the Steelmen as, 'Again the team of possibilities.'

The *Herald*'s preview continues: 'There seems little chance of the hope that some other teams will challenge the Old Firm's supremacy,' but adds that 'Motherwell – herein lies the great hope for the breaking of the Glasgow monopoly'.

So, as Motherwell, with a very experienced squad, travelled to Hampden Park on 8 August, to face Queen's Park in their opening league game of the campaign, hopes were high for another good season. The Steelmen were favourites, but a 5–1 success was the perfect start to the thirty-eight-match campaign. The Fir Park side made the early running, but, against the run of play, the Spiders went in front in twenty-eight minutes, McKenzie scoring. Their lead was short lived, however; just two minutes later Willie Macfadyen equalised, before putting his side ahead at the break with a goal that would never be allowed today. A cross was held by the Queen's Park keeper, who was immediately shoulder charged to the ground by Macfadyen, prior to the centre forward kicking the ball out of his hands and into the net. Macfadyen completed his hat-trick from a Ferrier cross; John Murdoch added a fourth, before Macfadyen had the last word with a great volley in the eighty-seventh minute. This victory immediately put Motherwell atop the league table, ahead of defending champions Rangers, who had kicked off with a 4–1 win over Dundee, after the new league flag was unfurled over a packed Ibrox. But Motherwell were deposed from the top of the table in midweek, as, on 11 August, Rangers entertained Airdrie at Ibrox and won 2–1.

The fixture list for the season had, however, decreed that Rangers' first away trip of the season should take them to Fir Park. On Saturday, 15 August 1931 Motherwell were ready for them. Sadly for the fans, Motherwell's Bob Ferrier and Rangers' 'Wee Blue Devil', the great Alan Morton, were both unfit, with Sailor Hunter drafting-in utility player Willie Dowall as Ferrier's replacement. Without the two best wingers in Scotland, this match was going to be won in central midfield, where 'Tully' Craig and George Brown of Rangers had the better of John McMenemy and George Stevenson in the early exchanges. The contemporary reports praise Craig's range of passing, while McMenemy and Stevenson were criticised for taking an over-physical approach to quelling the Rangers' midfield threat. Rangers' outside right Jimmy Fleming had the first real chance, in twenty-five minutes, but Allan McClory thwarted him. Two minutes later, however, in a repeat move, Fleming broke the deadlock, before hitting a post shortly afterwards. Gradually, Motherwell came back and in forty-three minutes, Dowall, who had hitherto appeared nervous, took advantage of a slip by Dougie Gray to get clear and his cross was buried by Murdoch to leave the sides level at the break.

Dowall was also involved in the game's key moment, in sixty-five minutes, when he sprang Rangers' offside trap to run unchallenged from halfway and put his side in front. Rangers were still seething when, a minute later, Stevenson sidestepped the challenges of Meiklejohn and McAuley to shoot past Jerry Dawson from twenty yards for Motherwell's third. But, you can never write off Rangers, and in seventy-two minutes Fleming got the better of a challenge on Ellis, and the loose ball fell to Jimmy Smith, who made it 3–2. But, Motherwell were in no mood to surrender their advantage and when Willie Telfer broke upfield, Macfadyen's clever run distracted Meiklejohn for Murdoch to nip between him and McDonald to head home the match-clinching fourth Motherwell goal. Such was the intensity and passion from both sides that the match was described in the press as more like a cup tie than a league game.

Motherwell: McClory; Johnman, Ellis; Wales, Craig, Telfer; Murdoch, McMenemy, Macfadyen, Stevenson, Dowall.

Rangers: Dawson; Gray, McAuley; McDonald, Meiklejohn, Craig; Fleming, Brown, Smith, McPhail, Nicholson. Mr J. Hudson was the referee.

The teams were again in midweek action, Sam English netting five goals as Rangers thrashed Morton 7–3, while Motherwell travelled to Somerset Park and beat ten-man Ayr United 3–1; Motherwell's goals coming from Macfadyen, Dowall and an own goal from United's Roberts. Ayrshire was again the destination on Saturday, 22 August, as 'the famous Motherwell,' as the *Kilmarnock Standard* describes them, travelled to Rugby Park to face a Kilmarnock side that had also made a good start to the season.

This was seen in Ayrshire as the first big game of the season and what wouldn't the present Kilmarnock management give for the 12,000 crowd who turned up to see a 'thrilling match' unfold. Right from the start Kilmarnock goalkeeper Sam Clemie was in the sort of inspired form which had made him the hero of Killie's Scottish Cup win in 1929. The local paper's report tells of the goalie being 'repeatedly cheered' as he made good saves from Macfadyen and the fit again Ferrier. But it wasn't entirely one-way traffic, Telfer was praised for a crucial tackle on Connell, before, right on half time, the home side broke through. Jimmy 'Bud' Maxwell's free kick was punched into the air by McClory, McEwan controlled the dropping ball and centred, for Maxwell, who had charged into the six-yard box, to poke the ball past McClory.

Kilmarnock's second-half tactics weren't pretty, but they worked and their quick, hard tackling upset the visitors. The *Kilmarnock Standard*'s reporter writes of Motherwell being 'rattled' in the second half and only rarely able to produce 'some delightful football'. Clemie continued to be inspired, denying Motherwell a point with a brilliant late save when Ferrier appeared certain to score. But it wasn't a one-man show; centre half Tommie Smith and right back Leslie were praised for their destructive tackling.

Rangers meanwhile bounced back from their Fir Park loss to beat

St Mirren 4–0 then win 3–1 at Ayr United, while Motherwell seemed to have a hangover from the Rugby Park reverse when they were held to a 2–2 draw on the short midweek trip to Broomfield to face Airdrie. However, they put the dropping of these three points in two games behind them with a 3–0 home win over Aberdeen, before Dowall got the crucial goal in a 1–0 midweek Love Street win over St Mirren.

The Scottish league then went into the first of its two derby week-ends on 5 September. The Old Firm clash of that day will forever be remembered for the tragedy of John Thomson's death at the feet of Sam English, an incident that contributed massively to the eventual 0–0 draw. At the same time Motherwell were at Douglas Park, facing Hamilton Academical. This was a typically hard-fought clash, with the goals delayed until the final seventeen minutes. Macfadyen broke the deadlock, but Wilson equalised for Hamilton five minutes later. Ferrier put Motherwell back in front with seven minutes left, and that goal looked like being the winner until, in the dying seconds, Wilson grabbed his second equaliser of the match, so late there wasn't time to re-centre the ball afterwards.

These results left Rangers ahead of Kilmarnock on goal average at the top of the table, both clubs having fourteen points, Celtic were third on thirteen points, with Motherwell fourth, also on thirteen points but with an inferior goal average. Battle had now been joined and by the end of the month Motherwell would have nosed a crucial point ahead of the defending champions, as they put together a run of four straight wins. They beat Falkirk 4–1 and Third Lanark 6–0, with Macfadyen scoring five goals, four from headers, both at Fir Park, then travelled to Shawfield and edged out Clyde by the odd goal in five; the Bully Wee staging a late fight-back from 3–0 down to make the final minutes very nervous for Motherwell, who were without Stevenson, who was on Scotland duty against Ireland at Ibrox. The Steelmen then completed a successful month by thumping Leith Athletic 7–1 at Fir Park.

That win – with Macfadyen scoring four of the goals and taking his tally for the season past the twenty-goals mark in a mere twelve games – was crucial. It elevated Motherwell to the top of the table for the first time since opening day. Rangers meanwhile beat Partick Thistle 4–1 at

Firhill, cruised past Aberdeen, 4–1 at Ibrox, but were held to a goalless draw by Hearts at Tynecastle and with Celtic stuttering in the tragic aftermath of Thomson's death, drawing with Queen's Park and Morton, before beating Falkirk 4–1 at Celtic Park, at the end of September, Motherwell led the table, on goal average, from Rangers and Kilmarnock. All three clubs were on twenty points, with Celtic, who had a game in hand, on seventeen.

It is now received wisdom that Celtic suffered in the aftermath of the Thomson tragedy. The facts back this up. In the seven games that season up until Thomson's accident, they had accrued 12 points at the rate of 1.71 per game; after the loss of their iconic goalkeeper, Celtic's points-per-game average dropped to 1.16 – 36 points from 31 games. Clearly, his loss was felt. However, the Thomson tragedy wasn't the only blow Celtic suffered that season: Jimmy McGrory missed several games with a recurring knee injury, while other regulars spent lengthy spells on the Celtic Park treatment table during the campaign.

There was a slight setback for Motherwell at the start of October, as without Stevenson, who was on Scottish League duty in Belfast, they were held to a 2–2 draw by Morton at Cappielow. Motherwell twice trailed that day and had McClory to thank for their point after he saved a Graham penalty, with Morton leading 2–1, before Macfadyen's second goal of the game garnered a precious point. The same day Rangers thrashed Cowdenbeath 6–1 at Ibrox and with Celtic beating Kilmarnock 3–2 at Parkhead, the defending champions were again out in front in the title race.

Rangers were on Glasgow Cup duty on 10 October, beating Queen's Park 3–0 in the final at Hampden and Motherwell took advantage of their extra game with a 5–0 Fir Park win over Dundee United, in which another Macfadyen hat trick enabled Motherwell to go back to the top of the table, by a single point. The following Saturday the Lanarkshire side consolidated their lead, beating Hearts 2–0 at Fir Park, while Rangers were slipping-up, losing 1–0 to Queen's Park at Ibrox. This was a huge turnaround in seven days. Perhaps Rangers thought they merely had to turn up to win: but not even being awarded two penalties could get them two points as Queens keeper Smith saved 'Doc' Marshall's effort, before Alan Morton hit the post with his penalty. Both teams kept up their momentum the following Saturday: Motherwell travelled to Central Park and crushed Cowdenbeath 5–1, with Macfadyen hitting another hat trick to take him past thirty goals for the season; while Rangers went to Douglas Park and beat Hamilton 2–1.

Motherwell then entertained Celtic on 31 October, but had to be content with one point, from a 2–2 draw. This match came on the Saturday after the 1931 general election, one that saw Motherwell chairman Thomas Ormiston CBE elected to Parliament as the MP for Motherwell and Wishaw. The game also saw Joe Kennaway's debut in goal for Celtic, as the long-term replacement for Thomson. Kennaway had already played international football for his native Canada and for the USA and he was to go on to win one cap for Scotland. He had mainly a watching brief in the early minutes as Charlie 'Happy Feet' Napier put Celtic in front in three minutes and added a second ten minutes later. However, between these Celtic goals Kennaway, in almost his first action in Scotland, had clutched a Murdoch shot on the line. The referee allowed play to continue in the face of Motherwell claims that, in saving, Kennaway had carried the ball over his own line. Douglas pulled one back for Motherwell before the break and a goal line clearance, with Kennaway beaten, kept Celtic in front at the break. In the second half, however, Dowall equalised in sixty-five minutes.

At Ibrox, Rangers were putting five past Dundee United without reply. So, at the end of the month, Motherwell still led the table, with twenty-eight points from their seventeen games, with Rangers two points off the pace with twenty-six points from sixteen games, the same total as Kilmarnock, while Celtic were three points further away.

This close race continued in November. On the seventh, Motherwell, Rangers and Celtic were all idle because of the annual Scottish League versus English League match, which Scotland won 4–3. A week later, battle was rejoined and the top two sides both dropped a point in 2–2 draws, Motherwell with Dundee, Rangers with Clyde, while Celtic, the same day, lost 2–1 at home to Partick Thistle. At Dens Park, on a heavy pitch and against a Dundee side who were in their faces from the off, Motherwell struggled to get their cultured passing game going. Two goals in the final fifteen minutes of the first half put the home side in front at the break, but, while Alec Troup was off the park having a dislocated shoulder reset, the seemingly inevitable Macfadyen goal got Motherwell going, with the prolific centre forward scoring the equaliser fifteen minutes from time. At Ibrox, Rangers appeared to be cruising as they led Clyde 2–0 at half time, but the Bully Wee staged a great second-half fight back to share the points.

Seven days later Motherwell put six past Ayr United at Fir Park, Macfadyen helping himself to four more goals, while down at Cappielow, Rangers triumphed by the odd goal in three and, at Tynecastle, Celtic slipped further behind after going down 2–1 to Hearts. Kilmarnock too were finding the pressure getting to them as they began the month with back-to-back 1–1 draws with Aberdeen and Hamilton Accies.

The league race was now at the halfway point, with Motherwell two points ahead of Rangers, who, however, had a game in hand; Kilmarnock were a further point away in third. The final matches of the month saw no change in positions at the top, Motherwell beating ten-man Airdrie 3–0 in the other Lanarkshire derby and Sam English netting a hat trick in Rangers' 6–2 stroll against Leith Athletic. Kilmarnock lost 2–0 to Queen's Park at Hampden and they and Celtic now faced a major task in making-up lost ground.

Into December and Motherwell showed no signs of cracking under pressure as they thumped St Mirren 4–1 at Fir Park, in a game memorable for Macfadyen missing two second half penalties. They then travelled to Cathkin to beat Third Lanark 2–0 in front of a 25,000 crowd, before posting a 4–1 home win over Queen's Park. This victory meant Motherwell had gone nineteen league games, half a campaign, without defeat.

Rangers were flagging slightly, they began December with a comfortable 4–0 Ibrox win over Falkirk, English bagging another hat trick; but the following week they were held to a goalless draw at Pittodrie and on 19 December they again headed out of Glasgow, to go down 4–2 to Dundee at Dens Park, in spite of scoring first. Kilmarnock had slipped further behind after losing 3–1 at Morton on 5 December, but a run of four straight wins, scoring nineteen goals for the loss of just two in the process, against Cowdenbeath, Third Lanark, Airdrie and Leith Athletic had brought Celtic right back into the equation.

Boxing Day would see a crucial encounter in the title race, with Motherwell heading to Ibrox to face Rangers. Rangers bagged first use of the wind and pegged Motherwell back from the off. It was no surprise therefore when English, whose display was described as 'outstanding', headed home a McPhail lobbed pass in twenty minutes. Motherwell survived until half time without further loss, but, after the change round they failed to harness the strong wind as well as their hosts and that English goal not only proved crucial, but also reduced Motherwell's advantage at the top to three points.

Ne'erday 1932 brought the usual round of local derbies, so while Rangers and Celtic clashed at Parkhead, the away team winning 2–1, Motherwell were entertaining Hamilton Academical, in front of a ten thousand crowd at Fir Park. Contemporary reports praise Motherwell's 'beautiful football', but they were unable to break down Accies' resistance in a blank first half. One minute after the break, however, Stevenson headed them in front, with the prolific Macfadyen adding a second seven minutes later. Ferrier made it 3–0, before Wilson pulled back a late consolation goal for Accies, so Motherwell's three-point advantage over Rangers remained. That Ne'erday match was played in very wet conditions, which continued the next day, as Motherwell travelled to Brockville to face Falkirk and won by three goals to two.

The weather was still anything but perfect on Saturday, 9 January, when Motherwell entertained Kilmarnock, the only side other than Rangers to have beaten them that season. On this occasion, the problem was a strong wind, which made controlled football difficult, if not impossible. Killie had first use of the wind and pressed Motherwell back from the kick off. But they found McClory in international form, saving everything the Ayrshiremen flung at him and the closest Killie came to a goal was when 'Bud' Maxwell hit the bar. A Stevenson 'goal' was disallowed in twenty minutes, but five minutes later Ferrier broke the deadlock, before giving his side a two-goal interval cushion from the penalty spot, in forty-four minutes. Wylie, standing-in at centre forward for the injured Macfadyen, made it 3–0 in forty-eight minutes and Ferrier completed an emphatic 4–0 win with his second penalty goal of the day, ten minutes from time.

The same day, Rangers were winning 2–0 at Love Street, so, when the league went into abeyance for the first round of the Scottish Cup, Motherwell still had that precious three-point lead.

Their cup experience – a comfortable 7–2 demolition of second division Stenhousemuir – did nothing to cramp Motherwell's style, although their next league fixture was by no means an easy one – a trip to Aberdeen in January is never one to look forward to. At Pittodrie, the Dons' tactics were simple: make it as difficult as possible for their high-flying visitors and, to be fair to them, they largely succeeded in spoiling Motherwell's cultured outfield play. However, left half Willie Telfer, one of the unsung heroes of the campaign, popped up midway through the second half to head home the only goal of the game to keep his side on-course for the title.

The following Saturday, the last in January, saw another detour down the road to Hampden in the Scottish Cup and that's exactly the road Motherwell took, travelling into Glasgow to comfortably see-off Queen's Park by two goals to nil. Marine Gardens, home of struggling Leith Athletic, was Motherwell's first port of call in February. Athletic were already heading for twentieth and last place in the first division and relegation. Over the season Leith shipped 137 goals, five of them in this game, in which their cause wasn't helped by having to play the entire second half with ten men after right back Allen broke his arm moments before the turn round. Macfadyen was absent for this game, but wasn't missed as stand-in Moffat, having given his side a 2–0 half-time lead, added two more in the second half, with Wylie adding the fifth.

The confidence boost these goals gave an already confident side was timely. Saturday, 13 February would see them playing hosts to Celtic in the Scottish Cup. This fixture attracted a record crowd of 36,000 and they saw Murdoch and Ferrier get the goals that put Motherwell into the last eight. The victory was relatively straight-forward, and most of the post-match headlines concerned a spot of crowd trouble before the start.

Macfadyen was back and back on the goals trail a week later as

Motherwell went to Tannadice to face a Dundee United team already on the road to relegation. The prolific centre forward added another four goals to his ever-growing tally, Murdoch bagged a brace to complete the Motherwell total, while Taylor got United's consolation goal from the penalty spot. The same day, Rangers had made the short hop to Cathkin to dump Third Lanark 3–1, so Motherwell's advantage remained at three points. But, Rangers fans fancied this gap might be closed on Saturday, 27 February, with the defending champions once again staying in Glasgow – surely the trip to Hampden to face lowly Queen's Park would not be a tortuous one for the Govan giants?

This proved to be the case, Sam English helping himself to four goals in a 6–1 demolition job. But, sadly for Rangers, a George Stevenson twenty-yarder, in the final minute of the first half, was enough to give Motherwell both points from a trip to Tynecastle. The three-point gap was proving difficult for Rangers to bridge.

March began with a clash of the top two, in the quarter-final of the Scottish Cup. Watched by a crowd of 80,000 conditions at Ibrox were tricky as constant, heavy rain fell on a pitch that had a frost on top. These underfoot conditions were better suited to Rangers' power foot-ball than to Motherwell's passing game and the home side were in the driving seat from the off. They snatched a first-half lead following a rare McClory mistake, failing to hold a shot to allow Murray to knock the ball home. However, the Steelmen had chances to get back on terms after the break, before Bob McPhail's eighty-third-minute second ended their cup hopes and put Rangers into the last four.

After this disappointment, Motherwell faced another test of char-acter. The next port of call was Celtic Park and, having seen their great rivals end their visitors' cup hopes, Celtic were determined to be equally dominant. Sadly for them, in a match which in many ways summed-up their season, their early delightful play wasn't crowned by goals and Motherwell took first blood when Murdoch scored in fourteen minutes. Alec Thomson equalised eleven minutes later, but Stevenson restored Motherwell's lead at half time. This was followed by two goals in three minutes, early in the second half: Murdoch netting again in fifty-five minutes, before Macfadyen scored his forty-ninth goal of the season, breaking Jimmy McGrory's Scottish record for a single season and although O'Donnell got a second for the Hoops before the close, Motherwell had overcome a potential banana skin and were still top of the heap. But, Rangers refused to give up the chase, beating Dundee United 5–0 at Tannadice.

On the nineteenth of March, Motherwell entertained Partick Thistle. The home side began well, moving the ball around freely and creating numerous chances. However, Thistle keeper Joe Jackson, a future Scotland back stop, was in inspired form and it wasn't until the eighty-seventh minute that Motherwell found a way past him, George Stevenson getting the crucial goal. On the other side of the Clyde, Rangers were still racking-up the wins, comfortably beating Kilmarnock 3–0. This championship race was going down to the wire.

The final Saturday of the month, twenty-sixth March, offered Motherwell a chance to open up a bigger gap on Rangers. While the Ibrox men were facing Hamilton Accies in the Scottish Cup semi-final, Motherwell had home advantage against Dundee in a league match. And the Steelmen made that home advantage count with a burst of goals late in the first half; counters from Stevenson, Moffat and Wales putting the match outcome beyond doubt, with forty-five minutes remaining. They eased off in that second period, forty-four of the forty-five minutes having elapsed before Moffat scored their fourth goal. Motherwell were now just three matches from the finishing line. If they could win all three, it was game over. Even if Rangers won their five remaining matches, Motherwell would still win the title by a single point.

But could they do it?

Based on form – they had won ten straight league games since that Boxing Day loss at Ibrox – Motherwell were favourites. But, there is many a twist twixt cup and lip and here, on Saturday, 2 April 1932, was another. Mind you, Motherwell might have known it was coming.

A mere two weeks previously Partick Thistle, their opponents that day, had defied them for eighty-seven minutes at Fir Park. Surely, at Firhill, they would prove no less obdurate and it would take all the wiles of Stevenson, McMenemy, Ferrier and Co to wrestle a win out of their hosts. Motherwell tried everything they knew, but, in front of a bumper 32,000 crowd, they had to settle for a share of the points after a 0–0 draw. The same day, Rangers were thrashing Cowdenbeath 7–1 at Central Park, so the gap was down to four points, with Rangers having two games in hand.

There were no league games on Saturday, 9 April, since most of Scotland appeared to be in London, where the annual clash between Scotland and England attracted a then record crowd for the fixture in England, with over 92,000 cramming into Wembley.

One Motherwell player who was there was Allan Craig, chosen at centre half for the Scotland team, which lost 3–0. If it was to be any consolation to Craig, twenty-three years would elapse before another Scottish team lost at Wembley in a home international.

Saturday, 16 April, offered Motherwell a chance to extend their lead at the top of the table. They entertained Cowdenbeath at Fir Park, while Rangers put the title chase to one side to face Kilmarnock in the Scottish Cup final at Hampden. The final finished all-square, 1–1, while at Motherwell, after a blank opening period, the home side got into their stride in the second half. Ferrier's fifty-third-minute opener eased the nerves, with McMenemy adding a second a minute later. Then, in the final minute, Macfadyen scored his fiftieth goal of the season to complete the victory.

Motherwell were idle on Saturday, 23 April, while Rangers, who had beaten Kilmarnock 3–0 in the midweek cup final replay, travelled to Shawfield to face a young and eager Clyde team. The relatively untried Bully Wee weren't expected to put up too much of a challenge to the newly crowned cup holders. However, the match didn't go according to plan and when the final whistle sounded on a 1–1 draw, the news quickly filtered across to Motherwell: the title was theirs, since Rangers could no longer match their tally of sixty-four points, regardless of what happened in Motherwell's final match.

As luck would have it, this game, on Saturday, 30 April 1932, pitted Motherwell against the same Clyde team that had just trumped Rangers. Fir Park was en fete before the kick off. The burgh band played 'See the Conquering Hero Come' as Motherwell took the field and after this big build-up, the only question was: would the occasion get to the home side? There was no chance of that. Macfadyen settled the nerves with a fifteenth-minute opener, before McMenemy added a second, eight minutes later. Time to turn on the style: Macfadyen, who had earlier missed a barrow load of chances, completed the scoring with his fifty-second goal of the season. The final whistle sounded, Motherwell were champions, crowned in front of a massive home crowd. The happiest man in Fir Park, however, had to be Allan Craig, who had chosen this match as his benefit, in recognition of his decade of service to the club.

In the course of a historic season Motherwell had withstood all the pressure from Glasgow; they had turned promise into reality. For the first time in twenty-seven years the league flag would not be unfurled in a Glasgow stadium. Rangers were particularly frustrated: if they had taken the title in 1932 it would have equalled Celtic's record of six-in-a-row, set between 1905 and 1910. A delighted Motherwell town council gave the club a well-deserved civic reception, before the team headed off for an end-of-season trip to France and Belgium.

Despite Motherwell's continued good form for the rest of the Thirties the 1932 league season was not the dawn of a more competitive age in Scottish football. Sadly, it would be a further sixteen years before, in 1948, Hibs – inspired by the 'Famous Five' forward line – broke the Old Firm duopoly. That is a measure of just how much the marvellously talented Motherwell players and their formidable manager, John 'Sailor' Hunter, achieved. Legends indeed.

Terence Murray

5

Home Before the Postcards: Scotland in the 1954 World Cup

Terence Murray

The word disastrous might have been specially minted for Scotland's 1954 World Cup campaign in Switzerland. The organisation of the campaign was marred by incompetence, infighting, apathy and arrogance. The manager, amid allegations of bad faith and treachery, resigned during the tournament. The players who made up the squad were derided for lacking not only the high-level skills required of the international footballer but also for their lack of application. Other players, who should have been in Switzerland, opted not to go for reasons that in today's world would be greeted with incredulity. And let's not forget that the Scotland team suffered the heaviest defeat in its long and distinguished history.

The result was that Scottish football, which prided itself on having produced some of the greatest players in the annals of the game, was shown up as parochial, petty, backward looking and disunited.

None of this was necessary. Scotland could have avoided the humiliation visited on our national game in the land of fine chocolate and cuckoo clocks. The team might even have emerged from the group stages and taken its place in the quarter-finals. It wasn't to be. A mixture of poor planning, vicious infighting, a cynical disregard for the national interest and, inevitably, a large slice of bad luck were all factors in the debacle that was 1954.

*

In his great novel *The Go-Between*, L. P. Hartley writes that 'The past is a foreign country; they do things differently there.' That was certainly true of Scotland in 1954. This country, like the rest of the United Kingdom, was in the final stage of recovery from the Second World War, which, although it had ended nine years earlier still cast a shadow over the lives of ordinary Scots. Perhaps surprisingly, food rationing was in force, nearly nine years after the great conflict had ended and, in another link to wartime, all British citizens were required to carry identity cards.

For many historians it was not just an age of austerity but also an age of conformity, in which the working class, then numerically dominant, deferred to their social 'betters'. Manufacturing and other heavy industries still dominated Scottish business: steelmaking, shipbuilding, mining and engineering. Social mobility was made more difficult by the rigid nature of the economy. Most Scots, away from work, were looked after from cradle to grave by the state. Born in an NHS hospital, educated at a state school, resident in a council house.

There were of course many popular leisure pursuits: the pub, the local picture house, trips 'doon the watter'. But most of all it was to sport and the heroes it produced that people looked to for their entertainment. And what heroes they were in 1954. Rocky Marciano was world heavyweight champion, and would twice defeat Ezzard Charles in that year. Len Hutton opened the batting for England against Pakistan in the Lord's test match. At the tender age of eighteen Lester Piggott won his first Derby on Never Say Die. Roger Bannister became the first man to run a mile in less than four minutes on 6 May.

For the Scots however it was football, always football. The post-war boom in attendances might have been levelling off but the game was still the beating heart of a nation. Club football was in rude health, not least because it was so much more competitive by comparison with the inter-war period, which was dominated to an even greater extent by the Old Firm, and particularly by Rangers. In fact of the twenty championships between the end of the First World War and the suspension of the Scottish league at the end of season 1938/39 Rangers won a quite incredible fifteen. That trend would not be repeated in the years after the Second World War. In the eight seasons from

1946/47 to 1953/54 Rangers garnered four championships, Hibs three and Celtic one. Nor were the cup competitions an Old Firm closed shop: East Fife won the League Cup three times, in 1948, 1950 and 1954, while Dundee won it twice, in 1952 and 1953. Motherwell too lifted the League Cup, in 1951, and for good measure added the Scottish Cup in 1952, while Aberdeen triumphed in the Scottish Cup final of 1947. It was a pattern that would be repeated throughout the 1950s, especially with the rise of the great Hearts team in the second half of that decade.

There was great pride too in the national team. The dark blues won three of the eight home-international championships from the end of hostilities in 1945 up to 1954 (one was shared with England) and were runners-up three times, an impressive record given that Scotland was competing against a country with ten times its population. So this was a strong football nation, with passionate fans and fine traditions, one that should have looked forward with optimism to taking on the best the world had to offer.

Although Scotland made its World Cup debut in 1954 the team could have gone to the 1950 finals in Brazil. The SFA, however, chose not to compete. A decision had been taken that the team would only travel to South America if it won the home-international championship of 1949/50 (the home internationals doubled as qualifiers for the World Cup). It was a question of national pride. Scotland would not go as second-class citizens and in any case the powers-that-be were confident that its players were good enough to take the British title. Scotland after all were the reigning champions, having beaten the other three home countries on the road to the 1948/49 title, with a comprehensive 3–1 victory over the old enemy at Wembley the highlight of an impressive campaign.

After two rounds of the 1949/50 home internationals it looked like another title was in the bag. Scotland thrashed Northern Ireland 8–2 in Belfast then comfortably defeated Wales 2–0 at Hampden. As Scotland were the reigning champions the rules of the competition stipulated that all that was required for the men in dark blue to retain the title was a draw against England at Hampden on 15 April 1950. But in a hard-fought game watched by a crowd of 133,300, England took the lead through Roy Bentley and despite the Scots coming agonisingly close to an equaliser when they hit the bar minutes before the final whistle England held out for the win.

Many associations would have rescinded their previous decision and sent a squad to Brazil. The SFA, and more specifically its autocratic secretary, Sir George Graham OBE, DL, JP, refused to budge. But then George Graham was not a man known for budging. Despite the fact that he was a paid employee of the SFA – albeit its highest-ranking employee – he ran the place like a personal fiefdom, using his detailed knowledge of its arcane regulations and convoluted committee structures to get his own way. It did not pay to cross this knight of the realm and former Grandmaster of the Grand Lodge of Scotland. Many historians, especially those of a Celtic-minded persuasion, believe he orchestrated the so-called 'Eire flag flutter' of 1952, in which Celtic were ordered by the SFA to take down the Irish tricolour that flew over Celtic Park. Whatever the rights and wrongs of the flag debacle it is clear that Graham would have carried through on his threat to shut Celtic down had not a compromise been reached.

So when George Young, the Scotland captain, approached Graham at the post-match dinner and argued that the decision not to travel to Brazil should be rescinded he got short shrift from the SFA secretary, despite their close professional relationship. Young had an ally in Billy Wright, the highly respected captain of England, who put it to Graham that Scotland, with its magnificent traditions in association football, would enhance the finals. Wright also reminded Graham that England had pledged to take part even if they had finished second in the home internationals. It was to no avail. George Graham was not for turning.

The decision was not just disappointing for the Scotland players but also for millions of Scottish fans. In his book *Captain of Scotland*, (published in 1951) George Young notes that he received shoals of letters from 'Scots at home and abroad' expressing disappointment that their team would not be taking its place among the leading football nations in South America.

Perhaps mindful of the events of 1950 the SFA took a more flexible stance by the time the World Cup of 1954 came around. With the home internationals again having a dual role as British championship and World Cup qualifiers it was decided that Scotland would participate even if the team could only manage second place. And second place, in a year in which all three games were played at Hampden, is where Scotland finished. Northern Ireland were defeated by three goals to one while a hard-fought game with Wales ended in a draw. In the championship decider on 3 April 1954 Scotland lost 4–2 to the Auld Enemy, despite being cheered on by a Hampden throng of 134,544.

That game with England was notable, not for the result or the performance – both were awful – but because for the first time in its history the country employed the services of a manager: Andy Beattie. Beattie had a distinguished record, on and off the field. A hard-tackling, yet skilful, left back Beattie would undoubtedly have won more than seven Scotland caps had not the Second World War taken away his peak years as a player. Along with his more famous compatriot, Bill Shankly, he was a member of the formidable Preston side that won the FA Cup in 1938. Like Shankly he went into management when his playing days were over and gave solid service to a number of sides. At the time of his appointment in February 1954 he was manager of Huddersfield Town, where he was enjoying considerable success. In 1952/53 he had guided the Yorkshire club back to the first division, then the top tier of English football, and in 1953/54 he took them to third in that division, which remains Huddersfield's best league finish of the post-war years. His credentials when it came to the international game were therefore solid but as we shall see it was not an appointment that met with universal approval in the cloistered world of Scottish football.

With qualification for the World Cup in the bag it might have been expected that the various branches of the Scottish game would pull together for what was, after all, the nation's first tilt at the biggest prize of all. Nothing of the sort happened. The biggest problem was arguably the attitude of Scotland's leading clubs and, it must be said, of their players.

Although it seems incredible from the vantage point of the twenty-first century, clubs in Scotland and their star players considered that close-season tours to foreign climes were more important than the World Cup. For the summer of 1954 both Rangers and Hearts had arranged tours, to Canada and South Africa respectively. Rangers took the view that all of the club's stars should be on the boat in order to make the tour matches as attractive as possible to the Canadian public.

From the early months of 1954 there was a running club-versus-country battle between the SFA and Rangers. The governing body, no doubt in an attempt to find a compromise that would be acceptable to the Ibrox club, stipulated that a maximum of two players would be required to attend the pre-World Cup training camp in Ayr, which had been scheduled for May. Even this was too much for Rangers. At a meeting of the SFA executive, held in February 1954, the members voted seventeen to fifteen against a motion that would have allowed Rangers players to miss the training camp, tour Canada and then fly home in time for the World Cup. Tom Reid, chairman of selectors for the international team, insisted it was essential for the Rangers players to get along to Ayr for what he described as 'special training' and that it would be detrimental to team bonding and morale if they joined up after the tour.

At the meeting Rangers were represented by chairman John Wilson and director George Brown. Although Brown had no less than twenty-four Scotland caps to his name his presentation to the SFA hierarchy that day speaks volumes about the attitude of Scottish clubs to the game outside of Britain and more specifically to the World Cup.

> But you are going to take part in a continental circus and play Scottish
> club players against eleven freak players who are trained only for
> political prestige. It is something entirely foreign to British football.

Brown wasn't a lone voice in the wilderness at Ibrox. He was strongly supported by Rangers chairman John F. Wilson. Wilson felt strongly that the game in this country was based on the clubs, which he felt were the best in the world.

It wasn't just Rangers, or Scotland's other elite clubs, who felt this way. One man who was widely tipped to be in the squad for Switzerland was the brilliant Hearts centre forward Willie Bauld. It was Bauld who had struck the England crossbar at Hampden in 1950, a shot that had it gone in would have sent Scotland to the World Cup finals in Brazil. He was the fulcrum of the great Tynecastle attacking trio of Conn, Bauld and Wardhaugh and a prodigious talent. Despite his laid-back, almost lackadaisical, attitude he was a goal machine. During his sixteen years at Hearts he scored an astonishing 355 goals in 510 games, helping the Tynecastle side to two league titles and a Scottish Cup.

For a player like Bauld, who at twenty-six was at the peak of his powers, a World Cup would surely have been the crowning glory of a wonderful career. Not so. On 20 April 1954 when a reporter from the *Scottish Daily Express* put it to him that he was likely to go to Switzerland, Bauld's response was clear and telling. 'I would rather have seven weeks on tour with Hearts in South Africa than two weeks in Switzerland,' the Hearts man insisted. Bauld was not misquoted. This is confirmed in the *Sunday Mail* of 2 May 1954, when he gave a near-identical reply to a reporter who told him that his name had been added to the list of World Cup probables. The *Mail* man notes that Bauld 'got a fit of the shakes' when he heard the news because 'he has been looking forward to his trip with Hearts to South Africa'.

Nor did the hostile attitude of the clubs towards participation in Switzerland provoke a media storm. Most newspapers and commentators thought it perfectly natural. Commenting on Bauld's preference, and the determination of Rangers to have a full squad, the *Scottish Daily Express* opines that 'World Cup honours are all right, and something every player would be proud of, but a club tour such as Hearts in South Africa or Rangers in Canada would, naturally, be preferable.' (20 April 1954)

The end result was that no Rangers or Hearts players were considered for inclusion in the Scotland squad. Look at the talent Andy Beattie was deprived of. Chief among the ranks of those he had to do without was George Young, one of the most-redoubtable captains ever to pull on a dark-blue jersey. A powerful man at six-foot-two and fifteen stones – huge for the 1950s – 'Corky' Young was a formidable right back or centre half, and a mainstay of the famous 'Iron Curtain' defence of Brown, Young and Shaw, McColl, Woodburn and Cox that helped Rangers to so many honours in the immediate post-war period. He played fifty-three times for his country, forty-eight of them as captain, and his most famous outing in Scotland colours was probably the 3–1 win against England at Wembley in 1949. Despite an injury-plagued season in 1953/54, which forced him to ask to be excused some Scotland games, Young informed the SFA that he wanted to play in the World Cup finals, club commitments permitting.

Scotland missed the dominant figure of George Young in Switzerland as much for his leadership qualities as his playing ability. A number of his Ibrox colleagues would also have added much-needed steel and experience, not least fellow 'Iron Curtainers' Sammy Cox and Willie Woodburn. Cox was a left-sided player of exceptional technical ability and moreover someone who could play anywhere down the left side. He had proved himself at the highest level for Scotland, enjoying great success against right wingers of the calibre of Stanley Matthews and Tom Finney. Willie Woodburn's reputation has been overshadowed by the *sine die* ban he received from the SFA in the autumn of 1954. But the fact remains that he was a marvellously talented centre back and a man who took defeat almost as a personal insult, qualities that would have served Scotland well in Switzerland. In attack Willie Waddell was a player who would have given Scotland more options. A frequent provider of goals for his Rangers teammates, 'Deedle' was also a regular scorer for both club and country.

It is worth noting that both Rangers and Hearts swept almost all before them on their summer tours. Even allowing for the quality of the opposition their performances were impressive. Rangers won seven, drew one and lost one in Canada. That solitary defeat was to Chelsea, who would go on to become champions of England in 1954/55, and it was part of a sequence of three matches against the Stamford Bridge club in which Rangers also won one and drew one. Meanwhile, in South Africa, Hearts were scoring goals as if they were going out of fashion, notching thirty-six in ten games to leave them with a record of nine wins and a draw. It is instructive to look at the main source of their goals: twenty-eight of the thirty-six were scored by the deadly trio of Conn, Bauld and Wardhaugh.

The absence of Rangers and Hearts players was bad enough. But Scotland's World Cup hopes would be hit further by a combination of poor judgement and sheer bad luck, which meant the squad that eventually travelled to Switzerland was effectively a second string. The decisions made about who should be included showed a distinct lack of good judgement. Men of proven quality, and who would have been delighted to go, were not even considered. Men like Billy Liddell. The Fifer – who inspired Liverpool to the English title in 1946/47 and an FA Cup final in 1949/50 – was such a hero in Liverpool that the fans renamed the club Liddlepool. Liddell was that rarest of beasts: a flying winger who also scored more goals than his striking colleagues. He had been a Scotland regular up to 1953 and, in a distinction he shared with one other player, Stanley Matthews, he was picked for the Great Britain sides that took on firstly the Rest of the World and then the Rest of Europe. Given that Liddell would play for Scotland until 1956 his omission now seems inexplicable. It may be that the selectors were influenced by Liverpool's relegation to the second tier of English football at the end of season 1952/53. But Liddell continued to perform brilliantly for the Merseyside outfit in the lower league and would surely have been an asset in Switzerland.

The decision to leave Frank Brennan out, if not quite so seismic as the exclusion of Liddell, was nevertheless an error. Brennan, at six-foot-three and thirteen stones, was, like Corky Young, a colossus by the standards of the day. As the 1954 World Cup came around he was at the peak of his considerable powers. A dominant centre half, Brennan was the rock upon which Newcastle United built its FA Cup-winning sides of 1951 and 1952, performances that made him a Scotland regular in 1953 and early 1954. But when Scotland played poorly against England at Hampden in April 1954, losing 4–2, Brennan was made a scapegoat, and he was not helped by his status as an Anglo.

Some of the selection decisions were less clear cut. Billy Steel was a great footballer, one of the best inside lefts Britain has ever produced, a man who had twice been transferred for record fees. With thirty Scotland caps he had also been selected alongside legends like Stanley Matthews, Wilf Mannion and Tommy Lawton for the Great Britain team that played the Rest of Europe in 1947. In this so-called 'match of the century', which was played at Hampden in front of 135,000 spectators, Steel scored a quite spectacular goal. Although season 1953/54 was his last in Scottish football (he emigrated to the United States in 1954) Steel was only thirty-one when Switzerland came around and someone of his calibre would surely have been an asset. Many informed observers bemoaned the fact that he was not considered for the squad, including Alan Breck of the *Evening Times*.

Then there was bad luck. Lawrie Reilly contracted pleurisy in early 1954 and could not be considered for selection. That was a hammer blow. Reilly's goals fired Hibs to successive league titles in 1951 and 1952; form that he replicated at international level. He was in terms of his goal-scoring ratio the deadliest striker – among those who played a statistically significant number of games – ever to pull the dark-blue jersey over his head. He scored 22 in 38 internationals (0.58 goals per game), compared to Denis Law's 30 in 55 (0.54) and Kenny Dalglish's 30 in 102 (0.29). Reilly was prolific against England, scoring against them in 1949, 1952, 1953 and 1955. His two late goals against the Auld Enemy in 1953, which gave Scotland an unlikely 2–2 draw, earned him the nickname Last-Minute Reilly. The Hibs man would have been a star in any company, even at a World Cup.

Reilly's colleague Bobby Johnstone – another member of the Hibs 'Famous Five' forward line – was luckier. He was selected for the finals and travelled with the rest of the squad to Switzerland. But Johnstone's luck ran out. He picked up an injury. A wonderfully gifted schemer, who laid on innumerable goals for his Easter Road colleagues, Johnstone was also a prolific scorer for both club and country. He was transferred to Manchester City in 1955, where he enjoyed great success, becoming the first player in history to score in successive FA Cup finals.

Then there was the greatest Famous Fiver of that illustrious quintet, someone whom many good judges regard as the greatest player Scotland has ever produced. His name was Gordon Smith. Smith's achievements are unprecedented. He not only won five league titles with three different clubs – none of which were either half of the Old Firm – but also played in three European Cup semi-finals with those same three clubs (Dundee and Hearts were the other two). With his 364 goals in all competitions Smith will always be remembered for that aspect of his game, but it was his artistry that had the purists salivating. Such was his close control and skill that he was often compared to Stanley Matthews and Tom Finney. The Hibs faithful adored him and 76,000 of them came out for his testimonial match against Manchester United, a game that Hibs won by seven goals to three. He would have been a match for any forward in Switzerland but he had endured an injury-plagued season in 1953/54, turning out only twelve times for his club. Those injury problems, combined with the selectors' inexplicable scepticism about Smith in a Scotland jersey, meant that this wonderfully gifted individual did not make the 1954 finals.

So Scotland would have a first tilt at the greatest tournament on earth minus a host of wonderful talents. These were players who had proved themselves at the highest level. They were experienced internationalists, trophy winners in both England and Scotland. They could not be replaced. Yet somehow they had to be.

*

The thirteen brave souls who left Scottish shores for the 1954 World Cup finals were a decidedly mixed bunch. Some it has to be conceded were out of the top drawer. Wille Ormond and Bobby Johnstone were both members of the Hibs Famous Five forward line and marvellous players in their own right. Bobby Evans of Celtic was a hardened and capable internationalist who had formed an excellent half-back partnership for Scotland with George Aitken (another mysterious absentee from the squad of thirteen).

After that star quality is hard to find.

The keeper was Fred Martin of Aberdeen, who had supplanted the previous incumbent, George Farm of Blackpool, another who had fallen out of favour after that 4–2 defeat to England. It is fair to say that Martin was very surprised to be included in the squad given that he had only two caps – both awarded for friendly internationals – to his name.

Partick Thistle, the great unpredictables of Scottish football, had two representatives in Switzerland: Jimmy Davidson and Johnny McKenzie. Davidson, a midfielder-cum-centre-half, played for fourteen years at Firhill without being snapped by a bigger club. His colleague, McKenzie, was a speedy winger, known as the Firhill Flyer. He was a capable performer but not remotely in the same league as his positional rivals, Willie Waddell and Gordon Smith. Doug Cowie, like the two men from Thistle, plied his trade in Scotland, with Dundee. A fluent and elegant midfielder, who would win twenty caps for Scotland and play in both the 1954 and 1958 World Cup finals, Cowie might just about have been a candidate for inclusion in a 'first-choice' squad had it been made up of eighteen or twenty-two players.

A clutch of players came from what might be described as unfashionable clubs in the north-west of England. Two were employed by Preston North End: Willie Cunningham, who was appointed Scotland captain for the finals, and the man he replaced as skipper, Tommy Docherty. While Cunningham was an uncompromising full back and Docherty a dynamic right half it is doubtful if they would have been selected had other, more illustrious, names been available. Indeed Docherty felt he had no option but to leave Celtic for Preston in 1948 when he was unable to dislodge Bobby Evans from the first team. Another who earned his living in the north-west, Jock Aird of Burnley, had a distinctly modest playing career. It ended rather ignominiously at the age of twenty-nine when he found himself the third choice right back at Turf Moor. With no offers from senior clubs in the United Kingdom, Jock joined Eastern Union FC in New Zealand.

The last member of the Lancashire squad-within-a-squad was Allan Brown of Blackpool. Brown was a very capable, if injury-prone, striker who had been transferred from East Fife to Blackpool for £27,500, a huge sum for the time. He clearly had ability but not even his most fervent admirers would have mentioned him in the same breath as Lawrie Reilly or Willie Bauld.

That leaves Celtic's two other representatives, Neil Mochan and Willie Fernie. Both were members of one of the more modestly endowed Parkhead sides, albeit one that managed to win the league-and-cup double in 1953/54. Mochan, a left winger, played his best football in that double-winning season but would win only three Scotland caps, two in Switzerland and the other in a friendly, indicating that when alternatives were available Mochan was dispensable. His teammate Fernie, an inside forward, won twelve caps but scored just once. His record after being transferred to Middlesbrough in 1958 for a big fee was little short of disastrous: he notched just three goals in sixty-eight games. Jimmy McGrory he was not.

To paraphrase Winston Churchill this was a modest squad with a lot to be modest about. On the other hand modest squads have been known to succeed. With good organisation, careful planning, considered tactics and total commitment a group of players can become more than the sum of its parts. Look at Greece, the complete outsiders who won the European Championships in 2004. They fulfilled all of the said criteria and reaped a rich reward. Sadly, the same could not be said for Scotland in 1954.

The first decision of course was that a squad of just thirteen would be taken. Some have attributed this to a desire to save money but this is not a satisfactory explanation. After all Scotland took eighteen players on the mini tour of Scandinavia that immediately preceded the World Cup. Given that the staff and travel costs for Switzerland would have been in the same ballpark it does not appear that cost was the only factor. The decision to take such a small group was heavily criticised in the press, and the reaction of the *Daily Record* is typical. The paper describes the squad as 'far too small', even for a 'maximum of two games'.

The situation when the Scotland players got together for a pre-tournament training camp in Ayr was even more ludicrous. Andy Beattie did not have enough bodies to organise a full-scale training match and urgently had to get on the phone to Celtic and Partick Thistle and beg for players to make up the numbers. The *Scottish Daily Express*, perhaps the most influential Scottish newspaper of the time, describes this as 'unbelievable' and when it came out that the two Hibs players – Ormond and Johnstone – were on tour with their club in Germany when they should have been at the training camp the *Express* understandably describes the situation as 'farcical'.

It was certainly a good example of Beattie's lack of power in the Scotland set-up. An even more telling example was his role in the selection process. Beattie had not picked the squad of thirteen. That was done by a three-man selection committee made up of chairman of the SFA selectors, Tom Reid of Partick Thistle, George Carroll (Airdrie) and A. W. Beattie (Albion Rovers). Messrs Reid, Carroll and Beattie (no relation to the manager) were not even football professionals; they were directors and club officials, men involved in the business and administrative side of their clubs. It was an antiquated, dysfunctional system, one that most pundits regularly fulminated against. The *Scottish Daily Express*, for example, argues that the manager should have had full power to pick the squad, instead of being handed 'a ready-made short leet from which our team must be chosen'.

*

The contrast with Scotland's group opponents, Austria and Uruguay, could not have been starker.[1] These were countries that had a burning desire to win the World Cup and were prepared vigorously to plan and execute their campaigns with that aim in mind. Among other things that meant taking all of their star players to the finals. Austria named a squad of twenty-two for Switzerland, among them two of the best players in the history of the Austrian game: Gerhard Hanappi and Ernst Ocwirk. With ninety-three caps Hanappi, the captain, is regarded as the greatest player ever to wear the jersey of his national side. Indeed such is his status that Rapid Vienna's ground has been named the Gerard Hanappi stadium in his honour. There were other great talents, not least Ernst Ocwirk, who was generally regarded as the best centre half in world football. Scotland had good reason to fear the Austrians: they had lost 4–0 to them in Vienna, a game the Scottish press had described as a 'Donnybrook'.

---

[1] Although there were four teams in the group FIFA decided that the top two seeds, Austria and Uruguay, would play only the bottom two seeds, Scotland and Czechoslovakia.

It is hardly surprising that the talent available to Scotland's other opponents was also exceptional. Uruguay were, after all, the world champions, having beaten Brazil in the deciding game of the 1950 World Cup finals. The Brazilians, playing at home in the newly constructed Maracana stadium, had been red-hot favourites to win their first World Cup in front of 205,000 of their adoring fans, the biggest crowd ever assembled for a football match. In fact, so fancied were they that the winners' gold medals had already been inscribed with the names of the Brazil players, while the Rio newspapers had printed special supplements proclaiming their favourites as world champions. Against the odds, however, it was the skilful Uruguayans who prevailed, coming from behind to win by two goals to one. The shock was so great in Brazil that the country's greatest playwright, Nelson Rodrigues, describes it as 'an unredeemable national catastrophe, something akin to Hiroshima'.

Six of the victorious Uruguay team of 1950 would go on to face Scotland in 1954, including two who were considered among the leading players in world football: goalkeeper Maspoli, nicknamed 'the Barrier', and the giant centre back, Varela, or *El Negro Jefe* (the black chief) as he was often known. A wonderfully gifted, ball-playing centre back it was Varela who had inspired Uruguay to victory in the 1950 final, exhorting his teammates 'Now it is time to win,' in the Maracana cauldron after Brazil had taken the lead. Varela is to Uruguay as Pele is to Brazil and Maradona to Argentina.

There were many rising stars in the Uruguayan ranks, most notably their wingers, Abbadie, who played on the right, and Borges, the outside left. With world-class players throughout the squad Uruguay would once again be genuine contenders for the biggest prize in football. The Scots got an early warning of what they were likely to come up against thanks to the wonders of cinema. In the middle of May, just a few weeks before the World Cup started, Scotland's cinemagoers were treated to a film entitled *World's Soccer Champions*. It is a documentary about the Uruguay national team and it shows the fabulous ball skills of their players, which included incredible feats of ball juggling and keepy-uppy. As the *Sunday Mail* notes 'All this wasn't achieved overnight. It took hours of practice through boyhood and adolescence.' The *Mail* also bemoans the fact that this did not happen in Scotland noting, with a degree of frustration, 'that our kids did not practise enough with the ball'.

That dedication was mirrored by the incredible attention to detail demonstrated by the Uruguayan football association. To ensure effective acclimatisation the squad arrived in Switzerland not the week prior to the start of the tournament, but a full month beforehand. Nor had anything been left to chance when it came to choosing the training camp and accommodation. Uruguayan officials had scoured Switzerland for four months before plumping for a base in the tiny village of Hilterfingen on the banks of the Lake of Thun. As the *Scottish Daily Express* rather wryly notes the plan was to 'keep the players away from casinos, dance halls and of course from the lovely *senoritas*'. Discipline was strictly, often harshly, enforced and one player was sent back to South America simply for missing a roll call. Even the Uruguay kit was chosen with summer football in mind; it was lightweight, ultra-thin and comfortable.[2] Nothing was left to chance.

Given the disparity between the efforts of the Scots to prepare and those of their opponents the wiseacres of the Scottish press did not look forward to Switzerland with even a scintilla of optimism. Some indeed feared it would be a catastrophe and urged the SFA to pull out. Rex, previewing the World Cup for the *Sunday Mail*, notes that Scotland had been 'heavily criticised all season' and pronounces himself 'very pessimistic' about the team's prospects. While that level of pessimism was par for the course among the fourth estate one leading journalist, Waverley of the *Daily Record*, went much further. He argues in an article published on the eve of the first game that 'Scotland should not have entered for the World Cup,' simply because of the huge handicap they faced against sides that 'put country, not club, as their first consideration'.

So Scotland would go into its first World Cup finals with a second-

---

[2] By contrast, Scotland's jerseys were heavy and uncomfortable, 'like playing in Crombie overcoats,' quipped Tommy Docherty.

string squad, a powerless manager, farcical levels of preparation and an unenthusiastic, even indifferent, press corps.

The omens were not auspicious.

*

The Scotland team to play Austria on 16 June 1954 was much as expected, with perhaps the only real surprise the exclusion of Celtic's Bobby Evans. For their part the Austrians were a little surprised when, during the customary exchange of banners before the game, they received nothing in return from Scotland skipper Willie Cunningham. It was a small, yet telling, incident, one that said much about Scotland's lack of commitment to the whole enterprise.

Scotland: Martin, Cunningham (c), Aird, Docherty, Davidson, Cowie, McKenzie, Fernie, Mochan, Brown, Ormond

To everyone's surprise, perhaps even their own, the men in dark blue made a decent fist of that opening match. Scotland dominated the first half an hour or so, with the half-back partnership of Docherty, Davidson and Cowie performing particularly well. Chances were created but alas not taken and as so often happens in these circumstances misses come back to haunt the team that squanders them. Probst, completely against the run of play, scored after thirty-five minutes and the Austrians went in at half-time leading 1–0. In the second period the Scots again acquitted themselves well and steadily increased the pressure on the Austrians as the half progressed. In the last ten minutes, desperate for the equaliser, the dark blues had their opponents pinned right back and came agonisingly close to scoring when a fine move gave Neilly Mochan a great opportunity to score. Alas, his shot was brilliantly saved by the keeper and the match ended in the narrowest of defeats for Scotland.

As the post-mortems began the players pronounced themselves cheated, not only because of the number of chances spurned but also because they felt a penalty should have been awarded when Mochan was unceremoniously barged off the ball inside the box. Nevertheless, after all the negativity, it was better than had been expected. Andy Beattie, as managers always are, was keen to highlight the positives, telling reporters: 'I am very pleased with our display. It was even better than I expected. With a little luck we should have been two up at half-time.' The watching Stanley Matthews agreed, insisting that 'The Scots played very well. I thought they were unlucky.' Even the Austrians acknowledged that they had been lucky to win, with the president of their association taking the view that his team would be unlikely to have a harder game in the tournament. It meant that everyone connected with Scotland now looked forward to the encounter with the world champions with a degree of optimism.

Until, forty-eight hours later, the roof fell in.

On 18 June, the day before the game against Uruguay, Andy Beattie told the world he had resigned. There is a little confusion about what he meant by the word *resigned*. It certainly did not mean that he would walk out before the Uruguay clash. The only question was what would happen if Scotland qualified for the next phase. According to the *Daily Record*, Beattie would leave Switzerland immediately after the game with Uruguay, whether or not the team got through to the quarter-final, which was still mathematically possible. However, by contrast, the *Evening Times*, published on the same day, reports Beattie as saying that 'I will see the team through the World Cup,' which implies that he would relinquish his position only after Scotland were knocked out. No matter his precise day of departure it is evident that Beattie was deeply dismayed by his lack of power and the hostility he faced from many in the game. Beattie told the *Times* that his appointment had not gone down well 'in certain quarters' and the paper agrees, pointing out that 'the appointment of a team manager had not been generally approved in Scottish football'.

While the Scottish public may have been shocked by Beattie's decision those in the know were not. Waverley of the *Daily Record* 'had known for months' that things were not as they should be and he also felt that Beattie would be a big loss to the team because 'he is a real straight shooter . . . who from a collection of units has welded together a team.' As George Reid, the chairman of selectors, had been behind Beattie's appointment we can only assume that it was George Graham, the autocratic secretary of the SFA, who, perhaps resenting a diminution in his power and influence, had put the knife into Beattie. It is certainly true that in the days before Beattie was appointed Graham and George Young, the Rangers and Scotland captain, had dealt with tactics and other team matters, the selection of personnel aside.

Whatever the precise circumstances of Beattie's resignation the timing could hardly have been worse. Scotland needed to beat the world champions if there was to be any chance of reaching the next phase of the competition. A very difficult task had been rendered well-nigh impossible.

Scotland made no changes to the eleven that had performed so creditably against Austria for the game with the South Americans in Basle. But that is where the similarities end. They were crushed by a team of all the talents playing at the very top of their game. The Uruguay wingers, Borges and Abbadie, were outstanding. Borges, on the left wing, got a hat trick but that was far from his only contribution. He ripped the Scotland defence to shreds time and again giving Scotland right back and team captain Willie Cunningham the worst ninety minutes he had ever experienced on a football pitch. On the other flank Abbadie out-played Jock Aird to such an extent that when asked after the game what he thought of Uruguay's right winger the bewildered Scot replied: 'I don't know. I never saw him.'

It was 2–0 at the break, not yet a disaster, but in the second half the South Americans, sensing that the game was done and dusted, relaxed and began to play a very open and expansive game. Faced with sublime footballers playing with complete freedom the Scots crumbled and lost a further five goals. That 7–0 drubbing is the biggest margin of defeat ever suffered by a Scotland team, either before or since.

Despite the misgivings about the whole enterprise in the weeks leading up to the finals the reaction from the Scottish press was nevertheless savage. The *Scottish Daily Express* got the ball rolling, declaring that 'The Scotland team are recovering from the worst humiliation they have ever had on the football field.' The *Daily Record* was no less scathing, arguing that 'We are an old country in football terms but now we play like old men.' Alan Breck in the *Evening Times* was part of the consensus, and emphasises how far Scotland had fallen behind: 'The

Uruguayans played football not in our world . . . . They have a team of superlative athletes . . . and are unsurpassed in making the ball do the work.' Harry Swan, president of the SFA, no doubt devastated by the debacle he had just witnessed, was grateful for small mercies, insisting that it could have been a cricket score 'if the Uruguayans had really pressed home their advantage'.

They say that laughter is the best medicine and we are fortunate that Tommy Docherty was on hand to give us the benefit of his undoubted wit. Bearing in mind that the game was played in extremely hot cond-itions the Doc would later reflect that Willie Cunningham had spent all afternoon trying to catch Carlos Borges and ended up with a sun-burnt tongue. The other full back, Jock Aird, Docherty believes, lacked only one thing: ability. While keeper Fred Martin was 'like a crocus' because he only came out once a year. (Perhaps Docherty wasn't too wide of the mark when it came to Martin. In 1955 he again lost seven goals while playing for Scotland against England.) It was no surprise, concludes the Doc that 'we were home before the postcards'.

However, it was no joke for the Scotland players or the SFA and it was doubly unfortunate that the Uruguay game was the first to be broadcast live to the Scottish nation. After a defeat of that magnitude lessons should have been learnt. They were not. Club football would continue to be given the highest priority at the expense of the national team. Scotland would not appoint a manager with real authority over team matters for another decade. The basic skills, practised so assidu-ously by the South Americans, would continue to be ignored, a failure that has continued to this day.

Is it realistic to suppose that the national team could have avoided the indignities heaped upon it in Switzerland? After all Uruguay were the world champions and would go on to beat England in the quarter finals before being eliminated in the semis by the tournament favourites (and eventual beaten finalists) Hungary. Austria too were excellent, fielding the strongest side in their history, which enabled them to finish in third place in 1954.

Failure however was not inevitable. Given proper preparation, a manager with real authority over team matters and unity within the football establishment the outcome would have been significantly different. And that is without factoring in the most important element of all: the unavailability of such a large number of leading players, whether through injury, club commitments or poor decision-making by the selectors.

Surely a team like this would have beaten Austria and surely a team like this – not one of whose members played in the finals – would have beaten Austria and made a game of it against Uruguay.

Scotland: George Farm (Blackpool), George Young (Rangers), Sammy Cox (Rangers), Willie Woodburn (Rangers), Frank Brennan (Newcastle United), Billy Steel (Dundee), Gordon Smith (Hibs), Lawrie Reilly (Hibs), Willie Bauld (Hearts), Bobby Johnstone (Hibs), Billy Liddell (Liverpool)

I rest my case.

Ronnie Esplin

6

Nearly Ten Past Haffey:
England 9, Scotland 3

Ronnie Esplin

On 12 April 1961, Yuri Gagarin became the first man to travel in to space. The Russian cosmonaut struck a major blow for the USSR in their Cold War race against the USA to put a man on the moon. If Scotland had had the capability, both superpowers may have been beaten in their quest by eleven Scottish footballers just three days later following their 9–3 trouncing by England at Wembley. There is no black hole in the universe darker than the mood which enveloped a country proud of its place in football history in the wake of that defeat.

However, as is often the case with disasters, football or otherwise, it is humour that is used as an antidote to the pain. In terms of that day in London, it has centred around keeper Frank Haffey. It was claimed that the Celtic number one, then aged twenty-two, wouldn't catch the orange ball and that the Rangers players, Bobby Shearer, Eric Caldow and Davie Wilson, wouldn't kick it. And what time was it? Nearly ten past Haffey, of course. Scotland striker Denis Law returned to the dressing room to find the apparently unconcerned Glaswegian singing in the bath before waving at angry Scotland fans as the team coach left the stadium. Anecdotes polished and embellished over time? Who knows, but what is certain is that Scotland lost by a record score-line to the Auld Enemy in what remains our heaviest defeat since a 7–0 drubbing by Uruguay in the 1954 World Cup.

Yet after fifty-five minutes a star-studded England side led only

3–2 and with twelve minutes or so remaining it was 5–3, a respectable if disappointing score-line. However, the game spun out of control late on and left the visitors – and Haffey in particular – with an unwanted legacy.

So what went wrong?

The 1960s had just started to swing when Scotland travelled to north-west London for what was a home-international championship decider. The round-robin tournament, which involved Scotland, England, Northern Ireland and Wales, with games played over the course of the season, had begun in 1883/84 and was an important part of the football calendar. Traditionally, Scotland had always measured itself against England. It had little choice in those more parochial times. The World Cup had not yet grown into a sporting behemoth while the European Championships had begun as recently as 1960 (as the European Nations Cup) and had only four teams in its inaugural finals.

Scotland could have gone to the World Cup finals in 1950. FIFA had decreed that the top two teams in the 1950 home internationals would be guaranteed a place in that year's World Cup finals to be held in Brazil. However, the Scottish Football Association decided it would only send a team if the national side topped the group and refused to relent when it came second to England. FIFA kept the same qualification criteria for the 1954 World Cup and Scotland again finished second in the home internationals. This time the SFA relented and for the first time Scotland sent a team to the World Cup finals. It was hardly an auspicious debut because, after losing narrowly to Austria, Scotland then went down to that humiliating 7–0 defeat to world champions Uruguay.

Although results in the home internationals did not count when qualification for the 1962 World Cup in Chile was decided the games against Northern Ireland, Wales and above all England retained a high degree of importance for most patriotic Scots. With the Scottish National Party growing but still on the fringes of mainstream British politics, and with the Second World War still in living memory, most of Scotland remained comfortable with a dual Scottish/British identity. The football field, rather than the political arena, was the place for any nationalist frustrations to be released.

Britain was working its way through the austere post-war years and had yet fully to embrace the more liberal attitudes that would characterise the sixties. Deference to authority remained deep-rooted in the British psyche and that sense of place and position was neatly encapsulated by SFA councillor Tom Paterson, whose assessment of the Wembley mauling focused on the antics, rather than the ability, of the Scottish players. The patron of the Football Association, Her Majesty The Queen, and His Royal Highness The Prince Philip, Duke of Edinburgh, past president of the Football Association, had witnessed a tetchy performance from those in dark blue, which led Paterson to claim that it had been a 'most unhappy show from the point of view of playing and conduct. It reflected poorly on us before the Queen and the Duke. Some of the players couldn't take it.'

Hierarchical power structures were as important in football as they were in society but the Scotland players had no one to keep them in check. After effectively finishing his career with Rangers, Ian McColl had been installed as manager of the national team but it was a nominal appointment. An SFA selection committee picked the side. It had been thus since the beginning of international football although the national manager would in time assume total control.

Ian St John, one of three Motherwell players who played on that fateful day at Wembley, recalls the shambolic nature of international football when he began his Scotland career.

> People will think it was weird that selectors picked the team and that there was no manager but that's the way it was. When I started playing for Scotland we had no manager and Dawson Scott was the trainer, as in the man who treated the injuries and so on. He was actually a medical man so that put him up a level from most of the other trainers in the game but there was no coaching, no preparation and no team talks.
>
> The captain had a bit of responsibility in the dressing room but as far as training was concerned we would just get the ball out and play five-a-sides. Ian McColl came in but he had no coaching experience and no power. It wasn't fair to put him in that position. The England manager was Walter Winterbottom, who was head of the

coaching at the FA, so he was more advanced and knowledgeable. Ian had just finished playing for Rangers and Jim Baxter was still calling him by his first name, there was no 'boss' or 'gaffer'. At training Baxter would say, 'come on Ian, let's get the ball out'.

The day before one game we had a wee training session at one end of the pitch where we practised attacking free-kicks. We went through a few simple routines and then Ian said, 'That's enough of the attacking free kicks, let's go down to the other end and try defending free kicks.' It was a wee bit embarrassing.

It wasn't just that kind of thing, we were so far behind everyone else in so many ways. The first time I went with Scotland to Ireland the players brought their golf clubs with them! I wasn't into golf then so I didn't have clubs. So you had the situation where the day before an international game, the Scotland players were out playing golf.

The selectors didn't bother. All they wanted was a jolly, although they were tight with our expenses and the players were kept in their place. When I was at Motherwell I had to get the bus into Glasgow for international games and get a bus back home with the fans. When I later went to Liverpool I had to get second-class train tickets up from England.

When we played Northern Ireland the whole Scotland party got the boat to Belfast along with the punters. The SFA were too tight to fly us over. Most of the Scottish supporters were on the bevvy and marauding all over the place. I was sharing a bunk with Eric Caldow and we had to stay inside.

If the method of team selection in the 1960s appears outdated then the typical 2-3-5 tactics of that era look positively antiquated but it was a time when football was mostly about entertainment. The accent was on attack, which invariably led to goals. In the 1961 home internationals there were forty goals scored in six matches, a ratio of 6.66 goals a game, a statistic that would give modern-day coaches heart failure.

Rangers legend Caldow now works in the hospitality suites at Ibrox on match days and he mourns the way football has changed.

I'm not a fan of modern-day football, especially in Scotland. It's rubbish to watch. It's ridiculous the difference in playing styles from then until now. In my day it was attack, attack, attack. Teams play with just one striker these days but we played with five forwards. What chance has one striker got?

It must be easy for defences now. If you are a full back you haven't got a job to do because teams don't play with wingers. When I played you had wingers in every team and good wingers who took you on. It is too defensive now. These days goalkeepers are lucky if they have six saves to make in an hour and a half. I wouldn't pay to watch it.

Plenty of people, though, were watching football in Britain in the 1950s and 1960s. The healthy post-war attendances were still holding up and 100,000 crowds were the norm at big games at Wembley, with even bigger attendances at Hampden. Those fans keen on international football got their money's worth that season. On 8 October 1960, England began the home internationals with a 5–2 thrashing of Northern Ireland in Belfast, with Jimmy Greaves (2), Bobby Smith, Bobby Charlton and Bryan Douglas on the score sheet while later in the month Wales beat Scotland 2–0 at Ninian Park in Cardiff. In the next round of fixtures, played in November, Scotland also beat Northern Ireland 5–2, at Hampden. Rangers striker Ralph Brand grabbed a double with Alex Young, Denis Law and Caldow's penalty completing the scoring. England again scored five against Wales at Wembley thanks to Greaves (2), Charlton, Smith and Johnny Haynes with the wonderfully named Ken Leek scoring for Wales.

Three days before the Scots travelled to Wembley for the decisive match in that year's championship, Wales beat Northern Ireland 5–1 at Windsor Park.

There were positive signs for Scotland in the lead-up to the Wembley game. On 22 March, a Scottish League select beat their English counterparts 3–2 at Ibrox. Both countries fielded sides close to the ones that would appear at Wembley weeks later. There was another boost for the Scottish game when Rangers beat highly fancied Wolves 2–0 in the first leg of their European Cup Winners Cup semi-final at Ibrox, and later completed the job at Molineux with a goalless draw. (The Light Blues would lose the two-leg final to Fiorentina.) However, the *Glasgow Herald's* Cyril Horne warned against reading too much in to the inter-league result, arguing that 'the lethargy of Greaves and Charlton had to be seen to be believed'.

Live televised press conferences before international games to announce twenty-two-man squads or suchlike was for the future. Caldow remembers how he found out if he had been selected. 'The team would be picked, for instance, on a Wednesday night and you read it the next day in the papers. That was how you found out if you were playing or not.'

On 2 April 1961, the *Sunday Mail* reported that the SFA selectors would meet in private the following day to pick the team, and journalist Willie Allison claimed that Rangers' precocious new talent, Jim Baxter, was 'still a long way from the tough tackler needed for this match'. Slim Jim would never become a tough tackler but he would in time make his mark on the fixture. The *Glasgow Herald* claimed that the England selectors had picked their team in less than an hour. There was to be one change to the side that had thumped Wales 5–1, Ron Springett returning in goals at the expense of Alan Hodgkinson (a future Scotland goalkeeping coach). It was also noted that England had called upon only twelve players in their previous five games, a consistency that had not occurred since the Second World War.

Cyril Horne was right to urge caution. Scotland had not beaten England in a decade and were about to face some great players who were beginning to cash in on their fame and talent. The wage cap in English football – which meant the best players in Scotland were often better remunerated than their English counterparts – was in the process of ending. When it did, Johnny Haynes's earnings at Fulham famously rose from £20 per week to £100 per week, making him the first player to earn a three-figure sum for a week's work, something that shocked the nation. At a time when you could buy a new house in Bishopbriggs, Glasgow, for £2,285, the *Glasgow Herald* appeared to recognise the early-warning signals for football's finances and in an editorial muses that the twenty-two players who would be on show at Wembley were worth 'hundreds of thousands of pounds,' citing Greaves's £73,000 move to AC Milan and calling it 'all very strange'.

But it was a far cry from the money-obsessed game that football

The resignation of manager Andy Beattie, in the midst of the 1954 World Cup, Scotland's first venture in that august competition, was yet another body blow in what turned out to be a disastrous campaign. (courtesy Mirrorpix)

(*left*) The great Queen's Park team, which, quite incredibly, went unbeaten for almost a decade.

Geniuses all.
(*clockwise, from left*) Hughie Gallacher, Alan Morton and Alex James were not only Wembley Wizards but also three of the greatest players in football history. (courtesy Colorsport)

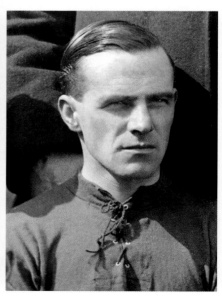

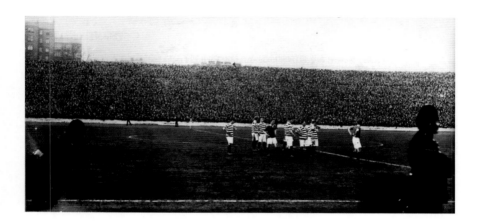

There were no winners. The 1909 Scottish Cup was withheld after Celtic and Rangers fans rioted after the final at Hampden. (*above*) The teams leave the field at the end of the game. (*below*) The match report from the *Daily Record and Mail*. (courtesy Mirrorpix)

Motherwell are champions. In 1931/32 the Fir Park side achieved what many thought was impossible by taking the league title away from Glasgow. (*above left*) The legendary Motherwell manager John 'Sailor' Hunter in the late 1920s. (*above right*) Hunter in later life. (author collection) (*below*) The Motherwell team that won the title. (*back row*) Johnman, Wales, Craig, McClory, Telfer, Hunter (*front row*) Murdoch, McMenemy, McFadyen, Stevenson, Ferrier (courtesy Mirrorpix)

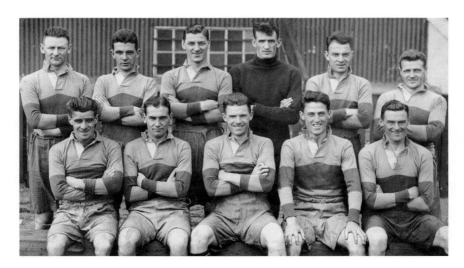

(*above left*) Ally MacLeod in confident mood in May 1978, a few weeks before the start of the World Cup finals in Argentina. (*above right*) Ally MacLeod in the depths of despair as Scotland's World Cup hopes crumble. (*below*) The great Hampden send-off: in hindsight this event, which took place before a ball had been kicked in Argentina, must be filed in the unwise category. (courtesy Mirrorpix)

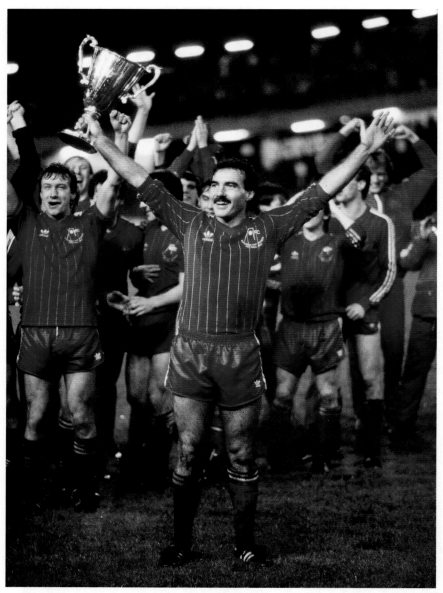

Willie Miller holds aloft the European Cup Winners' Cup trophy for 1983. Aberdeen had just beaten Real Madrid by two goals to one in Gothenburg. (courtesy Colorsport)

Jock Stein's death in Cardiff on 10 September 1985 was a shattering
blow for Scottish football. It was scant consolation that the 1–1 draw
Scotland achieved would set the nation on the road to the World
Cup finals of 1986. (*above*) In the dugout Stein (*seated, second left*)
with, among others, Alex Ferguson. (*below*) Stein suffers a fatal heart
attack. (courtesy Colorsport)

The appointment of Berti Vogts as Scotland manager in 2002 was hailed as a bold and innovative move. Sadly, it did not work out either for *der terrier* or for Scotland. (courtesy Colorsport)

would become. It was the thought of beating England on their own patch that got the Scottish media salivating and there was no better prospect for the Scotland support. The 'Wembley weekend' was the Scottish male working class at play, even if, as St John recalls, 'it was mostly Rangers fans who supported Scotland at that time'.

The Empire stadium, to give the famous ground its proper name, was as much a shrine to Scots fans as Hampden Park and the Big Smoke had long held a fascination for people north of the border. Tens of thousands of supporters, shaped and hardened by the shipyards, coal mines and steelworks of industrial Scotland, would contribute their weekly subs to the local Wembley club and looked forward to the raucous and alcohol-fuelled trip south.

That week in April, while the world gasped at the new frontiers that were being bravely explored by Gagarin, Scotland's focus remained firmly on north-west London. It emerged that three players were doubts: first-choice keeper Lawrie Leslie, Bert McCann and Caldow; as a result Haffey and Kennedy (both Celtic) and Baxter were put on stand-by. As it transpired, Leslie failed to recover from an eye injury and the Parkhead keeper was handed only his second cap. Haffey had made his debut twelve months earlier in a 1–1 draw against England at Hampden and had saved a Bobby Charlton penalty. Despite those heroics he did not appear to be brimming with confidence. 'I don't like the idea of last-minute call-ups. It would be better if we knew the Monday before the game . . . I hope to do Scotland justice,' he told the press.

Caldow recovered from a knock to take his place in the side as skipper and McCann also made the starting eleven after a rather unusual ailment threatened to cost him his place, as the former Motherwell player explains.

> I had an operation the night before the game to stop my nose bleeding. Only a couple of people knew about my problem. It was cloak-and-dagger stuff and at first the doctor we visited didn't want to operate in case it got worse. Eventually he was persuaded but it was late when I got back to the hotel, about two o' clock, and I was up at eight for a fitness test.
>
> The trainer Dawson Scott thought I wasn't fit but Ian McColl said

I had to play and, as he wasn't keen to make another change, I did. But there was more than that which wasn't right about the whole game. We had journeyed down overnight on the train and we couldn't sleep.

Our hotel was not as close to the ground as it should have been so the journey to Wembley was long and arduous. The roads were blocked with cars and buses and we staggered off the coach not feeling at our best. England looked fresher and fitter.

Turning up at Wembley fresh and fit would not have been a priority for the travelling support, which helped pack the stadium to capacity to see Scotland line up as follows: Haffey (Celtic), Shearer (Rangers), Caldow (Rangers); Mackay (Tottenham Hotspur), McNeill (Celtic), McCann (Motherwell); MacLeod (Hibernian), Law (Manchester City), St John (Motherwell), Quinn (Motherwell), Wilson (Rangers).

It was a very inexperienced side. Shearer, McNeill, MacLeod and Quinn were making their debuts. Wilson was playing for the third time while McCann and St John were earning their fifth and seventh caps respectively. Caldow was Scotland's most experienced player with twenty-eight appearances.

Winterbottom's England lined up: Springett (Sheffield Wednesday), Armfield (Blackpool), McNeil (Middlesbrough); Robson (West Bromwich Albion), Swan (Sheffield Wednesday), Flowers (Wolverhampton Wanderers); Douglas (Blackburn Rovers), Greaves (Chelsea), Smith (Tottenham Hotspur), Haynes (Fulham), Charlton (Manchester United).

Jimmy Greaves, a legend at both Spurs and Chelsea, was in the England squad that won the World Cup in 1966 under Alf Ramsay but he maintains that Winterbottom's side were better.

In 1960/61 Walter Winterbottom was creating an England team I felt was good enough to go on and win the 1962 World Cup in Chile. . . . The team of 1961 was actually better than the team that won the World Cup in 1966 . . . but lost three top players, Peter Swan, Bobby Smith and Bobby Robson. . . . A great run of results began in October 1960 with a 5–2 win over Northern Ireland in Belfast. A fortnight later we won 9–0 in Luxembourg and a week later a 4–2 win in Spain came before a 5–1 win over Wales. We weren't just beating teams, we were steamrollering them. In six weeks, in four games, England had scored twenty-three goals . . . but the best performance was still to come.

By contrast, Scotland were going through a fallow period and aside from their decade-long famine against England, they had only won seven out of their previous twenty-five games.

The slim and rather formal match programme, which cost one shilling, had been published too early to acknowledge the change in Scotland's last line of defence but it confirms that three of the greatest players ever to wear an England shirt – Greaves, Charlton and Haynes – were fit and on form. Fine players like Bobby Smith, future England manager Bobby Robson and Jimmy Armfield were more than able confederates.

The *Scottish Daily Express*'s 'Voice of Football', John Mackenzie, profiled the Scotland team with Leslie described as an 'automatic choice' while it is revealed that Shearer was making his debut after ten years as a senior player. Caldow was making his third appearance at Wembley while Dave Mackay, somewhat presciently, is described as the 'controversial character of the Scottish side. Some want him in – some don't . . . [he is] classed by many as the best wing-half in Britain today.' MacKenzie describes debutant McNeill as a 'stalwart 21-year-old' while McCann was revealed to be a student of languages. MacLeod, apparently, had made sure of his trip to Wembley with 'another clever game' against the English League the previous month at Ibrox. Law had just become Britain's most expensive player when he was transferred from Huddersfield Town to Manchester City for £53,000 and, MacKenzie notes, 'carries the burden with complete unconcern' and his 'super-confident, restless style stamps him, and although still young enough for the under-23 side, as one of football's greats.' St John, a 'restless bundle of energy' had 'form and favour' while Quinn, winning his first cap, was hailed as brilliant while the versatility of outside left Wilson was noted. Curiously, there is no mention of either Winterbottom or McColl.

Traditional British pomp and ceremony permeated the pre- and post-match events. The detailed timetable included two renditions of the national anthem, before and after the game. Some community singing suggested a sporting contest between two allies, as opposed to two enemies, but French referee Marcel Lequesne and his two assistants had been flown in to oversee proceedings. However, there was no hint of the Auld Alliance helping Scotland as England eased to a three-goal lead by the interval. Robson scored the opener after nine minutes with a drive from outside the box. Greaves's first goal was taken in his usual calm fashion and his second on the half-hour mark came from just a few yards after Haffey had palmed a shot into his path.

It looked all over at the interval but three minutes into the second half Mackay's powerful free-kick from eighteen yards reduced the deficit before Wilson's diving header at the back post in the fifty-third minute made it 3–2. Any thoughts the Scotland fans might have been entertaining about a glorious comeback lasted only two minutes. Moments after Law hit the crossbar, Haffey fumbled Bryan Douglas's shot for England's fourth. The goal came after the award of a dubious free-kick by Lequesne, who allowed Greaves to take it quickly and not from the right place. If at that point the scoring had ceased then maybe Scotland would have had cause to gripe but the controversy surrounding the free kick soon became little more than a moot point.

The game continued to swing from end to end. In the seventy-fourth minute Smith gave Haffey no chance with a shot from the edge of the box to make to made it 5–2 before Quinn scored a debut goal to keep the visitors within touching distance. However, four late England goals changed the course of history. As Scotland disintegrated, Haynes scored twice within four minutes. With seven minutes remaining a trademark finish saw Greaves bag his hat-trick before Smith completed the rout with the ninth after eighty-five minutes.

It was a defeat of cosmic proportion and the recriminations would be bitter and lengthy.

*

The front page of the *Sunday Mail* showed Haffey walking off the pitch under the headline 'Saddest Man at Wembley'. However, the Celtic keeper was not the focal point of some scathing press criticism. It was the Anglos in the Scottish side, Law and Mackay, at whom much of the vitriol was aimed although, in Rex Kingsley's ratings, the latter was highest marked of all the Scots with four stars. Haffey was awarded three, along with Shearer, Caldow, McNeill, MacLeod, Quinn and Wilson, while Law and St John got two.

In his report Kingsley's reference to Haffey is not so much critical as sympathetic, and he is also quick to highlight the inadequacies of the ten outfield players. 'If ever a side needed coaching, this was it. In comparison, our forwards were like a bunch of wee boys who were promised an orange if they could somehow worm the ball through the human maze their own dull wits had created and in to the net.' But Kingsley, with reference to Gagarin, kept most of his powder dry for Law, asking: 'Where was Denis Law all the time? Now THERE'S a question. He was on the field, I saw a jersey with a number eight on it but if this is the form of a £53,000 player, my granny's a cosmonaut.'

The *Glasgow Herald*'s sub-headline: 'Anglo Scots' Bad Tactics' introduces what is in essence an attack on Law and Mackay. The paper's man at the match, Cyril Horne, who had warned against Scottish complacency, opines: 'Not for the first time Mackay and Law must be charged with putting their own whims and fancies before the good of the team as a whole . . . Law lucky not to be sent off for flagrant fouling . . . if that was good enough then I am the Queen of Sheba.'

Waverley in the *Daily Record* blames Haffey for three of the goals but turns his sights on the SFA selectors: 'Scotland were disgraceful and the chief responsibility lies with the selectors.' But there was no hiding place for the Anglos in that organ either. Under the headline 'Mackay causes big mix-up' the article reads 'Mackay usurped the powers, whatever they are, of his manager at Wembley. In doing so, he had an upsetting influence on several of the other Wembley Scots.'

After crashing to earth with a bump, Scotland fans dusted themselves down and registered their complaints. Andrew McDonagh from Glasgow wrote to the *Daily Record* in the following terms: 'Sack the selectors. Only one has a connection with any club that could be called an asset to Scottish football, Motherwell.' (This, as St John admits, may have explained the three Fir Park players in the team.)

However, James Young, from Coatbridge, continued the attacks on Law, insisting: 'Denis Law should be barred from any Scottish team until he stops behaving like a child.'

Mackay would go on to enjoy success as a player and manager in England but he remains philosophical about the criticism he took in the aftermath of that infamous defeat: 'It was easier to have a go at the Anglos. Everybody took stick but especially the Anglos. We knew it was going to be bad and it was.'

St John moved to Liverpool and became an Anfield legend. However, he remains perplexed and peeved about the anti-Anglo attitudes that pervaded the Scottish media when he was a player.

> After I was transferred to Liverpool the poison pen turned towards me. It was crazy. We were thought of as deserters because we were leaving to better ourselves in many ways but, of course, financially. The Scottish press picked on Anglos and they were out of order. There was always a better player in Scotland who should have played in your position. Players like Eric Caldow would not have got as many caps had he played at a club like Aston Villa. I'm sure of that.

Haffey dodged much of the early flak. He raised his head above the parapet just a week later as Celtic drew 0–0 with Dunfermline – then managed by Jock Stein – in the Scottish Cup final at Hampden. 'I went out there and forgot about Wembley,' the Parkhead keeper said. 'I was given what amounted to a hero's welcome home from Wembley by those who wanted to help me and I was determined not to let them down. I'm happy I can tell you.'

However, he didn't help his bid for redemption in the replay, which Celtic lost 2–0, his mistake allowing Charlie Dickson to score Dunfermline's second goal minutes from time. Haffey's star, such as it was, continued to wane. After injuring an ankle against Partick Thistle in November 1963, he left Celtic the following October to play for Swindon Town and following a short spell in England he moved to Australia in 1965 where he continued his football career with St George Budapest and then Sydney City Hakoah before becoming a part-time cabaret singer.

Years later, in an interview for *FourFourTwo* magazine, Haffey claims that he had left Celtic 'a sad and disillusioned man' after boss Jimmy McGrory had tried to enforce a wage cut on him. In his absence, or perhaps because of it, Haffey became the fall guy for the 9–3 game and teammates and opponents were happy to add to the legend. No book, magazine or newspaper interview involving the Wembley participants is complete without a comical reference to the goalkeeper.

Jimmy Greaves's autobiography includes the 'nearly ten past Haffey' joke although he prefers to focus on England's performance.

> It's true that he had a poor game but Frank wasn't the only one who didn't perform well that day. I don't think any international team could have lived with England that day. Johnny Haynes was outstanding. To my mind it was his greatest performance in an England shirt and that's saying something considering his track record at international level.

In Sir Bobby Charlton's autobiography, the Manchester United legend also makes use of the 'nearly ten past Haffey' joke but is more sympathetic: 'Only the shortcomings of Haffey are remembered – the ultimate cruelty of football.' *The Only Game: the Scots and World Football*, written by Roddy Forsyth, makes reference to Haffey singing in the bath afterwards. Law is quoted as saying: 'The rest of us were trying to drown ourselves. As a matter of fact, we were trying to drown him!'

It is not surprising, therefore, that even people with a limited knowledge of Scottish football associate Scotland's most infamous result with Haffey.

However, for the game in this country the earth did not stop spinning on 15 April 1961. In fact, the Wembley defeat ushered in a golden era at club and international level and the decade ended with Neil Armstrong, an American astronaut with Scottish roots, becoming the first man to set foot on the moon.

McColl remained as Scotland manager although five players were dropped for the next game on 3 May, a 4–1 home win over Eire in a World Cup qualifier at Hampden and from then on Scottish fortunes improved still further. Revenge over England was gained the following year at Hampden through goals from Davie Wilson and Eric Caldow (penalty) as the Scots won the home-international championships for the twentieth time. And Scotland were unlucky not to reach the 1962 World Cup finals, beaten in a play-off in Brussels by Czechoslovakia, who went on to reach the final in Santiago, losing to Brazil.

Scotland were best of British again in 1963 when Baxter scored twice as the dark blues beat England 2–1 at Wembley, despite the loss of Caldow, who suffered a broken leg in the second minute. That same year also saw a 6–2 victory against Spain in Madrid and a 6–1 win against Norway at Hampden Park. Ian McColl was sacked in 1965 and became manager of Sunderland as Jock Stein took over for a short period before achieving legendary status at Parkhead. But by that time club football in Scotland was also resurgent. Rangers had reached the semi-finals of the European Cup in 1960, lost the Cup Winners Cup final a year later to Fiorentina and had made the quarter-finals of the European Cup in 1964/65. Celtic chalked up two appearance in the semi-finals of the European Cup Winners Cup, in 1963/64 and 1965/66, but it wasn't just the Old Firm who were flying the Lion Rampant in Europe. Dundee reached the semi-final of the European Cup in 1962/63 where they lost to AC Milan. Dunfermline made the quarter-finals of the European Cup Winners Cup in 1961/62 and the quarter-finals of the Fairs Cup in 1965/66 while Hibernian made the semi-finals of the Fairs Cup in 1960/61 and 1962/63.

Scottish football's finest hour, though, was 1966/67.

It was Bobby Brown who led Scotland to that most famous of Wembley victories, the 3–2 win over world champions England, the first time Ramsay's side had been humbled since they had won the Jules Rimet trophy against West Germany the previous year. That achievement was usurped by Celtic, who became the first British side to win the European Cup when they beat Inter Milan 2–1 in Lisbon. A week later, Rangers fell at the last hurdle of the Cup Winners Cup to Bayern Munich in Nuremberg. Just as noteworthy was Kilmarnock's feat in reaching the semi-finals of the Fairs Cup while Dundee United beat then Fairs Cup holders Barcelona home and away before losing to Juventus.

That campaign of 1966/67 was the high water mark for Scottish football. The 9–3 defeat by England had been an embarrassing blip albeit one that the players have never been able to forget.

Bert McCann continued his successful club career with Motherwell before going into education when his playing days finished. Recalling that afternoon in London, when his brief international career came to an end, he argues that Scotland simply came up against a magnificent England side.

> The whole Wembley thing was very unfortunate as far as I was concerned not least because I was unfit to play. They had Johnny Haynes, Bobby Charlton and Jimmy Greaves and that's why they scored nine goals. Haynes was the big difference, he was clever, the star man of the English team. Charlton was difficult to stop because he had a burst of speed and could shoot and of course Greaves was a goal-scorer and he was on top form.

Like most of the Scottish team that day, the former Fir Park player remains sympathetic to Haffey.

> Frank took most of the heat. I'm not sure that is what necessarily should have happened. About half the Scotland team didn't play well that day. I'm quite happy to take my part in it seriously. I would never make out that one or two others were more to blame than me even though they might have been. I didn't play well. I didn't do enough. Frank was larger than life but I think he was as nervous as the rest of us. He maybe tried to cover it but, regardless, England were just too strong.

McCann is happy that the passage of times means only people of a certain generation can recall the game.

> Young people, of course, don't remember the game, so it is fathers and grandfathers who bring it up. So you can't put it behind you. So I usually bring the topic up before they do! But when someone mentions it, I think of my performance. It wasn't too good. I think about how I did this wrong and that wrong. Everyone likes a chance to put right a wrong and I hoped that I would get the chance but I didn't play again for Scotland. I knew there would be scapegoats and I was one of them. But Scotland recovered quickly – we beat England at

Wembley two years later – but you could say that it didn't matter with regards the 9–3 game. It was different teams by then.

Dave Mackay prefers his trips down memory lane to take a detour around Wembley, 1961 but insists the whole team has to share the blame.

> To get beat 9–3 was terrible but it wasn't just Frank's fault. It was the fault of eleven players. To lose nine goals means there is something very wrong with the team. People ask me if I played in that game. I tell them that I didn't play but I was on the field. It was a terrible result. England had an excellent team and we had a disaster. It was one of those really bad days and I still don't like to think about it. I have seen a few of the Scottish players from that day over the years but we don't talk about it.
>
> It is a game that I would rather forget.

For his part, Caldow refuses to blame Haffey for an afternoon of misery.

> You can't just blame the keeper for that result. What about the defence? To lose 9–3! I haven't seen Frank since but the players didn't blame him. In fact, I never heard of one man getting blamed for a defeat in any team I played for. You had to blame the eleven players. I've heard all the jokes over the years, 'ten past Haffey' and the story that Davie, Bobby and myself wouldn't kick the orange ball and Frank wouldn't catch it. England was always our hardest game but that day they were different class. We had one or two players winning their first caps and we all tried our best but we couldn't do much about it.
>
> But it's forgotten. It was something that happened and it will never happen again.

Caldow was to have another nightmare at Wembley two years later when he broke his leg before ten-man Scotland (there were no substitutes allowed) went on to win 2–1 but he refuses to let the 9–3 thrashing detract from a remarkable career.

> It was still enjoyable. To captain Scotland at Wembley was a great honour and I was delighted to have won forty-odd caps. I'm the only British player who played over 550 games and never got a yellow

card or red card. Some games you didn't have the players available and other times we did and then we got some great results. But I always enjoyed playing for Scotland.

Former Scotland manager Craig Brown, who watched the game from the Wembley terraces as a youngster, recalls how the late Bobby Shearer would explain his international debut.

> I was friendly with Bobby. I used to get a run in to Ibrox from Hamilton with him when I was a young player at Rangers. He would say to me, 'We might have got beat 9–3 but I'll tell you something, Bobby Charlton didn't score.'
>
> I would say, 'Bobby, he laid on seven of them!' But Bobby's stock reply was, 'That was fuck all to do with it.' That was the rule at Rangers at the time; you had to eliminate your immediate opponent. If you were a centre half, the centre forward wasn't to score.

Ian St John confirms Brown's recollection of the Rangers and Shearer defensive philosophy.

> We had Shearer and Caldow as the full backs and Billy McNeill making his debut in the middle. The full backs stuck with their men and if they didn't score then they thought that they had done all right! Big Billy was left trying to deal with Bobby Smith and Jimmy Greaves. Frank lost nine goals but he was entitled to ask what was happening in front of him. We scored three goals and the record books will show that few Scottish teams have done that at Wembley, but there was just a total lack of organisation.

It was the erratic nature of international football that ultimately led to St John's departure from the international scene.

> It was my fault, me and my big mouth. The selectors would change the team all the time. I played and scored in the 2–2 game at Wembley in 1965 and then I was left out. I was angry and disillusioned. I told them they could stick it up their arse, called them clowns, and said that I didn't care if I didn't play for Scotland again. I never did. I regretted it years later. We had some great players like Henderson, Wilson, Law, Mackay, Baxter and McNeill. But Scotland were good

despite the SFA. Shankly was the first man to talk to me about the game and about tactics. What a pity he never got to manage Scotland. We could have gone to the 1962 World Cup finals if Shankly had been the manager.

Scotland fan Donald Campbell remains philosophical about arguably the most depressing afternoon in this history of the national team.

The country was traumatised, it hurt deeply. But we are resilient. We got over it and bounced back off the ropes. England were better than us in every respect. They were fitter, cleverer, and the pace of the football was far superior. Haffey could only be blamed for a couple of goals but he liked to poke fun at himself; that was the type of character he was.

As noted, Haffey moved to Australia but had Armstrong taken him to the moon and left him there, it would not have been far enough away from Wembley, 15 April 1961. Every discussion and debate about that game inevitably comes back to the former Celtic keeper. In 2005 he returned to Scotland for the first time in forty years and *Daily Record* journalist Neil Cameron made his way to Celtic Park to meet the man who lived up to his reputation as a larger-than-life character. Cameron's recollections about their meeting make for fascinating reading.

The piece about Frank Haffey in December 2005 began with how the interview had ended. Our conversation that afternoon had been easy, friendly, had lasted roughly half an hour and yet there was an elephant in the corner so big that it would have covered half of India. So I had to ask what the former Scotland goalkeeper remembered about that day in 1961 at Wembley. Turned out Frank remembered a lot.

In fact, he said to me; 'I'm glad you asked me that,' and then joked that he hadn't slept a wink since that night. It was difficult to believe. He had a twinkle in his eye and carried himself like a man who hadn't a care in the world.

Since becoming a sports journalist in 1995, nine years of them spent with the *Record*, this was by far and away my favourite interview. And the response I got from readers who had waited a long time to hear from the man was amazing.

I had to hang around the lobby of Celtic Park for a good couple of hours waiting for Frank to arrive, his first visit to the ground – indeed to Scotland – since he left for a new life in Australia.

Lisbon Lions Bertie Auld and John Clark were part of the welcoming committee and spoke with genuine warmth about their old teammate, telling me that he was a happy-go-lucky guy, genuinely popular in the dressing room. They said, albeit under their breath, that he wasn't much of a goalie, but he was as delighted to see them as they were to clap eyes on a man who looked a good ten years younger than his age.

Frank had spent much of his time down under as a cabaret performer, not difficult to believe having met him. He was brilliant company, full of life and full of himself. He spoke with great self-deprecation about the 9–3 match, although he made the point that there were ten other Scotland players at Wembley that day.

Frank won just one other Scotland cap, against England at Hampden a year before his Wembley appearance, when he saved a penalty from Bobby Charlton in a 1–1 draw. I told him that we would speak about that next time he was in town.

I'm still waiting.

Graham McColl

7

'The Old Men of Peru'

Graham McColl

There was a good reason for Ally MacLeod to be wary when he arrived at the San Martin theatre in downtown Buenos Aires for the televised draw for the 1978 World Cup. On arrival in the Argentine that mid-January, MacLeod had discovered there were strong rumours that Scotland were to be grouped with West Germany, the holders, and would face the Germans in the opening match of the tournament, a prospect the Scotland manager was understandably keen to avoid. There were several others that he also wished to dodge: a talented Hungary side, Brazil, Argentina and Austria.

A practice run-through had MacLeod frozen in his seat when it placed Scotland in a formidable group along with Brazil, Austria and France. Even though this was a dummy run, thoughts of how to deal with the multifarious talents of Zico, Hans Krankl and Michel Platini flashed scarily through MacLeod's mind and brought home to him just how tough Scotland's group might be. So when the tiny, three-year-old hand of Ricardinho Teixeira Havelange – grandson of Joao, president of FIFA – deposited the Scots in a group with Holland, Peru and Iran, the Scotland manager's assessment of the genuine article was tinged with relief, followed swiftly by euphoria.

It was, MacLeod believed, 'a dream section' for Scotland. 'Ally, your luck is in,' he thought to himself as he sat in the theatre that afternoon. Not only the opposition itself, but also the sequence of the fixtures looked favourable, with Scotland opening against Peru and then facing Iran.

'We really couldn't have asked for any better,' MacLeod said in the immediate aftermath of the draw. 'We have a nice start against Peru and it could be that the Dutch and ourselves will have the section settled by the time we meet. That could leave us simply deciding who would be first and who would be second.' The San Martin theatre had been named after the Argentinian general who had liberated Peru during the nineteenth century but knowledge of that would have instilled no trepidation in MacLeod, given that his own sense of liberation, at being drawn against that country, was now running rampant.

A week later, after touring Argentina to arrange hotel accommodation, MacLeod and Ernie Walker, the secretary of the Scottish Football Association, arrived back in Britain, disembarking at Gatwick airport on the Saturday evening of 21 January after a twenty-three-hour flight and looking as if they were 'feeling the effects of their journey,' as one onlooker put it. The Scottish press had not attended the draw as such extravagances were rarely contemplated by the fourth estate at that time. So it had been almost a fortnight since the media-friendly MacLeod had held court and when he saw the familiar faces of journalists with whom he had become friendly during his dozen years of club management at Ayr United and Aberdeen, he became positively effusive. 'I'm certain that we'll be among the medals and if we get the right break of the ball then who knows?' His bullish forecast was a terrific story for the half-dozen Scottish pressmen who had flown south to meet him off the plane.

Some results have shaken the followers of Scottish football for days or weeks or months or years but Scotland's defeat by Peru at the 1978 World Cup was different. It sent a seismic shock through not just the Scotland team's devoted supporters but also through every strata of Scottish life like no football match before or since. The entire nation, it seemed, had been drawn to the television at 8.45 p.m. on the Saturday evening of 3 June 1978 to see the Scots set about the South Americans. It wasn't just committed fans who tuned in but also those who might previously have been described as football agnostics: grannies, poets, professors, children in sheltered middle-class ghettoes; all sorts of people with little or no previous interest in the game had been overwhelmed by the extravagant promises of World Cup glory that poured from the mouth of Ally MacLeod during the last six months. With Ally promising Scots the earth – or at least its cup – the game with Peru was pitched to the nation as a mere overture for the greater glories to come.

The frenzy whipped up was such that, as John Hagart, MacLeod's assistant manager, puts it, 'If you went into a supermarket, there would be two old women talking about the World Cup coming up. Everybody was completely hooked and captivated by the whole thing.'

MacLeod's promises of World Cup victory in early 1978 were quickly backed up and put to music by Rod Stewart in 'Ole Ola', the official World Cup song, and by Andy Cameron, a Glasgow comedian, in 'Ally's Tartan Army'. Both singers insisted, in bombastic style, as Ally did, that Scotland were certainties to win the great trophy. The nation was happy to believe them and each of those singles sold more than a quarter-of-a-million copies, making them top-ten hits in the United Kingdom.

Scotland had qualified for the 1978 World Cup in some style, principally through two stirring victories, over Czechoslovakia and Wales, in the autumn of 1977, but it was not until that snowy January of 1978 that Ally MacLeod fully warmed to his task of whipping the nation into a frenzy and it was Peru, unwittingly, in their faraway, junta-ruled land, that helped ignite the flame.

Underpinning MacLeod's exuberance was the opening fixture with Peru. Holland, World Cup finalists in 1974, were seen as serious rivals from whom no points could be guaranteed. Iran, World Cup debutants, were quickly labelled as the whipping boys for the rest of the group. So MacLeod's certainty about Scotland's progress was pinned almost entirely on taking full points from the match with Peru, points that would, he believed, almost certainly eliminate the South Americans and advance the Scots into the last eight. He was not alone in such sentiments. Following the draw, William Hill, the bookmakers, had immediately reduced the odds on Scotland winning the World Cup from 11/1 to 8/1.

Such a blithe dismissal of the Peruvians was very strange. They were, after all, the reigning South American champions and even teenage fans would surely have recalled the television images beamed back to Scotland by satellite from the 1970 World Cup in Mexico. Peru, even on the black-and-white sets prevalent at the beginning of the decade, were hard to miss because of the distinctive, diagonal sash of red that they wore across their all-white shirts. In the 1970 finals Peru had been sublime contributors to a fine tournament and were stopped by mighty Brazil in the last eight following an enthralling 4–2 defeat.

'Peru were excellent,' Roberto Rivellino, the Brazil midfield player said of their 1970 team. 'They had movement, speed and quality.' Helmut Schoen, manager of West Germany, had declared Peru, early in the 1970 tournament, to be playing the best World Cup football since the Brazilians of 1958 and they had, indeed, been widely described as 'the new Brazil'. It was reasonable to expect that a seasoned football man like MacLeod would have seen those captivating images of Peru manoeuvring their way stylishly through opposing defences and have duly banked such knowledge in his memory.

It might also have been expected that Scotland's professional football writers would reach for their recollections of the 1970 finals when assessing Peru's potential. Yet those relatively recent achievements were barely mentioned in Scotland after the World Cup draw as commentators fell over themselves to do down the South Americans. Peru were summarily dismissed as 'old men', with one newspaper rubbishing their standing as South American champions by noting that Argentina and Brazil had 'lined up players from obscure country sides' in the 1975 tournament; a statement that was misleading and thoroughly un-researched.

Denis Law, who had played in Scotland's sole encounter with Peru prior to 1978, at Hampden Park six years earlier, was quick to join the fray. 'I don't think Peru will be able to stand up to Scotland,' he argued. 'None of the Latin teams are particularly clever at crosses coming into the box. Peru will be the same. I can see us getting a few goals in the opener.' Peru, he added, had moved the ball around nicely at Hampden but had offered little threat near goal. Law did concede that the Peruvians, on tour in Europe that spring of 1972, had jetted into Glasgow from Romania only shortly before the game, which Scotland had won 2–0, and he did say that he had particularly liked one of their players: his name was Teofilo Cubillas.

Law also made great play of the Peruvians' supposed elderliness and this caricature of Scotland's first opponents as a team of ancients was perhaps the most damaging of the various pieces of propaganda that were being spread in Scotland during the early part of 1978. The general impression given in the press was that several Peruvian players were in their late thirties, with some even nudging forty or having already reached that age. The highest bid for a Peruvian's age, asserted in cavalier fashion by Alex Cameron of the *Daily Record*, had Hugo Sotil at forty-six. This was simply crazy; rumour passed off as fact, but there was no alternative source of information. During the 1970s, the press held a near monopoly on dispensing information about football and, with most Scottish reporters uninterested in the intricacies of the game outside the United Kingdom, it was inevitable that misinformation would spread like wildfire. 'Against Chumpitaz, Cubillas, Melendez and Sotil, it will be nice for Don Masson, Bruce Rioch and myself to see so many players older than us in the one team,' Archie Gemmill, then aged thirty-one, stated.

Despite MacLeod being a football man to the tips of his toes and someone who should have known better, he did little to contradict this misreporting of the Peruvians' qualities or, as the press would have it, lack of them. Ally characterised Cubillas, the South American footballer of the year in 1972, and a star of the 1970 World Cup, at which he had won the Bronze Boot, as being 'short and tubby now' with no-one in the mood to question how he might have declined in height across eight years, along with the more common affliction of piling on the pounds. It was as if the Peruvian was some sort of geriatric totem wheeled out on to the park when, in fact, he was a mere twenty-nine-years old in 1978, having been a precocious pup, nicknamed 'The Baby', in 1970.

With the challenge of Peru having been so brusquely dismissed, the country could get down to the more important business of worshipping at the feet of MacLeod, who was routinely, almost casually, described in the tabloid press during early 1978 as 'our soccer Messiah' and 'the king of the Scots'. On 'Ally's Tartan Army', Andy Cameron's World Cup single, the comedian sang not about the strengths of the Scottish team but of the sheer potency of Ally MacLeod, as if it were the 47-year-old manager who was going to fill the Peruvian net with goals. MacLeod's infectious optimism – he was rarely pictured without an enormous smile on his face – did much to fuel this personality cult. He had been Scotland manager only since May 1977 and the aura of invincibility that enveloped him owed much to his excellent record in the job. Scotland won the home-international championship in June 1977 after a rousing 2–1 win over England at Wembley, followed by the exhilarating, Ally-inspired victories over the Czechoslovakians and the Welsh in the World Cup qualifiers. It was a near-flawless record and 1977 was arguably the most successful year in Scotland's history at international level. It helped cement the idea that with MacLeod at the helm Scotland were just about unbeatable.

Far from backtracking from his initial assessment that Scotland would return from the World Cup among the medals, MacLeod enthusiastically developed his theme, repeatedly insisting that his players would come home not with bronze or silver but with gold medals. His promises of glory resounded almost unchallenged around the nation as if it were an echo chamber specially designed for him to bounce around his thoughts. At the draw in January he had mused aloud: 'If we are going to win the World Cup, there is no point in being afraid of any team'; in May, as the tournament approached, it was, 'Willie Johnston is a key player because he can help us lift the Cup.'

MacLeod's message was particularly potent because of the humour with which he laced his pronouncements. 'Once we win the World Cup, we'll return to tour every town to show it off – starting with Southampton,' he said as the tournament neared. In the period before leaving for Argentina – when players and management would be allowed several days at home with their families – MacLeod would, he informed the nation, be carrying out home improvements: 'I'm putting in a new corner unit to hold the World Cup.'

After losing 1–0 to England in the final match of the 1978 home internationals – which saw the Scots deposed as British champions, but playing well despite defeat in their last international before facing Peru – Ally was undaunted. 'We go with this warning to England,' he said. 'Enjoy your reign as champions because we want our title back next year. We fancy the home-international trophy will look well at Park Gardens [the Glasgow address of the Scottish Football Association] even if it could be dwarfed by the World Cup.' This blend of easy nationalism and couthy confidence – from a man whose Scottishness extended to preferring fried clootie dumpling over cake to celebrate his birthday – was hugely enjoyable for his fellow Scots.

It is sometimes tempting to dismiss MacLeod as a pied piper, a supercharged salesman – he had once worked as a rep for a pharmaceutical company – who captivated a spellbound nation in those heady months but underpinning the froth was a considerable degree of substance. When an assessment is made of the talent at his disposal it is clear that there was a real basis for his confidence even if he did go over the top.

Shortly before Scotland and Peru had been drawn together in January, Joe Jordan, the Scotland striker, had been transferred from Leeds United to Manchester United for a record fee between English clubs of £350,000, a record broken within hours when another Scot, Graeme Souness, a midfield player, moved from Middlesbrough to Liverpool, the European Cup holders. The £440,000 transfer of Kenny Dalglish, Jordan's settled partner in the Scotland attack, from Celtic to Liverpool in August 1977, had set a new British record and Dalglish finished the 1977/78 season as top scorer in England's top flight, with thirty goals, rounding it off in style by scoring the only goal in the European Cup final against Bruges after latching on to an artful pass from Souness. It meant that Liverpool had spent almost £1 million on Scots – Dalglish, Alan Hansen and Souness – in a single season. That record British fee, for Dalglish, was subsequently broken in February 1978, when Gordon McQueen, the Scotland centre-back, followed Jordan from Leeds to Old Trafford for £500,000. Scottish players were the most sought after commodity in one of the world's leading leagues and MacLeod's would be one of the most highly valued squads – at least in terms of transfer fees – at the finals.

The quality of those whom MacLeod could afford to ignore in his final squad for Argentina also reflects the talent at his disposal. Alan Hansen – who had the vital role of anchor man in the Liverpool team that had won the European Cup at Wembley three weeks before the match with Peru – was not included and there was not a squeak of protest from either the press or the fans at such an omission. The range and depth of players available to MacLeod meant that Hansen was not even considered, principally because he was still in his early twenties and not yet an established international.

Souness was well aware of the strength of the squad. 'I'll be trying to break into the finest midfield in European football and you cannot get any harder than that,' he said in February 1978 of his hopes of being chosen by Ally. 'I'd settle for being a sub in Argentina and I hope being with Liverpool will increase my chances of going there with Scotland for the World Cup finals.' Andy Gray, the Aston Villa striker, who would score twenty goals that 1977/78 season in England's top division, was another who spoke in humble terms of how he hoped that he might be considered good enough for inclusion. In the event, MacLeod could afford to overlook him. Tommy Craig, the clever, 27-year-old, Glasgow-born midfield player – who moved to Aston Villa from Newcastle United for £270,000 in early1978 – was not even the subject of consideration for the squad. Omitted too were John Wark and George Burley, FA Cup winners with Ipswich Town that spring of 1978. British football was teeming with so many able Scots that MacLeod could pick and choose freely of them.

'I have never known so many talented Scots to be available for the national team,' said Tommy Docherty, who had been manager of Scotland in the early 1970s. The Doc named five whom he considered world class: Kenny Dalglish, Joe Jordan, Danny McGrain, Gordon McQueen and Don Masson. Billy Bremner, Scotland's captain at the 1974 World Cup – and now winding down his career at Hull City – was equally effusive. 'Scotland can win the World Cup. They are that good. Individually and collectively, we have the best team in the world at the moment. I just cannot see anyone beating the Scots in South America if we get it right on the day.'

Dissenting voices were only to be found outside of Scotland and its diaspora. Sir Alf Ramsey, the England manager who had guided his country to glory in the 1966 World Cup, struck a note of caution. 'The big danger to Scotland's qualifying chances will come in their opening match against Peru. I remember Peru from the 1970 finals in Mexico. They had some very good players who had clearly modelled themselves on the Brazilians. My impression is that they have been progressing since then.' No-one in Scotland, however, wanted to listen to the opinions of Sir Alf, shrewd observer that he undoubtedly was. Nor, particularly, to those of Claudio Coutinho, manager of Brazil, who suggested, 'Peru have always been a team who knew only how to attack. They didn't know anything about defensive football. They were a little lazy too. Not now. They have improved.' Such was the mood inside Scotland at the time, though, that such opinions were snowed under by opinions to the contrary, like solitary voices suggesting the merits of temperance at a Hogmanay party.

Peru were considerably less high-profile than their opening World Cup opponents. All their players bar one were attached to clubs in the Peruvian league as transfers to Europe were a rarity in the 1970s. Cubillas, who was perhaps understandably the exception, had spent time with Porto and Basle in European football following the 1970 World Cup but by 1978 was back home with Alianza Lima. This was handy because in early February 1978 Peru did something that has never been an option for a Scotland team: the entire home-based squad left their club sides and took up residence at a training camp twenty miles from Lima, where they would remain sequestered together until the finals began in June. Juan José Munante, then with UNAM of Mexico, was the only player who did not join them but that problem was solved in April when the Peruvian FA obtained his release from UNAM and he belatedly joined his squad-mates. It is one of the admittedly few advantages of living under a military junta that there are no club-versus-country arguments when national prestige is at stake. Denuded of their international players, Alianza Lima and Sporting Cristal, the country's two most prestigious clubs, plummeted to the bottom of the Peruvian league.

No fewer than fourteen friendly matches were arranged for the team between February and May so Marcos Calderon, the manager who had led Peru to the 1975 South American championship, could feel certain that his team had bonded. MacLeod, in comparison, had arranged only one friendly match – against Bulgaria in February – between qualifying in October 1977 and the three home internationals in May 1978. That gave him four preparatory games but with the exception of the clash with England he used the games to experiment with personnel and formations.

One minor problem did face Peru as they prepared to leave for the World Cup – they discovered that they could not afford to go. The Peruvian government had become effectively bankrupt and so, before they could set off for Argentina, FIFA had to provide a loan of $100,000 to cover the team's expenses at the finals.

Marcos Calderon had no doubt that his team would be too good for the Scots: 'We will beat Scotland,' he insisted on arrival at the World Cup. 'Scotland kick too much and don't play with their heads. We will try to wear them out with our short passing.' MacLeod was equally bullish. Before leaving Scotland, he had placed Iran and Peru in the same category as Zaire, the African team Scotland had beaten at the 1974 World Cup in West Germany, and which had conceded fourteen goals in three games without finding the net themselves.

Such was his confidence that MacLeod expected his team to 'chase goals' in the matches with Peru and Iran and he was, he said, expecting to bring on Lou Macari, the attacking midfield player, and Joe Harper, the striker, as substitutes in those matches to assist the team in that fun-filled pursuit. 'We will go into the game against Peru thinking of attack. I want to have players pushed up because in the videos I have watched of the Peruvians I had the feeling they were suspect at the back.' Willie Johnston, hours before kick-off, said he was expecting a very hard match on the basis that Scotland were expecting Peru to be 'defensive'.

There were, despite MacLeod's belligerence, some reasons for caution as Scotland prepared to face Peru after all the months of hype. The Scotland team had been booed for its poor standard of play in the 1–1 draw at Hampden Park against Northern Ireland in the home internationals and in the next match with Wales, again at Hampden, had been forced to settle for another 1–1 draw when Willie Donachie put through his own goal in the dying seconds. The performance against England, with a team close to MacLeod's favoured eleven, had been much better although Scotland had lost 1–0 and at the end of that game the fans had refused to shift from the terraces until MacLeod and his team emerged to indulge in a lap of honour.

Five days later, the Scotland squad was back at Hampden Park for a send-off prior to leaving for Argentina, an occasion that would in later years wrongly be characterised as an example of hubris, coming as it did before a ball had been kicked in the finals. It was no such thing. In fact it was an event that Ally had opposed. The celebration, or send-off, was held on the early evening of 25 May 1978, when a crowd of around thirty thousand filed into the national stadium to wave their flags and chant their support. Nor was the Scottish Football Association keen on this exhibition of euphoria. It had actually been insisted upon by Strathclyde Police, which, understandably, had public safety and not nationalistic support for the football team in mind. The police, with their elephantine memory, remembered what had happened at the previous World Cup.

In 1974, when Scotland had returned unbeaten from the World Cup in West Germany, the squad had been surprised by the welcome they got when they landed in Glasgow. Thousands of Scots were at the airport and, in scenes reminiscent of VE Day, the city centre too had been thronged by thousands of wellwishers, anxious to express their gratitude for the plucky displays against Zaire, Brazil and Yugoslavia. The police were therefore keen to avoid that kind of chaos when the 1978 team left for Argentina. On a less savoury note, they also had in mind the night at Anfield when Scotland had qualified for the 1978 finals. After that match bottles had rained down from the terraces after the Liverpool police had refused to allow MacLeod and his team to emerge from their dressing room for a lap of honour.

Strathclyde Police, in an attempt to exert as much control as possible, agreed on Hampden as a focal point for the departure of MacLeod and his squad. This perhaps explains the manager's demeanour that evening. The habitually extrovert MacLeod looked bashful as he and his players took to the turf and waved to the crowd before twice going round the Hampden track swathed in an outsize Argentine flag. While some in the squad and in the media may have had their doubts about the whole exercise, it is worth noting that there were no dissenting voices at the time. Instead, it was viewed positively as yet more Ally-inspired fun.

From Glasgow's south side, the squad travelled down through Ayrshire, to discover a route lined by wellwishers. When they got to Prestwick airport, the point of departure for Argentina, there were scenes that Gordon McQueen describes as reminiscent of Beatlemania. They were similar in many ways to the hysterical scenes at Kennedy airport, New York, in February 1964, when the arrival of the Beatles in the USA was met by sheer delirium.

Astounding as these events of May 1978 might have been, they were symptoms, and not causes, of the over-confidence that had spread to every corner of Scotland. The groundwork had been carried out assiduously by MacLeod in the five months up to that point and the scenes at Hampden and in Ayrshire were merely barometers of how successfully he had raised the temperature to fever pitch.

*

The opening match of the World Cup produced a dull, goalless draw between Poland and holders West Germany but three other matches in the tournament's early days between the opener on 31 May and Scotland's encounter with Peru on 3 June had ended in surprise results: Tunisia beat Mexico 3–1, becoming the first African country to win a match in the World Cup finals; Hungary pushed Argentina all the way and were defeated only because of a series of questionable refereeing decisions; while Sweden and Brazil drew 1–1 thanks to Clive Thomas, the Welsh referee, blowing his whistle for full time just as Zico was heading the ball into the Sweden net for what would have been a Brazil winner. It all suggested that, in the World Cup, form can go out of the window.

The 'old men' of Peru were looking remarkably fresh-faced as they sprang on to the turf in Cordoba to face Scotland. Of the team picked by Calderon, only one, Hector Chumpitaz, was over thirty but so exquisite were the central defender's skills that, even at thirty-five, his inclusion in the national side was mandatory. He and Jaime Duarte, at twenty-three, were the only members of the Peru side not in their mid-to-late twenties. The team had an average age of just over twenty-seven and most of its members were in their football prime.

And here was the rub. The Scotland team that started the match was, despite all the hype of the preceding months, slightly older than that of Peru. The eleven Scots had a combined age of 305, compared to 299 for Peru. It meant that the average age of the Scots was 27.7, whereas Peru's was 27.2. Additionally, Scotland fielded no fewer than three players who had already celebrated their thirtieth birthdays: Willie Johnston, Don Masson and Bruce Rioch.

That said there was a freshness about Scotland in the opening exchanges. The defenders and midfield players looked sharp and aggressive; Dalglish, in attack, was alert and lively, difficult for the Peru defenders to pin down. The team's play was also penetrative: a magnificent pass from Dalglish sent Asa Hartford in on goal but his left-foot shot went veering wide. Then a pacy move that began in the Scotland half saw Rioch find Dalglish and when his pass was headed forward intelligently by Stuart Kennedy, Don Masson was set fair for a twenty-yard shot at goal that was saved well by Ramon Quiroga, the Peru goalkeeper. Another clever move saw Asa Hartford and Dalglish conveying the ball cleverly to Masson inside the penalty area, where he smartly manoeuvred himself away from two hard and fast tackles to shoot low towards Quiroga, who again grasped the ball securely.

Peru were almost like extras at this point, playing to perfection the role in which MacLeod and others had cast them. None of this would be any good without a goal to show for it, of course, and, right on cue, Scotland obliged. It was a fine goal too; eight quick, clever passes conveying the ball smoothly across the midfield and then up the left wing before Rioch's shot was parried by Quiroga, but only to the feet of Jordan, who nimbly prodded the ball into the Peru net. Fourteen

157

minutes had passed and things could hardly have been better for Scotland.

Within a minute of the goal, a Hartford shot tested Quiroga but with the 1–0 lead in the bag, Scotland, although apparently still in control, appeared a little less urgent in their play. They were still robbing the Peruvians with impunity in midfield, and José Velasquez became the first player to be booked by Ulf Eriksson, the Swedish referee, when he chopped down Joe Jordan close to the Peruvian penalty area, but the game had slowed to some degree.

Then, suddenly, Peru came alive. A five-man move that began on the halfway line concluded with Cubillas through one-on-one with Alan Rough. The keeper did well to block the striker's shot at close-range, even managing to turn the ball off Cubillas for a goal kick. The most alarming thing about this segment of play was that the Peruvians had used no width at all, instead threading the ball delicately through the middle of the field and being met with little resistance.

The game had changed and with half an hour played, Peru had mutated from seeming slugabeds into a powerful attacking force, with Munante, Cubillas and Juan Carlos Oblitas especially fast and dangerous. Scotland were failing to adjust and, rather than redoubling their defensive efforts, were still pushing forward at every opportunity. This was playing into the hands of Peru, who were brilliant exponents of the counter-attack.

Tactics can throw up questions in a match but players always have the final say in how it finishes. For all Peru's new threat, Scotland still carved out a superb chance when Masson's expert pass found Jordan inside the penalty area and he headed down for Dalglish in front of goal. Quiroga was smartly off his line to pat down Dalglish's attempt at a lob. It had been a superb opportunity to establish a two-goal lead. On such moments a match can hinge. It was only the first of two chances to arrive in quick succession for Dalglish. Jordan soon got to the goal line and did well both to keep the ball in play and in the same movement to cut it back to Dalglish. This time he scooped his shot over the crossbar.

At last, a ten-minute lull in the game arrived, which gave both sides some breathing space. The Scots took the steam out of the game, through ploys like taking an eternity over throw-ins. Peru too looked as if they needed a second wind. Scotland appeared on course to reach half-time and get the chance to regroup until, three minutes before the break, a Peru move involving eight successive slick passes saw Calderon's side again slice their way directly through the centre of the Scottish defence. This time Cesar Cueto clipped a low shot past Rough and into the net for the equaliser.

Scottish heads did not go down despite losing a goal so near to the interval. In fact they began the second half almost as brightly as they had the first. A Joe Jordan header, seconds after the restart, clipped the outside of Quiroga's post. Chumpitaz deflected a Dalglish shot over the bar. Quiroga got both hands to a fierce goalbound shot from Jordan and somehow managed to send the ball up and over the cross-bar from almost directly underneath it.

A sustained period of Scottish pressure, close in style and tempo to that with which they had opened the game, was capped after sixty-two minutes when Kennedy crossed and Jordan headed the ball down to the running Rioch, who appeared to have knocked the ball too far ahead of him when he was fouled by Chumpitaz. Ulf Eriksson, the referee, quickly awarded a penalty. Half a dozen Peruvian players protested to the Swede in vain and Quiroga, in protest, stood on the penalty spot to prevent Masson taking the kick. Only the threat of a yellow card finally forced the Peru goalkeeper back on to his line. Then Calderon delayed matters further by, unconventionally, making a substitution before the spot kick was taken, replacing Guillermo la Rosa with Hugo Sotil. Masson did not look too discomfited by all this but his penalty, when he did finally strike it, was a poor one, to the goalkeeper's right and at a comfortable height for Quiroga to ease gently across his goal and push the ball round his post.

Peru, who had been subdued in the second half until then, suddenly became aroused. Now, instead of working the ball painstakingly through the middle, as had been characteristic of them in the first period, they brought Munante and Oblitas, their wingers, into play. An uncertainty could be seen in the Scottish players following the penalty and Peru began to make the most of it, picking away steadily at the Scottish defence.

With twenty minutes remaining, Quiroga clutched a cross from Kennedy and quickly threw the ball out to Munante who eased it on to Duarte to find Cueto who, in turn, fed Cubillas, thirty yards from goal and slightly left of centre as he looked towards the penalty area. There was no Scotland player in the vicinity as he took a first touch to get the ball firmly on his right boot, a second to nudge the ball nicely in front of him for a shot before, with a third, lithe movement, he swiped the ball smoothly and high into the top-left-hand corner of Rough's net.

MacLeod responded by substituting Rioch and Masson with Lou Macari and Archie Gemmill but one of Gemmill's first acts was to hit a woefully short pass in the direction of Jordan. Duarte easily intercepted and pushed the ball in Cueto's direction. Again Peru turned defence into attack in a nanosecond as Cueto curved an elegant long pass to Oblitas only for the Peruvian, with Rough's goal in his sights, to be sent tumbling after a hefty, clumsy challenge from Kennedy, the Scotland right-back who, in the absence of the peerless but injured McGrain, was making only his fourth appearance for Scotland.

The free kick was from the same area as that from which Cubillas had worked his deadly magic six minutes before and he was one of four Peru players who ambled around the ball in their relaxed style. Cubillas looked least likely to strike the ball, given that he was positioned incorrectly to bend it round the wall. That was to reckon without his exquisite skills and it was indeed Cubillas who, in unorthodox fashion, took the shortest of runs at the ball and, instead of attempting a bend, simply brushed the ball with his foot and pinged a delicate shot over the near end of the defensive wall and up into the same corner of Rough's net that he had found minutes before.

As the dust settled after the 3–1 defeat Ally MacLeod was certainly not willing to carry the can.

Don't blame me. I did all I could in the match preparations but the team were toothless tigers. How the hell it happened I do not know.

We were a shambles. I cannot understand it. In the opening fifteen minutes I was sure we were on the way to World Cup glory.

I am quite satisfied the players were properly briefed about Peru. I said they were a good team going forward – as in fact they were – but had faults in defence. Frankly, I wouldn't care to put my finger exactly on what went wrong with us but we were playing well for twenty minutes and looked sure to win. When things started to go wrong we didn't tighten up in the middle – and we were a fraction of a second late in moving. The team played well for the first twenty minutes and they also made a good start to the second half. Both times, when they played well, it was after I spoke to them.

Calderon was as outspoken post-match as he had been before it. 'Only a baby would leave Cubillas and Cueto unmarked. We have always thought that Scotland played with more brawn than brain but they did not even have that.'

Such emotional words from the managers are understandable in the immediate aftermath of such a vital match. Both MacLeod's defensiveness and Calderon's self-aggrandisement fit the formula that a manager's degree of post-match bombast is always closely related to the score on the day. Looked at more dispassionately, the match between Scotland and Peru was a good, entertaining joust between two well-matched teams. Both had good chances to win the game, the difference was that Peru put theirs away. A draw might have been the fairest result for the contribution both sides made to a contest that had swayed one way and then the other.

Peru had lived up to their pedigree; albeit a pedigree that was almost entirely ignored in Scotland. Marvellously talented players such as Cueto, Cubillas, Oblitas and Munante had the potential to worry any defence in the world. Nor had Scotland been that bad. Certainly, the lack of marking and cover at the second and third Peruvian goals had been poor but, before then, Scotland had created chances aplenty; scoring efforts that were denied by a combination of the woodwork and excellent goalkeeping from Quiroga. It was only after those chances were blown that Scotland were hit with two severe blows from a world-class footballer. Dalglish, Scotland's nearest equivalent to Cubillas, had played well but had never, on the day, reached the heights of the South American.

Even after their victory, it was still the fate of Peru to be grossly underrated in Scotland. Rather than giving credit to the South Americans, the setback was regarded as self-inflicted and the witch-hunt began. Stories began to seep out of a dispute between the players and the Scottish Football Association over bonuses. The players would complain that the Hotel Sierras, in Alta Gracia, where they were cooped up for the first fortnight of the tournament, was woefully substandard. MacLeod, of course, was instantly demoted from hero to villain, castigated for his lack of tactical nous and for not having watched Peru prior to the World Cup. Yet Calderon had not watched Scotland. Joe Harper also confirms that despite one or two discomforts at their base in Alta Gracia, the team 'were pretty upbeat' for the match against Peru. Rioch describes the bonus dispute as unfortunate but only a minor distraction in the approach to the match with the Peruvians.

For his part Willie Johnston argues that Scotland would have done much better if only the players had been briefed about the opposition.

> We weren't bad as a team against Peru but we didn't know that Cubillas would be the one to bend the ball round the wall. . . . If Don Masson had scored with his penalty we would have beaten Peru. We played all right but, with the two goals that we lost to Cubillas . . . if we had known about the boy we would maybe have been better.

The most rational explanation for the defeat was that Scotland were beaten by a good side that played to its capabilities and took its chances when they came along. But, given the pre-tournament bally-hoo, rational explanations simply could not be countenanced. All sense of perspective had been placed in a state of suspension for the opening half of 1978.

The ramifications of this defeat lingered longer than for any match in Scottish history. Scots may like to party but they also like to reproach themselves for over-indulgence. Never again would the nation invest such belief in its football team and the response of the SFA would be to ensure that every future World Cup was approached in a distinctly low-key fashion. It was a reaction as drastically out of proportion – and probably more damaging in the long term – as MacLeod's incessant trumpeting of impending glory.

Within forty-eight hours of defeat to Peru, Willie Johnston would be on his way back to Britain, swiftly ejected from the Scotland squad after testing positive for fencamfamin, a stimulant that was on FIFA's list of proscribed substances. With the players reeling from the dual blows of that episode and the defeat by Peru, they were unable collectively to raise themselves for the next match, with Iran, which ended in a demoralising 1–1 draw. It was the first time a Scottish team had failed to defeat one of the world's true minnows. A spirited 3–2 victory over Holland in the final group game won the team back some pride and in the three minutes between Archie Gemmill putting Scotland 3–1 ahead and Johnny Rep reducing Holland's margin of defeat to one goal, there was even the tantalising prospect of Scotland winning by the three clear goals necessary to progress.

Johnston's expulsion and the shambles of the tie with Iran were, outside Scotland, seen as more disastrous than losing to a useful Peru side, while Rep regards Holland's defeat to the Scots as the hardest match the Dutch faced in a tournament in which they reached the final. None of those subsequent events, though, had the impact in Scotland of that initial defeat to the South Americans, which was similar to a runaway train piling into the buffers at seventy miles an hour.

Yet if you should visit Hampden Park for a twenty-first century international match, you will find that the most popular retro jersey is that from the World Cup of 1978. Time has healed the wounds of the Ally era and Scotland supporters now look back wistfully on the first six months of that year as the most enjoyable period that international football has given the nation. For a brief moment Ally made the country feel on top of the world and that, surely, has to be worth something.

It was good for business too. MacLeod's sheer charisma had brought out sixty thousand, pay-at-the-gate fans for the friendly with Bulgaria in February 1978; a match in doubt just hours before kick-off because of thawing snow. More than two hundred thousand had been drawn to the three home internationals at Hampden; double the number that might have been expected in any other year.

It seems fitting, not to mention comical, that while back in Scotland the nation had watched perfect, colour pictures of the encounter with Peru, Ally MacLeod was struggling to get a view. The lowdown dugouts at the Chateau Carreras stadium in Cordoba afforded only an ankle-level view and in the late 1970s football managers had not yet hit upon the idea of standing up. On discovering his unsatisfactory vantage point, Ally asked for a seat in the stand but was told that every place had been taken. It was characteristic of Ally. He had promised us such delightful sights, only to discover that his view was obscured when that perfect vision failed to unfold.

According to Weir, the most depressing aspect of the afternoon was sitting in the dressing room at half-time with this oddly cast team and wondering whether they had it within them to do anything about a situation that threatened to define me, the man of a two former European Cup winner with Borussia Dortmund twelve years earlier might have struggled to see this distinction supersede helming a Scotland team thrashed in the Faroes. For a while it looked as though this might be the case, with Petersen, a handsome geography teacher, looking as though he might score every time he took aim at the goalposts. His first goal, after just six minutes, came via a header after a cross had evaded Christian Dailly. His second, with a barely credible twelve minutes having elapsed, was clipped in with a degree of expertise by the same player, again from a cross from the Faroese right.

'A cross came over my head and it was great finish from the lad, to be fair,' recalls an honest Weir, whose recollection of the scene at half-time does not tally with the report of others. He recalls the goings-on at the time of the interview in terms of a sombre and shocked dressing room. Weir remembers a lot of shouting and needling from others, too. But most of all he remembers feeling a depressing sense of hopelessness as they contemplated the task that lay ahead.

'The story, which has grown arms and legs, is that Paul Lambert got up and had a real go at everyone during the interval. He and Berti were very, very close. He [Lambert] set himself apart a bit as the elder statesman, not that he was very old at the time. There were the players, then Paul, then the manager.

'There was obviously a realisation during half-time that it was not good enough. And it was a disaster, or at least a potential disaster. There was shock as well as a determination to get it right, but to be honest there was also a feeling of "I don't know if we are capable of any". It was probably the worst feeling of all.'

The two centre-halves that afternoon later had the blame pinned on them by Vogts in an interview with the German sports agency SID. Although the manager protested that his words had not meant to sound as brutal as those published, they pushed Weir over the edge. Dailly, Weir's partner in the centre of defence shared the blame. Notably, while Weir responded by retiring, with immediate effect, from Scotland, Dailly flourished in the months and years ahead under Vogts and became the unofficial mascot for the Tartan Army. But Weir, whose second son had just been born, wondered whether it was still worth

8

The Death of Jock Stein

Stephen McGowan

'Every manager dies a little during a game. I'd rather die in a dug-out than moulder away in a director's box.'

Jock Stein speaking in 1978.

From within Ninian Park, across the Welsh valleys and beyond, the news spread fast. There were no mobile phones and no internet connections, merely television bulletins and word of mouth. On a seismic night in the Welsh capital of Cardiff, Scotland's national football team had taken a major step towards qualifying for their fourth successive World Cup finals and a nation rejoiced.

Yet the celebrations didn't last long. Like revellers being doused down by a water hose, the Tartan Army fell silent as the news passed along the line. Jock Stein, a colossus who bestrode the Scottish football scene for the best part of three decades, was dead.

Around Scotland, from the Highlands and Islands to the sprawling conurbations of the central belt and onto the Borders, groups had gathered around analogue television sets. Stein's injury-stricken Scotland needed a solitary point against an up-and-coming Wales side to reach the holy grail of a play-off spot against the winners of the Oceanic group. When Wales took an early lead a nation's faith was tested. The temperament of substitute Davie Cooper, striking a critical penalty kick nine minutes from time, proved the answer to five million prayers. Stein, the modern-day Midas of the Scottish game, had prevailed one last time.

As the game drew to its conclusion there was a commotion. Medics and coaching staff crowded around the Scotland manager just seconds after a rogue photographer had been manhandled from the same area, the final victim of Stein's volcanic temper. ITV commentator Brian Moore had expressed the wish at kick-off that his words might make sense above the pulsating emotions reverberating around this modest Welsh arena. Setting speech to the pictures of Stein being carried from the technical area, however, Moore's soundtrack made no sense at all.

The experience of Scotland's first minister Alex Salmond, an avid supporter of the national team, echoes that of so many armchair viewers.

> I was sitting in my front room in Linlithgow and what I remember most was the complete contrast of emotions. I had been sitting there with my nose to the television, revelling in the qualification for the play-off. At the final whistle I got up to make a cup of tea as reports were coming over in a slightly garbled manner that Jock Stein had collapsed.
>
> In truth, the initial reports didn't especially convey the seriousness of it all.

As panic enveloped the tunnel area of Ninian Park, blind faith played out in the bars and front rooms of Scotland. Stein had been known as the Big Man since his epic reign at Celtic. The description transcended his mere girth and physical presence; it spoke also for the manner in which he conducted his glittering managerial career with an air of invincibility. Put simply Stein was akin to the godfather of Scottish football. When injury cut short his time as the steadiest centre-half at Celtic he became the best coach in the country instead. In 1975 he had also defied a life-threatening car crash near Lockerbie, emerging from a lengthy convalescence a wiser, if more circumspect, figure. Now, when the national team needed his guidance most, television pictures showed a man quite literally drowning as his lungs filled with fluid.

'It was unbelievable because Jock Stein was always like a rock,' ponders Salmond, a lifelong Hearts fan. 'He was all-pervasive in Scottish football and seemed almost indestructible.'

No one cared to believe, then, as he crumpled to the trackside watched by millions across the United Kingdom, that Scotland's manager already had one foot in the grave.

Ernie Walker, secretary of the Scottish Football Association for thirteen years, was Stein's colleague and a close personal friend. When he heard the news of the manager's collapse on the television in a VIP room, where he had taken respite from the tension of the game's final moments, Walker rushed down to the treatment room to seek assurance. 'I'm all right Ernie, it's only the cough,' said the hulking figure on the treatment table. But it was much more than a cough, as Walker explains.

> I was told later that he was virtually dead from the moment he hit the trackside. I spoke to our doctor Stewart Hillis the next day and told him Jock had managed to speak to me. But he said it was akin to a car running without a battery. The man was already effectively dead and nothing could have been done to revive him.

Stein's final words before his long-term heart-and-lung ailments combined in fatal fashion were spoken to Hillis. 'It's all right doc. I'm feeling better now.'

In football, as in life, hindsight is the only perfect science. In the public post-mortem that followed Stein's death there was much discussion of his demeanour in the hours leading up to the game in Cardiff. Some sensed all was not well. Scotland had lost to Wales in Glasgow earlier in the same qualifying campaign, a damaging 1–0 defeat thanks to an Ian Rush goal, placing a manager unaccustomed to public criticism in an uncomfortable position. Unchecked claims surfaced that the Scotland manager suffered a mild stroke after that game. What was never in doubt was that he was on medication to mediate the dangers of heart failure, yet had opted against taking his pills in the hours leading up to the Cardiff return; ostensibly to remain focused and unencumbered by possible side effects.

Ernie Walker confirms that even at that point Stein was not a well man.

> Jock was not very well the summer before he died. He had a cough, which was persistent and never really abated. He was also under a bit

of pressure to get us to Mexico from all quarters, mainly the press. There was an attack from the former Airdrie and Scotland forward Bobby Flavell in the *Sunday Mail*. Bobby was finished with the game by then, so the paper dug him up as someone prepared to say whatever was required for £50 or whatever he was paid. He basically suggested in his piece that Jock was never a good coach. It was typical of the kind of nonsense going on around Jock at the time.

He was under pressure and the knives were out for him.

Accounts vary on whether Stein was entirely himself in the approach to the game. In 1977 Ally MacLeod's Scotland had prevailed against Wales in a winner-takes-all triumph at Anfield and, with the Welsh seeking not only revenge but also their first trip to the finals since 1958, the hype for the game in Cardiff reached boiling point.

As Archie Macpherson reveals in his 2004 biography of the Scotland manager, *Jock Stein: the Definitive Biography*, Stein had invited his coaching assistants Alex Ferguson and future Scotland manager Andy Roxburgh into his hotel room the night prior to the game. Stein dominated the conversation, but not in the conventional manner. What followed instead was a verbal dissection of his remarkable career, the triumphs and the despair. Never before had Stein, who preferred to push his players to the fore, revealed so much of himself. 'What was that about?' asked Ferguson as they left the room later that night. 'That was very strange.'

It was far from a solitary portent. Former Celtic manager Gordon Strachan played on the left of midfield in Cardiff before being replaced by Cooper in Stein's last major managerial decision. Strachan remembers the day of Stein's death clearly, recalling this giant of world football as hot and bothered at times, ashen faced at others. During lunch at the team hotel, around mid-day, the midfielder noted a rare show of vulnerability in the great man's armour.

Physically he didn't look so well. I'd never seen him like that before. He was a bit grey. I understand now as a football manager how you can go a bit that way. But he was perspiring. He was a big man, I know that, but it was just a thought that went in and out of my head very quickly. 'Jock's no well today,' and I came back to that thought later when I sat down. Aye, he wasnae well.

Others, it should be said, dismiss such talk, chief among them the redoubtable Walker, now aged eighty-one, who led from the front at the SFA, earning him the moniker Ayatollah of Park Gardens.

Few had expected Walker and Stein to rub along together at the SFA. They had what might euphemistically be deemed 'history'. Neither was given to holding back and their combustible personalities were regarded as oil and water. Furthermore, Stein's voluble mistrust of Scotland's football establishment had been formed during an early brush with SFA officials. A temporary reign as Scotland caretaker manager in 1965 witnessed a late John Greig goal handing the nation a historic victory over Italy in a World Cup qualifier. Yet a 3–0 thrashing in Naples in the return game showed clearly that the blazers had short memories. On the flight home the performance drew little tactical appreciation from the SFA committee men and, disgusted by their attitude, Stein concentrated his energies thereafter on guiding his fledgling Celtic team to great things.

By 1978, however, circumstances had changed. After thirteen years in Glasgow's east end Stein had severed his ties with Celtic because of what he believed was an insult. In financial terms his reward for delivering the European Cup, ten Scottish League titles, nine Scottish Cups and six League Cups was trifling. Stein, an inveterate gambler, ended his time at the club on a basic salary of £12,100. From a Celtic board famed for keeping match takings in a biscuit tin, there was never much in the way of gratitude. A league-and-cup double in 1976 was a final flicker of defiance, yet mediocrity was becoming evident in the Celtic team. Wary of the backlash a public hanging might provoke, the Celtic board sugared Stein's severance pill with the offer of a post as head of the club's pools operation. Talk of a seat on the board never materialised.

Angered and wounded by the derisory offer, Stein opted instead to cut his losses, being lured south by Leeds United chairman Manny Cussins. But Stein was Leeds manager for a mere forty-four days before the sight of four walls in a Yorkshire hotel room began to grate. Home was calling and the departure of Ally MacLeod from the Scotland hot-seat presented a window of opportunity. Lobbying influential journalists and broadcasters, Stein whispered his availability in the ears of the powers-that-be at Park Gardens.

First, however, there was the matter of a potential clash of personalities to resolve, as Ernie Walker knew only too well.

It was a strange thing. We had known each other for a long time, but almost as adversaries. I was always identified by those within the game as being on the side of law and order. To Jock it seemed as if I was always appearing on the steps of Park Gardens making some sort of pronouncement, banning someone or other.

Neither of us was particularly adept at stepping back. So, yes, we had a number of confrontations, but to me it was no big deal. We respected each other, but it's fair to say there was no love lost.

Eventually, I became secretary of the SFA itself and Jock, in time, joined us. But before he did so he came to me directly and asked what I felt about his appointment personally. He had the feeling I might not welcome his arrival. I told him straight: 'Jock, you and I want the same thing – a winning Scotland team.' So with that he came aboard and we quickly began to understand each other. In time it became a strong friendship.

I was forever trying to push this change or that innovation through the committees and I would bounce things off him. He was a sensible, wise man and often he would tell me not to take so and so on – not to stick my neck out. Sadly, I was never very good at keeping my neck in.

But we would travel to matches together. He would drive us to Manchester, Leeds or wherever for a midweek game at high speed and because of that we became close. He appreciated being part of the SFA.

Financially, we had a system where every year we would increase salaries in line with the cost of living. It wasn't a fortune by any means, but I wanted to ensure that the salary that covered the cost of a loaf of bread one year still covered it the next.

So I told him one day his salary would be rising by 3 per cent. He nodded and left without comment, but the next day he put his head round my door and told me he had discussed it with Jean and that they couldn't ever recall receiving any kind of rise without having to ask for it. It was a small thing, but we offered some security and he appreciated that.

Walker and Stein, then, became football's equivalent of the Odd Couple, Oscar and Felix, until death wrenched them apart. For the last sixteen years Walker has fought cancer, a pioneering drug from the United States granting fresh hope where there was previously none. If the body is ailing, however, there remains precious little wrong with the mind or the memory cells. Walker is quite emphatic that Stein's health was, while certainly not perfect, far from critical.

Jock had been better, but no one was thinking in terms of him dying. So far as I was concerned he was fine going up to the match. On the way to the stadium we were all at the front of the bus, myself, Jock, Alex Ferguson, the doc Stewart Hillis and so on.

We were actually playing a quiz game to relieve the tension and everything was perfectly normal. No one would have said he was anything other than his normal self. Okay, he was under more pressure than anyone, but that was the manager's job. He had been there before.

To me he never seemed remotely distracted. We had worked together a long time remember. Of course a person can keep something inside them, we didn't talk about a number of things. But the nature of his death was so bizarre, before the eyes of the world, that he would never have wanted that. Dying like that would have been the last thing he'd have wanted.

Maybe the pressure did eventually tell. The magnitude of the game couldn't be overstated, he understood that. Everything rested on it.

In those days we would regard it as a national disaster if we failed to reach the World Cup finals; these days people just shrug their shoulders. But we were going for our fourth successive appearance that campaign, people now expected qualification.

An experienced Wales team forged by manager Mike England had triumphed in Glasgow the previous spring on a night that Scotland lost the physical battle. Quite simply the team was bullied. At Ninian Park Stein was determined to avoid a similar fate. Richard Gough was detailed to pay extra attention to the bustling Manchester United striker Mark Hughes. Roy Aitken and Alex McLeish also played, with Willie Miller sweeping behind. Within three minutes McLeish was booked for his second clash with Hughes in a demonstration of the no-nonsense approach that would typify this turbo-charged encounter. Yet in a fiercely contested first half the Scots could barely contain the Old Trafford striker and Hughes duly claimed his sixth goal in ten games for his country in the thirteenth minute, Peter Nicholas outmuscling Aitken and Steve Nicol before his low cross was thumped into the net.

In comparison, Scotland's unfamiliar strike partnership of Everton's Graham Sharp and the highly strung David Speedie looks an odd choice now, given they had but one cap between them. Many thought that Andy Gray and Maurice Johnston were better options, but they were on the bench. Few in the Welsh camp would have exchanged Hughes or Rush for either Sharp or Speedie. Stein had been hampered by the loss of key players: Kenny Dalglish was out through injury while midfield anchorman Graeme Souness and his Liverpool defensive teammate, Alan Hansen, were also missing.

By his own admission Gordon Strachan – a hugely talented player at Aberdeen, Manchester United and Leeds – never imposed himself on the game. His first-half contribution was anonymous and Stein emphasised the need for improvement at the interval. On television half-time analyst Jimmy Greaves was already predicting the worst for the Scots.

Greaves might have been even more emphatic with his prediction had he known of the chaos unfolding in the Scotland dressing room. Goalkeeper Jim Leighton had lost a contact lens in the first period and carried no spares with him. The matter proved a source of consternation to Alex Ferguson, Scotland's assistant manager and Leighton's club manager. Later Ferguson was to say that he had no idea that the taciturn Leighton even wore contacts. Nor did his teammates, as Maurice Malpas, at the time a young full-back with Dundee United, confirms.

> At that stage the players realised nothing. Jim Leighton had lost his contact lens and to this day I don't know if he just forgot to bring a spare pair, but Alan Rough went on in his place anyway. There was mayhem

in the dressing room when this emerged, but in terms of big Jock there was no indication that he was poorly. To my recollection he performed the half-time team talk for a start. But like all the players I was engrossed in the game, that's just what you do as a player.

Later, Ferguson would describe some rare and highly unusual signs of Stein's confused state of mind at the interval. It was the first real indication something might be going awry. In the past Stein would have commanded his half-time dressing room like a prowling bear, urging, cajoling and rebuking the likes of Leighton for their lack of foresight. Not this time.

Scotland began the second half with Cooper and Everton's Andy Gray warming up on the sidelines and struggled to make inroads. In truth, the Welsh looked in little danger, the hustle and bustle of a fairly dreadful game of football suiting their style perfectly. Then, on the hour mark, Stein acted, introducing the enigmatic Rangers winger Davie Cooper for Strachan on the left flank. Not before more confusion, however, as the board initially suggested Nicol would be replaced. Gordon Strachan, while manager at Celtic, reflected on Stein's decision. 'What Jock did summed up management. It's all about decisions, making the right ones. I'm glad to say I was part of his last right decision. He's taken me off; it was the last big decision he ever made.'

Cooper changed the game, injecting urgency, trickery and pace into Scotland's attacks. Suddenly, the Welsh looked vulnerable. In the eightieth minute a Steve Nicol cross was nodded down by Sharp to Speedie, whose attempt on goal was handled by Wales defender David Phillips. It was, by any reckoning, a harsh award. No match perhaps for the Joe Jordan handball that had robbed the Welsh in similar fashion in 1977, yet Dutch referee Johannes Keizer pointed immediately to the spot.

At Rangers Cooper was known as the Moody Blue, a nickname that reflected his mercurial nature. However, his left foot was never anything less than steady and predictable and despite the tumult around him Cooper produced an exemplary penalty, prompting a volcanic eruption among the Scotland fans packed dangerously close together on terracing behind the goal.

In some respects the goal served to increase, rather than reduce, the tension. For Scotland the need to close the game out was imperative. Ernie Walker's nerves, meanwhile, were being stretched as taut as piano wire in the grandstand above.

> I simply couldn't take it anymore. Only people within the SFA could understand or comprehend what this game really meant to us. I had been unable to relax on holiday the summer before. Qualification would grant us four years of peace from the media, with no one on our backs. Sponsorship would be easier to come by and revenue would be secure. All of this depended on some guy either scoring or missing a penalty kick nine minutes from time. It was a ridiculous way to run a business.

> Thankfully, the late Davie Cooper scored the penalty and I got up to walk out of the directors' box. I went into the corridor and there was Graeme Souness asking what I was doing there. I said I couldn't take anymore and he was the same. The captain of Scotland was telling me he couldn't f——— take it either. So we went to the boardroom.

Under instruction to keep the bar closed until the final whistle, a waitress refused to serve drink to her VIP guests. Walker duly directed Souness to another VIP room, where he tried to pour a gin and tonic. 'I was so nervous and shaky I couldn't pour a drink properly.'

Gordon Strachan, meanwhile, was wrestling with very different demons in the dugout. Born in Edinburgh the midfielder had been there on the Wembley pitch in 1977 when the Tartan Army had indulged its agricultural instincts at the Mecca of English football. Later, as the squad's injured captain, he would hitchhike his way to the European Championships in Sweden to watch his beloved country. Here, in a Cardiff pressure pot, however, Strachan was quietly imploding in the face of his own shortcomings on the evening, fuming internally even as his countrymen began to contemplate a trip to Mexico that had looked improbable just minutes earlier.

His self-absorption was disturbed briefly by a glance along the lengthy bench to where Stein was rising to his feet to remonstrate with an intrusive photographer. Reacting to the changing tide of the game's fortunes, the snappers had shuffled over to catch the reaction of the

Scotland bench to the final whistle. As always where press photographers are concerned, one of their number sought a final picture, as Strachan remembers.

> The guy was lying underneath him trying to take a picture looking up the way, which is annoying if you're a coach and you have someone crawling about the place. It's bad enough trying to handle the pressure without having someone taking pictures of you.
>
> There was a bit of a commotion, then it all calmed down again. Then, next minute, there were a lot of people around. I looked over and thought, 'What's going on here?' And that was it.
>
> The words I remember are, 'Jock's no well. There's something wrong with his heart.' That's what we were told.

Stein was carried down the wood-panelled, cramped tunnel by four uniformed policemen. Caught in the drama of the final whistle, however, many had little concept of the drama unfolding.

Blood and fists pumping, Scotland's players united with the vast bank of supporters in ecstatic acclaim on the final whistle. The tension was released with the realisation that the play-off had been reached. With it came the likelihood of an appearance in the World Cup finals.

Suddenly, the television cameras cut away to shots of a conscious Stein being carted into the treatment room.

'Jock Stein is being carried off there,' said commentator Brian Moore. 'Maybe Jock has been overcome by it all.' If only that had been the full extent of it. The taut faces of doctor Hillis and physio Brian Scott suggested something altogether more serious.

The players thronged back to the cramped dressing room of the old stadium to be met with the immediate sense of displacement. Something, they instinctively sensed, was wrong. Willie Miller was caught by ITV interviewer Martin Tyler in the tunnel, his facial expression visibly altering as the broadcaster confirmed the news of Stein's collapse. Maurice Malpas was in the dressing room and recalls how he discovered what had happened.

> Bizarre is the only word to describe it really. I was absolutely elated because to all intents and purposes we had qualified and for me it

would be my first World Cup. But, right away, we sensed something wasn't right.

The backroom staff would normally be there waiting to pat you on the back, but they had all disappeared. Someone, I think it was Alex Ferguson, came in to tell us Jock had suffered a heart attack and everything fell silent. I remember seeing Jimmy Steele, the masseur, who was really close to Jock and he was absolutely distraught.

Within ten minutes we learned the manager was dead.

In that period a human tragedy unfolded, the nature of which haunts the sprightly Ernie Walker to this day. His recollections are as fresh now as they were the morning-after-the-night-before some twenty-five years ago.

I remember there was a television on the wall and there was a guy reporting that Jock had collapsed in the dugout. I immediately ran downstairs to the treatment room and boarded up the door. It was pandemonium as the final whistle sounded.

Stewart Hillis, our doctor, had all the facilities he needed – his own hospital couldn't have done more – and Jock looked up at me and said 'I'm all right Ernie.'

Myself and Bill Dickie held him still while the doctor put a jag in his arm to relax him, which it did. The ambulance had arrived by now and the doctor was writing a note to tell the hospital what he had given Jock. I told David Will, an SFA colleague, that his wife Jean would be watching and asked that he call her immediately to tell her what was happening. The ambulance men were about to place him on a stretcher when he died. They tried everything, adrenalin, a defibrillator; nothing worked.

As Malpas concedes, it was a shattering and deeply contradictory end to a night of triumph, surely the greatest contrast of emotions in World Cup history.

We went from one extreme to the next. During the game we had no idea what was happening. Other people were prepared for the news by watching it unfold on television, not us. I was as high as a kite and now, suddenly, we were brought back to earth by life. Or by the end of a life, as it transpired.

All we had been preoccupied with was qualifying and now suddenly that seemed totally immaterial.

It didn't matter a damn.

Striker Graham Sharp tells a similar tale, rating that night in Cardiff as the worst experience of a decorated career in the English top flight.

> I remember going into the dressing room, coming from the joy of making it to the World Cup playoff, and then being told Jock had collapsed. They didn't say how bad it was at first, but looking around the staff you saw the faces. I knew then something was seriously wrong.
>
> I met my Everton teammates who had played for Wales, Neville Southall, Kevin Ratcliffe and Pat Van Den Hauwe, outside and there was just nothing to be said. I was staying with Andy Gray that night in Birmingham and I remember the drive back vividly because we sat in silence. There was no conversation whatsoever.

As news of the developing turn of events reached news desks across the United Kingdom journalists learned the grim extent of Stein's collapse when Souness emerged, eyes glistening, to state baldly: 'He's gone.' The late David Will had emerged from the treatment room seconds earlier to deliver the message to the captain via a sullen shake of the head.

Walker granted the media an impromptu press conference on the squad charter back to Edinburgh that evening, confirming that Alex Ferguson would take charge for the playoff games with Australia. Later, at Edinburgh airport, an early-morning hush descended over the party of players, officials and press men who collected their worldly goods before making for home. As the last holdall was lifted from the baggage carousel a solitary item of luggage remained, spinning forlornly on the belt.

An appeal from an airport handler found no takers. A cursory scan inside revealed a book, some pills, a bottle of white wine and a letter addressed to J. Stein esq.

As former *Scotsman* sports writer Mike Aitken puts it: 'We'd all just dictated his obituaries, but only then did it become real. Jock was gone.'

Ernie Walker drove straight to the Stein family home on the south side of Glasgow with Will and family friend Tony McGuinness, where he extended his condolences, finally leaving at five in the morning. 'It was a terrible night,' he sighs now with something approaching under-statement. Handed the task of reclaiming Stein's body discreetly and arranging a funeral it was, he concedes, a bleak episode.

Even the hardest of men found it hard to take. Alex Ferguson had learned at the feet of the master, regarding Stein as his mentor in the hard school of football management. He would later relate what Stein meant to him.

> I didn't shed a tear until I had flown from Cardiff to Glasgow and set out on the drive to Aberdeen. On the way up I pulled into a lay-by and broke down. For people like myself Jock was the precursor of all the deeds and challenges we needed to aim at. He would never take the praise himself. It was always about the players and how great the team were.
>
> For any man seeking to further his education in football Jock Stein was a one-man university.

Long before the 'Dianafication' of the United Kingdom the passing of Jock Stein had working-class men, shorn of their macho bravado, shedding a tear. Up to ten thousand men, women and children – many too young to have known his heyday at Celtic Park – lined the route to Glasgow's Linn crematorium following a service attended by the great and the good of British football. Wife Jean and daughter Rae were joined by son George, while friends including Lawrie McMenemy, Sir Matt Busby, Alex Ferguson, Bobby Robson and the entire board of directors of Rangers and Celtic delivered their own tributes.

'Jock was a man of dignity, a touch of class,' recorded Robson, a former England manager who passed away to comparable plaudits after a battle with cancer in 2009. 'No one is irreplaceable, but he will be one of the hardest.'

Supporters dressed in black suits and ties, others in tartan, and many in Celtic's green and white. A wreath from Celtic Football Club read, 'Mr Scotland, missed by everyone in football.' It was flanked by a similar arrangement from the Scotland squad, which stated simply, 'We will miss you boss.'

Newspapers carried messages of condolence from the secretary of state for Scotland, his Labour shadow, the convener of Strathclyde Regional Council, the lord provost of Glasgow, the general secretary of the Trades Union Congress, the director of the Scottish CBI, Archbishop Thomas Winning and many legends of showbiz, including the late Jimmy Logan.

In death, as in life, Stein's influence was, as Alex Salmond puts it, 'all pervasive'.

> I never met Jock Stein. But growing up he was everywhere. I was a Hearts supporter and he broke my heart when he signed Willie Wallace for what would become the Lisbon Lions. I also remember the sense of shock when he left Celtic and joined Leeds. Why would Celtic let him go? Well, perhaps we know the reasons for that now. But I could never understand why someone who had managed Celtic in such a way would move to Leeds.
>
> For me one of the minor tragedies of Scottish football is that he was not managing the national team in the 1978 World Cup. Stein in charge of a side with that talent might have taken us into the last four.
>
> So for me he became the Scotland manager just a little too late. By 1982 we had a good team, but not a potentially great one like 1978.

Shorn of the shackles of SFA responsibility Ernie Walker can be privately scathing over the Ally MacLeod-led shambles of 1978. Walker carried the public can for much of the fiasco of Argentina and, in retrospect, probably shares Salmond's view.

> Jock came in after Ally MacLeod and proved his opposite in every way. MacLeod would jump up and down when we were winning and prove exactly the opposite when we lost. He told people we would win World Cups. Jock wanted none of that nonsense; it was his intention to manage on an even keel.

And yet not everyone was as appreciative of Stein's record as Scotland manager. These days the record books, propped up by the shambolic reigns of the hapless Berti Vogts and George Burley, show Stein to have the second-best record of any Scotland coach. A run of 68 games brought 30 wins, 13 draws and 25 defeats, statistics bettered only by Craig Brown.

Yet it is also true that the Stein reign began slowly. In his first tilt at a major competition after taking over from Ally MacLeod in the autumn of 1978, Stein failed to guide Scotland to the European Championship finals of 1980. That said, the qualifying effort was hardly a disaster: in a difficult, five-nation group – consisting of Austria, Norway, Belgium, Portugal and Scotland – Stein's team won three, drew one and lost four, a sequence that included a 4–1 victory over Portugal. It is also worth noting that group winners Belgium were good enough to reach the final of the competition.

The 1982 World Cup campaign saw a significant improvement. Scotland's qualifying group was again made up of five teams, with Portugal, Israel, Sweden and Northern Ireland the opposition. The Scots not only qualified but also topped the group, which was by any standards a significant achievement. In the finals, held in Spain, the Scots beat New Zealand by five goals to two but then lost heavily to Brazil. It meant that the final group tie, against the Soviet Union, would determine which of those two nations would advance to the next phase. In a game that could have been won Scotland discovered whole new ways to fail on the major stage, with comical defensive blunders condemning the team to another first-stage exit.

If the two previous tournaments had produced rather mixed outcomes the qualifying campaign for the European Championships of 1984 was, without doubt, poor. Scotland – this time up against East Germany, Belgium and Switzerland – finished bottom of the four-nation group, winning only one game. For the first time in his managerial career Stein's Midas touch was proving elusive.

As Archie Macpherson recalls in his Stein book the cumulative effect of failing to qualify for two out of three finals – with the last campaign particularly disappointing – provoked a telling episode in Switzerland, where the draw for the 1986 World Cup qualifiers was hosted. Over an otherwise convivial dinner SFA president Tommy Younger, emboldened no doubt by alcohol, turned on Stein without warning, arguing that any other manager with a similar record would have been sacked. Younger's outburst required the intervention of a visibly embarrassed Ernie Walker as Stein drummed his fingers on the table, gazing into the middle distance as he did so.

Ach, I read that about a lunch where all this was said, but it was exaggerated. I don't know, maybe Tommy had a bottle of wine in him or something. The fact is that Jock had no enemies within the SFA, but we always knew, as it must, that his time would come to an end.

It may be far from improbable to suggest that had Stein made it to the Mexico finals then, at the age of sixty-three, it might have been his final hurrah as national manager. Walker however was not prepared to let him simply walk away from football.

We had an agreement that if the time came when he would be replaced then he would hear it from me face-to-face. He would never read about it in the pages of a tabloid newspaper first.

He appreciated that, but always insisted that I would never need to do that. He would know his time was up and would come to me. The fact was that he operated without a contract. I had one in my office safe from the day he joined to the day he died – just sitting there unsigned. Our relationship was one of trust.

I had plans for Jock when he decided he no longer wished to be manager. There was no way he was going to be cast aside by the SFA. It was my firm intention that he stay on as an ambassador for Scottish football. He was a good representative of our game and had great contacts. People knew him across the world and we couldn't waste his great knowledge and ability. He was wise, he was sage. I always had the feeling that whatever field he had turned his hand to he would have been a success. It wouldn't have mattered what career.

Across the Old Firm divide that once invigorated him, Stein's impact was no less pronounced. Walter Smith grew up a Rangers supporter, suffering the outrageous arrows thrown in the direction of Ibrox by their tormentor-in-chief. Smith equalled Stein's record of twenty-six Old Firm victories as manager of Rangers with a 1–0 win at Ibrox in March 2010, yet seems almost embarrassed by comparisons.

From my own point of view Jock Stein has been an iconic figure for any of us involved in management. Sir Alex Ferguson went on to Manchester United and the success he has had there perhaps makes him the best Scottish manager ever. But, within this country, Mr Stein is without doubt the best there has been.

Whether that recognition ever extended south of Scotland's rugged border remains a matter of contention. In a little country with a sprawling conceit of its past achievements on the world stage simmering resentment accompanies the knowledge that Stein died before joining the ranks of football's knights of the realm.

Sir Matt Busby, a working-class son of Lanarkshire like Stein, was knighted for winning the European Cup for Manchester United in 1968 – a full twelve months after Celtic. Alf Ramsay, architect of a sterile World Cup win on home soil for England, was also accorded the ultimate honour by the Queen. In the aftermath of leading Celtic to their second European Cup final in Rotterdam in 1970, however, Stein's reward was a mere CBE, a rather modest accolade in comparison with his English-based peers.

In July 2007 some light was shed on the reasons for the government snub to Stein when the Freedom of Information commissioner released documents originally intended to be kept secret until 2030. Whether they reveal sinister class snobbery or painfully slow bureaucratic foot-dragging is a matter of interpretation. It would hardly be an act of treasonable proportions to suggest that both were at play.

The papers show that Labour's former Scottish Secretary, Willie Ross, fighting an increasingly bullish Scottish National Party at the polls, lobbied his London superiors hard on Stein's behalf, believing that the persistent ignorance risked accusations of anti-Scottish behaviour. By the time Whitehall accepted the legitimacy of Stein's claim, however, Celtic had become embroiled in a shameful world-club championship defeat to Argentina's Racing Club, in which four Parkhead players were sent off for violent play during an infamous play-off in Montevideo, the capital of Uruguay. Sensitive to accusations that he might be condoning sporting anarchy, the Labour prime minister, Harold Wilson, withheld the honour. More than forty years later the recriminations of that decision rumble on.

In response to the matter first being raised in May 1967, three weeks before Celtic's European Cup triumph over Internazionale in Lisbon, Sir John Lang, government advisor on sporting honours, had suggested that Celtic chairman Robert Kelly be knighted instead, with Stein receiving an OBE. A knighthood, they deemed, was inappropriate for a club manager, an argument that was quickly discarded when Matt Busby won the same trophy with Manchester United.

The response from Willie Ross and the Scottish Office was stinging. 'We would regard an OBE as quite inappropriate,' the missive reads. 'Mr Stein is admittedly manager of an individual football club, but it is a club which has achieved something wholly without precedent in Great Britain.'

The battle appeared to be edging to a successful and satisfactory conclusion for the Scottish nation until Jimmy Johnstone, Bertie Auld, John Hughes and Bobby Lennox were all dismissed in the world's top club match in South America. Stein's name, already pencilled into the honours list at the top end, was swiftly erased with undue haste.

In those government papers a Scottish Office civil servant points to the less than glowing disciplinary records of Ramsay's and Busby's teams by way of protest. William Weatherston argues in a memo, not without merit, that it was 'important that recognition is given where it is deserved and that Scottish claims should not be seen to be less well treated than those in England'.

Not until Stein took his team back to the European pinnacle in 1970, however, did Scottish Office rage and frustration at perceived English bias explode. 'If Celtic win the European Cup for a second time on May 6,' writes Willie Ross, 'I really do not see how we can avoid an award for Stein.'

Alex Salmond, Scotland's first SNP first minister, has no doubts about why Stein was refused a knighthood.

As we now know a Stein knighthood was turned down for the most ridiculous and spurious of reasons. When you think about it in retrospect it really was an enormous snub.

The idea that Jock Stein should somehow be blamed for the provocative events against Racing Club in the world-club championship of 1968 is absurd. You have to see it now as being anti-Scottish, anti-working class and, indeed, anti-Celtic.

But I read the documents on this and when you see the Scottish Office letter which damns them over this it is almost grovelling in its apologetic nature. It was written before the 1970 European Cup final, which Celtic lost, and basically states that if Celtic had won that game then, 'oh dear, he will have to get some kind of honour'.

Such is the nature of party politics that there may be an element of exaggeration to such talk.

In an intriguing twist to the tale, however, Ernie Walker offers up a hitherto unsuspected and unaired side to the story.

> I read all the things about Jock being regarded as 'not the right sort' and so on and I don't know that all that was true. So far as I am aware he was offered a knighthood, but rejected it. I don't know precisely why. I can only guess that he felt he was Jock Stein and could never see himself as Sir Jock Stein. We did not dwell overly long on the matter, but Jock definitely told me he had been offered it and I recall it quite clearly.

If true then Walker's account borders on the mildly sensational. It has long been rumoured that Stein was dismissive of the knighthood idea, suggesting the name of his chairman Bob Kelly to officials instead. Yet, as Alex Salmond points out, conjecture on that scale casts up more questions than answers.

> I don't know if that can be the case. Why would he turn down a knighthood, yet accept a CBE in 1970 if that were so? Ernie is a great guy and was a very fine football statesman, I know him well. He also knows these things well and you can never fully know what happened.
>
> But whoever is right it's odd in a sense that the knighthood was never awarded because Harold Wilson, the prime minister of the period, had a sureness of touch where these matters were concerned.
>
> Either way it is quite an anomaly.

A decision in October 2009 to name a set of commemorative stamps after the late Sir Matt Busby to celebrate remarkable Britons brought some measure of compensation to Scots. And yet in any poll of great football managers in his homeland Busby would invariably run a poor third to Stein and his Manchester United protégé Sir Alex Ferguson, another whose work in the sphere of English football drew the ultimate honour from Her Majesty's government.

How a miner from Burnbank, Lanarkshire came to occupy Scottish Office and Whitehall mandarins to such a degree is a remarkable tale. One that challenges every preconception amongst 'football people' over the background required to succeed at the top level in football management. Stein certainly played the game, but his true talent lay in his brain, rather than his feet.

At first Stein was not that highly regarded at Celtic. Jimmy Gribben, a club scout who had the ear of the controlling and hands-on chairman Robert Kelly, recommended the defender as a stop-gap option for first-team cover after hearing of his unhappiness with Welsh club Llanelli. Yet Celtic had never bargained for the sheer force of his personality, which encompassed rampant self-confidence, cunning negotiating skills and a sharp wit. Those qualities would have made him a candidate for high office in the trade-union movement had football chosen to forsake his talents.

Stein would prove himself a remarkable troubleshooter at distressed football clubs, cutting his teeth at Dunfermline Athletic where he avoided relegation and won the Scottish Cup within a year. In 1964 it was onto Hibs where his tactical thinking and physiological innovations were revolutionary in the conservative Scottish game. Prodding the likes of the gifted, yet wayward, Willie Hamilton into line Stein won the Summer Cup and made himself impossible for Celtic to ignore. In March 1965 he returned to the east end of Glasgow as the club's first non-Catholic manager. He demanded – and received – absolute power over team selection and brooked no interference from the fiddling fingers of Bob Kelly. In return he delivered Europe and in the eyes of supporters, the earth and the stars.

To those who succeed him at Celtic, Stein is the benchmark; the man whose image glowers down on them from a vast painting in a lounge bearing his name. East of the lounge is an entire grandstand named in his honour. On the wall outside Celtic Park is the plaque that stood for over twenty years in Ninian Park, close to the dugout where he collapsed and died. Ninian Park is no more. It was bulldozed to make way for a soulless new arena across the road. Yet Stein's memory and legacy have stood the test of time and outlived mere bricks and mortar.

Gordon Strachan, the first Celtic manager since Stein to lead the club to three championships in a row, is well aware of Stein's legacy:

> Most legends die younger, you know. And some of the legends who hang on a long time can be disappointing. I'm not saying I'm glad it happened; just that he will always be a legendary figure. Nothing will ever change that. You've still got the image of a giant man with a sarcastic comment here and a witty remark there. Your vision is still that rather than of somebody who is frail and struggling around the place. That's what I remember. We'd sit down on the settee, have a cup of tea and talk about the game. He seemed to enjoy my company and vice versa. You know, I've met football legends in my time and they've sometimes been disappointing in terms of personality.
>
> But when Big Jock walked into the room you knew straightaway you were in the presence of someone special.

Rob Robertson

9

Aberdeen: the Road to Gothenburg

Rob Robertson

11 May 1983. The most celebrated date in the history of Aberdeen Football Club. A team put together by the man who would go on to be Britain's greatest manager of all time, featuring some of Scotland's greatest ever players, beat the mighty Real Madrid in Gothenburg to lift the European Cup Winners' Cup. It was a victory that sent shock waves through the world of football and put the team from the north-east city firmly on the map. It also meant that the names of manager Alex Ferguson, captain Willie Miller and goal scorers Eric Black and John Hewitt gained legendary status overnight.

The Dons victory over the Spanish giants will never be forgotten by the Pittodrie faithful, who no doubt would love such great days to return to their club sometime soon. Although that looks highly unlikely they will always have the memory of one of the most remarkable eras in Scottish football, which culminated in not just the European Cup Winners' Cup victory but also a Super Cup win over Hamburg six months later. 'That Aberdeen team is one of the greatest Scotland has ever produced,' remembers captain Willie Miller. 'It was a privilege to be part of it and I will retain the memories of Gothenburg until my dying day.'

Miller admits that at the start of the 1982/83 season even he could never have predicted the fantastic year the club was about to have. Miller, along with Alex McLeish and Gordon Strachan, had started training two weeks after everybody else because they had been away with Scotland at the World Cup in Mexico in 1982.

To add to the high drama Miller returned after the World Cup to find an offer on the table to join Rangers – and with the guarantee that he would captain the side from the moment he signed. Alex Ferguson knew he couldn't risk losing his most influential player and pulled out all the stops to ensure he stayed at the club. Negotiations dragged on to the extent that when McLeish and Strachan joined up with the team for a series of friendlies against the likes of Nairn County, Ross County and Inverness Thistle the club captain stayed at home, as he explains.

> The financial offer from Rangers ended up at being about the same money I was being offered to sign a new deal with Aberdeen, which meant my decision was based on where I thought there would be a better chance of on-the-field success. That was a bit of a no-brainer as the gaffer was one of the greatest coaches in the game. He was also a very persuasive type who convinced me to stay, although to be honest, he was pushing at an open door.
>
> I always remember he said to me we would win more trophies, and lift a European one, at some stage. But privately he told me he didn't think it would be straightaway as the entrants into the European Cup Winners' Cup that year included top clubs like Tottenham Hotspur, Paris St Germain, Inter Milan, Barcelona, Austria Vienna and of course Real Madrid.
>
> For once the gaffer was wrong, and I still laugh about it now. Also, sometimes I look back and think what a huge mistake I would have made if I had decided to move from Aberdeen to Rangers and had missed out on great moments like the night we beat Real Madrid.

With Miller signed up the Dons started the season full of optimism but because Aberdeen were one of the unseeded teams in the European Cup Winners' Cup they had to play a preliminary-round qualification game against Sion of Switzerland. It was a tie they romped home in. All the hard work was done in the first leg, in which they humiliated their Swiss opponents 7–0 at Pittodrie. Goals from Eric Black, Gordon Strachan, Neil Simpson, John Hewitt, Mark McGhee, Stuart Kennedy and an own goal from the Swiss defender Balet made the second leg a formality. Things got even better for Aberdeen in the return, which they won 4–1 with the minimum of fuss thanks to goals from Willie Miller, John Hewitt and two from Mark McGhee. Miller remembers Ferguson being more relaxed before the second leg than he had ever seen him, before or since. He even had time to say to him before kick-off how he had been impressed by the picturesque Tourbillon stadium, which was surrounded by high mountains dotted with chalets, whose lights lit up the mountainside.

The win over Sion didn't help Aberdeen's domestic form and they lost their first Scottish league game to bitter rivals Dundee United before losing to them again in the League Cup. At that stage there was no indication their season would end with a major European trophy in the Pittodrie cabinet. Being out of the League Cup allowed Aberdeen to concentrate on the league, where they beat Dundee, Kilmarnock and Dundee United with only a draw against Hibs stopping four wins in a row.

Back in form and full of confidence they were drawn against the unknown Dinamo Tirana of Albania in the first round of the Cup Winners' Cup proper. It was a nightmare draw because back in the 1980s Albania was well and truly cut off from the rest of the world, with visitors banned by the Communist regime. Because of that there were also all sorts of visa complications and red tape to be cut through. Even Ferguson, not a man known for giving up, threw in the towel when the Albanian authorities made it impossible for him to go on a spying trip. Maybe the fact that it was a 'spying trip' gave them the jitters as they wanted nobody spying on them, whether a football manager or someone from the British embassy.

That lack of knowledge of the opposition, something Ferguson never willingly allowed to happen, put him at a disadvantage. It meant that when Dinamo Tirana turned up to Pittodrie he knew next to nothing about them and Willie Miller noticed how uncomfortable his manager was.

That made the boss a bit nervous. He did his homework on every opposition team but he was left frustrated that he couldn't compile too much information on them. To be honest we were confident we would beat them as Albania was hardly a football stronghold. We certainly did not underestimate them but things turned out more difficult than we thought.

That turned out to be an understatement, with Tirana revealing themselves as a stuffy, uncompromising outfit. For all their best efforts Aberdeen struggled to break the Albanians down and out of all their Cup Winners' Cup matches that year this was the most frustrating ninety minutes they had to endure. It was a John Hewitt goal that finally separated the sides and unbeknown to Aberdeen at the time it would prove to be one of the most significant of their European campaign.

The fact that the Dinamo Tirana players ordered steak for every meal, including breakfast, and ate heaps of food suggested to the Pittodrie backroom staff they didn't get much variety in their homeland. Because of that the Dons took their own chef and their own food, including fifty Mars Bars, to Albania to make sure the players ate well. Taking only a one-goal lead to Albania made it a nervous journey but at least Ferguson had the benefit of knowing a bit about their players, a luxury he didn't have before the first leg. Tactically, he set his side up well and what was even more important was their stamina late in the game.

The match was played in blistering heat of more than ninety degrees and with Willie Miller and Alex McLeish marshalling the defence the Dons restricted Dinamo to just a few speculative efforts. Ferguson was slightly concerned that coming from the north-east of Scotland his team might fade as the heat got to them late in the game. He need not have worried. All the training they did on the beach near Pittodrie meant they were in top condition and lasted the pace. Indeed they were in such good physical condition that it was the home side that started to fade near the end. Even so Aberdeen were delighted to hear the final whistle sound as the 0–0 score-line meant they scraped through to the next round.

Next up was Polish side Lech Poznan and the first thing Ferguson did when he heard the draw was to ensure that his assistant Archie Knox saw them in action. That was easier said than done as Poland was still dealing with the fall-out from the uprising at the Gdansk shipyards led by Lech Walensa and the whole country was gripped by martial law. Around the time Aberdeen were due to play in Poland the government were clamping down severely on the Solidarity union and would go on to arrest ten thousand of their activists. In consequence, foreign visitors were frowned upon, as they had been in Albania.

Because Knox would be there on football business he was reluctantly given the green light but only if he agreed to have an official from Lech Poznan by his side at all times. His shadow followed him everywhere and watched him taking notes on the players. He even gave a new meaning to man marking when the pair ended up sharing a room, as Knox recalls.

> It was all a bit weird. He was a nice enough bloke but he would not let me out of his sight. He met me at the airport and from that moment on he was my shadow. I was there for a couple of nights and he told me that as the hotel we were due to stay in was full we would have to share a room. I mean we had just met, but I went along with it, but I must admit I was a bit sick of the sight of him, and probably him of me, when I left to go back to Aberdeen.

Despite the close attention of his new Polish pal Knox had clearly still managed to do his homework on the Polish team. Lech Poznan were outplayed in the first leg at Pittodrie and, although they managed to keep Aberdeen at bay, goals from Mark McGhee and Peter Weir saw the home side record an easy victory. Where there had been trepidation before the previous match in Albania this time the team travelled to Poland quietly confident of victory.

They got a shock on their arrival because, thanks to the political upheaval in Poland, when they touched down they saw manned anti-aircraft guns on the tarmac and soldiers patrolling the airport terminal. On seeing what was going on Knox joked that it was the welcoming committee laid on by his pal from Lech Poznan. Although the whole atmosphere in Poland was tense the Aberdeen players found peace on the pitch and easily won the match 1–0 through a Doug Bell header, which gave them a 3–0 aggregate victory.

The Dons may have been delighted to have qualified but at the airport on the way home full back Stuart Kennedy was detained by the police and nearly arrested. It was left to the team interpreter to explain that the player was leaving Albania with much more of the local currency than he arrived with because he had won a few rounds of cards and not, as they had suggested, because he had robbed a bank. After half an hour of delicate negotiations Kennedy was finally allowed to get on the plane, much to his relief.

Unlike nowadays when European ties come thick and fast, back in 1983 the quarter-final draw was made in December for the matches in March. That meant Ferguson could watch their opponents, the mighty Bayern Munich – managed by former Hungarian internationalist Pal Csernai who had Uli Hoeness as his general manager – as often as he liked.

On hearing the draw there was huge excitement among Aberdeen fans, not only because their team had made the last eight, but also because they would be able to watch the superstars of that era, men like Paul Breitner, Klaus Augenthaler and the best of the lot, Karl Heinz Rummenigge, in action. The club had introduced a voucher system, which meant that fans who attended every home game from the quarter-final draw onwards would get preference when it came to buying tickets for the second-leg against the West German giants at Pittodrie. The Dons faithful enthusiastically embraced the offer and crowds approaching twenty thousand saw Aberdeen beat Hibs and Kilmarnock in successive weeks by two goals to nil.

It was Ferguson himself who made the journey to watch Bayern in action in early January and saw them at their irresistible best. The West German outfit beat Karlsruhe 6–0 but he didn't learn much that he didn't already know. Not surprisingly their star men were Rummenigge and Breitner with centre back Augenthaler and full back Wolfgang Dremmler also catching Fergie's eye. It was Rummenigge though that caused him the most sleepless nights. He was the Bayern danger man, the one who had the ability to change a game with a single piece of magic. Up to a few days before the first leg Ferguson was unsure how to play him, as Willie Miller remembers.

Going into the first leg in Germany I had never seen the gaffer so wound up about a player. He made it clear to us Rummenigge was the man to stop but didn't think it would work to man-mark him all the time. In the end we decided to let the nearest midfield player pick him up in the middle of the park. Whenever he got anywhere near the box I was to get in his face and not let him out of my sight. I knew it was going to be a tough assignment and I knew the way I played him would be vital to us.

The heat ahead of the first leg in West Germany was turned up by former Bayern Munich player and ex-West Germany captain Franz Beckenbauer who, when asked his opinion of Aberdeen by Scottish newspapers, paid them no respect whatsoever. The legendary defender, who had no links at the time with Bayern Munich, gave the Scottish team no chance and his arrogant comments were used by Ferguson to fire-up his team. 'Aberdeen are technically inferior to Bielefeld [a team in the German league] who Bayern Munich beat 5–0. I expect Bayern to outplay them. As soon as the Scots set foot outside their country, they are only half as good as they are at home.'

In that first, away leg on 2 March 1983 Aberdeen went with a bold 4-4-3 formation. Out of all the areas it was the midfield that had the most responsibility as they were told to hang on to the ball, keep passing it around and try and take the sting out of the match. Wide man Peter Weir was also given an important role: to keep Dremmler – who Ferguson had singled out on his spying mission as one of their best players – on the back foot as he was concerned that his surging runs from right back could upset the balance of the game.

Everything went like a dream for Aberdeen who closed down the Bayern midfield and whenever Rummenigge got anywhere near the box he was covered by Miller, who never gave him a sniff at goal. Neither side looked like scoring, which was good news for Aberdeen who were delighted to come away with a 0–0 draw. Miller was named man of the match, which wasn't surprising, although he nearly lost one thing of importance over the ninety minutes.

Near the end, when Bayern were getting desperate, Rummenigge tried a bicycle kick but missed the ball and hit me full in the face. He

197

took out my front teeth out in the process but to be fair to him at the end of the game he helped me search in the mud for them. I must admit it was a bit weird searching about on the ground with one of the world's best players for my front teeth!

Coming away with a 0–0 draw from the Olympic stadium was a superb result for Aberdeen but Ferguson wasn't getting carried away. He knew that the West German side was more than capable of scoring at Pittodrie and he tried his best to lower the expectations of the Aberdeen fans, who were expecting a night to remember. He named ten of the eleven players who started the first leg with Doug Bell making way for Gordon Strachan, who had not been risked in the first match as he had been carrying an injury and in consequence had been left on the bench.

In front of a capacity 24,000 crowd on 16 March1983 Bayern came at Aberdeen right from the get-go. Clearly, they couldn't believe Aberdeen had had the temerity to draw with them on their own turf and were determined to make them pay. With captain Breitner driving his side on the Germans took control of the match early on, and quite frankly, things looked bad for Aberdeen when Bayern took the lead from a free kick, albeit a controversial one. To this day Ferguson believes it was a soft award and television pictures suggest there was minimal contact between Alex McLeish and Dieter Hoeness. As it turned out Breitner took the free kick on the edge of the box and tapped the ball to Augenthaler who slammed the ball home with a tremendous shot that left Jim Leighton with no chance. Just ten minutes gone and the Germans were one up.

It took Aberdeen another ten minutes to fight their way back into the match, much to the fury of Ferguson. Before kick-off he had drilled into his players that they had to show resilience and calm if Bayern took the lead. Instead they lost their shape, and for a moment their drive and composure, as they struggled to pull themselves together. It was clear that it would take something special to get back into the game and so it proved. With half-time fast approaching the game turned on its head thanks to a magnificent move that led to the equalising goal. Stuart Kennedy played the ball to Gordon Strachan, who had pulled out wide. The midfielder put in a cross to the back post that was met by

Eric Black, who knocked it back for Neil Simpson to bundle the ball home. Aberdeen were level after the first forty-five minutes and it was no more than they deserved.

With Aberdeen only too aware that Bayern's away goal meant they had to win the game, Ferguson decided to commit more players to attack. His reasoning was that with stalwarts like goalkeeper Jim Leighton and central defenders like Miller and McLeish he had the men at the back to take that risk.

It was a sound idea but what Ferguson had been concerned about was Bayern's ability out on the right side, where their winger Karl Del-Haye was giving left back Doug Rougvie real trouble. The manager had warned Rougvie about the threat but the big defender had no answer to the little winger whose crosses were a constant nuisance to the Aberdeen defence. One was met by McLeish who got a decent enough clearing header on the ball, or so he thought. It fell at the feet of Hans Pflugler who volleyed it home from twenty yards out to put the visitors 2–1 up.

When that goal went in, Ferguson thought his side's European dream was over. They had thirty minutes left to score two goals against one of the best sides in Europe. It was a tall order and changes had to be made to make it happen. The manager made two of the bravest substitutions of his time at Aberdeen. He put on striker John Hewitt in place of midfielder Neil Simpson while midfielder John McMaster came on for right back Stuart Kennedy. In another tactical switch Neale Cooper dropped to left back to control Del-Haye, who was seeing lots of the ball, and this allowed Doug Rougvie to move to right back to neutralise the tall Pfluger, who was cutting in from the other wing and causing all sorts of problems. Peter Weir dropped back into midfield, which left Hewitt to play alongside Black and McGhee. Within minutes Aberdeen were level when a well-rehearsed free kick saw McMaster give the false impression he was about to put the ball into the box. His antics momentarily wrong footed the Bayern defence allowing Gordon Strachan to put a chip into the box, which was met by McLeish to make it two apiece with fourteen minutes left.

With the Pittodrie crowd roaring their side on things got even better when Aberdeen took the lead just a minute later. McMaster put in a pinpoint back-post cross to Eric Black. Although he is by no means the biggest striker in the game Black could always out jump big defenders because of his excellent timing. It looked like his header was going in but Bayern goalkeeper Muller made a great save and pushed Black's header out. Unfortunately for the German the ball fell to John Hewitt, who rammed it home to give Aberdeen a 3–2 lead. It would not be the first important European goal he would score from the bench that year.

There were now thirteen minutes left, the longest in living memory for many Aberdeen fans. With no more substitutes available Ferguson had to rely on the players out on the pitch to pull off what would be a famous win. It wasn't going to be easy as his players had run themselves into the ground, especially Black up front, which meant the Bayern defence could push up in the search for the equaliser. Not for the first time it was left to the triumvirate of Leighton, Miller and McLeish to defend for their lives and despite an overhead kick from Rummenigge that came close the German giants failed to breach the Aberdeen rearguard. At the final whistle Pittodrie erupted. It was as if the Cup-Winners' Cup itself had been won the way the fans celebrated.

In the semi-final the draw was kind to Aberdeen. From their three potential opponents of Real Madrid, Austria Memphis and Waterschei it was the side from Belgium that the Dons wanted, and got. The Belgians had no star players and the only major asset was their astute manager Ernst Kunecke, who had transformed the fortunes of the provincial club. His side played a 4-2-4 system and the fact it had managed to beat Paris Saint Germain in the quarter-finals meant there was no room for complacency.

The first leg was at Pittodrie and the Aberdeen hero that night was midfielder Doug Bell, who played the game of his life. It was his run and pass within the first two minutes that led to a goal from Eric Black and this was closely followed by a great solo goal from Neil Simpson just two minutes later. In the second half Waterschei did their best to get back into the match but another great run by Bell set up a goal for Mark McGhee in the sixty-seventh minute. With Bell pulling the strings there was a further strike from Peter Weir before Waterschei got their only goal. McGhee put the seal on a magnificent Aberdeen perform-ance with his second goal of the night to round off a comprehensive 5–1 win. It was a real blessing that the Dons had won the first leg so comprehensively because before the return they were involved in a bruising Scottish Cup semi-final match against Celtic, in which a Peter Weir header won the day.

Ferguson had the luxury of being able to rest key players in the second leg in Belgium, knowing the tie was sewn up. Andy Watson made a rare European start, Ian Angus came off the bench and Willie Falconer made his European debut. The second leg at the small stadium in a suburb of Genk was always going to be academic, with most fans in the small crowd being Aberdeen supporters who wanted to be with the club every step of the way to the final.

Alex Ferguson hadn't been impressed by the hotel facilities in Genk and decided to base his players in Maastricht in the Netherlands and bus them across the border on the day of the game. His team may have been 5–1 up from the first leg but he was not leaving anything to chance. Although a goal by Waterschei striker Eddy Vordeekers separated the sides the game will be remembered for a serious injury picked up by right back Stuart Kennedy. Nobody realised it at the time but that game in Belgium would be his last for the club and he would be forced to retire soon after.

The morning after the game in Genk Ferguson flew to Spain to watch Real Madrid in the second semi-final against Austria Memphis, which the Spanish side won 3–1 after a 2–2 draw in Austria. It was a heavy pitch, which made it difficult to play good football, but even so there was nothing he saw that frightened him. A trip by Archie Knox to watch Real play Valencia, in a game they lost 1–0, merely confirmed his view that Aberdeen were more than a match for the men from the Bernabeu.

What was vital was keeping the players fit from the 19 April semi-final until the final in Gothenburg on 11 May. Ferguson had two major injury doubts, with Eric Black and Doug Bell both touch and go and as he didn't want to take any chances he arranged a behind-closed-doors friendly with Hibs on the Sunday two weeks before the final to check their fitness. Fortunately for Black he came through with flying colours but things did not go so well for Bell. The midfielder, who had been such a vital player throughout the European campaign, was left heart-broken after failing to finish the match.

Without Bell and Stuart Kennedy it meant the Aberdeen team for the final pretty much picked itself. In goal was Jim Leighton with the back four being Doug Rougvie at right back, the usual centre-back partnership of Willie Miller and Alex McLeish with John McMaster at left back. The midfield was equally strong with Gordon Strachan, Neil Simpson and Neale Cooper while up front Mark McGhee, Eric Black and Peter Weir looked a potent strike force. John Hewitt was among the substitutes.

The SFA did its best to help Aberdeen's chances in the final and gave permission to bring forward the league match they won 5–0 against Kilmarnock to midweek, rather than the Saturday, to allow them more time to prepare.

Even before Aberdeen had qualified for the final the game had captivated the whole north-east of Scotland. Travel agents Harry Hynds reported that after the Dons had beaten Polish side Lech Poznan in the fourth round he booked the first few Aberdonians into hotels in Gothenburg on Cup Winners' Cup-final night. After the quarter-final win over Bayern Munich he had booked enough Aberdeen fans on flights to Gothenburg to fill six aircraft. Then, following the 5–1 first leg semi-final win over Waterschei, Hynds booked more than a thousand extra hotel bedrooms in Gothenburg. And of course that number didn't include the tens of thousands of fans who got there under their own steam.

Demand for tickets was huge and the fact that Aberdeen were due to play Real Madrid – surely the world's most famous side – only added to the allure. More than fifteen thousand Aberdeen fans officially booked up for Gothenburg for a match they would never forget. To the rest of Europe the game looked very much like a mismatch. Here you had a team from the north-east of Scotland, managed by a relative novice, taking on the mighty Real Madrid, six times European Cup winners, managed by the legendary Alfredo Di Stefano.

Although the rest of the Continent had already written Aberdeen off the support from the north-east of Scotland was overwhelming. The team even made a record called 'The European Song', with the B side being their version of 'The Northern Lights Of Old Aberdeen'. It didn't make the charts and suffice to say the players' singing abilities never matched their quality on the pitch. In the run-up to the game all the shops and offices in the city put good luck messages in their windows. There were insufficient supplies of red ribbon to make rosettes and the corner shop in Raeburn Place, Aberdeen, which made most of them, struggled to keep up with demand.

There was real excitement in the air but Ferguson also knew there would be huge pressure on his players the closer it got to kick-off. He made a conscious decision to try and relax everybody around the club, even to the extent of getting the wives and girlfriends involved in what turned out to be a bit of fun, although Ferguson being Ferguson, it also had a serious point. He called all the ladies to Pittodrie for a cup of tea and to give them their travel itineraries. Assuming they would go by plane and be put up in the best hotels Ferguson told them they would be going by coach and sleeping in a dormitory in an old army barracks on the outskirts of Gothenburg. Just as the shock was about to register he laughed loudly and told them it was all a big joke and that they would be well looked after. Realising he had them onside Ferguson then made a serious point: he did not want his players bothered, either by the wives and girlfriends who were going to Gothenburg or those who were staying at home. Any problems and the girls had to contact the club, not their partners.

There was also huge interest from the press and on the Sunday before the game Ferguson convened a packed press conference at Pittodrie. Men who became his close friends – Glen Gibbons, Hugh McIlvanney and Gerry McNee – attended along with other top writers and broadcasters of the time, like Jeff Powell, Archie Macpherson, Ian Broadley, Mike Aitken, Allan Herron, Alastair MacDonald, Ron Scott and Ken Robertson.

Many of those journalists had joined up with Aberdeen's run only in the later rounds as most were the 'number ones' (as they are called in newspaper circles) and had been following Celtic in the European

Cup that year. Mike Aitken, who was chief football writer at *The Scotsman*, was one of the men sent to cover Aberdeen matches from the quarter-final stages and regards it as a privilege to have had an insider's view.

> The run-up to Gothenburg and the final itself is a time in my journalistic career I will never forget. Here you had a small provincial Scottish club going up against one of the greats of Europe and coming out on top. I remember at the press conference Alex had on the Sunday, the day before we all left for Gothenburg, he seemed very relaxed. He chatted with a lot of us and was clearly hoping if he appeared relaxed his players would not get stage fright and go into the game and perform to the best of their ability.
>
> We all went to the final fancying Aberdeen to win mainly because of the way Fergie had them playing. European football was always about counter-attacking and Aberdeen were experts at that. You also needed a strong defence and I remember speaking to wee Jim McLean, the manager of Dundee United, who always publicly talked up his centre-defensive partnership of David Narey and Paul Hegarty. But that year, when Aberdeen won the Cup Winners' Cup, he admitted Miller and McLeish were better. But that was not for public consumption. Wee Jim would have hated that to come out at the time.

The team and the coaching staff flew to the final and were joined in the departure queues by tens of thousands of their fans, who proved to be the thirstiest travellers ever to pass through the airport. In the run-up to the final, Aberdeen airport reported record duty-free sales of whisky and beer, one that has not been beaten to this day. There were 59 flights in total carrying 5,000 fans over a period of three days, with 28 flights and 2,500 leaving on the day of the final, which, because it was an evening kick-off, made the journey to Gothenburg very convenient. As Ferguson joked afterwards the Aberdeen fans were celebrating even before a ball was kicked: according to an inventory carried out by airport officials, sixty-six bottles of champagne were bought in duty-free as were 2,000 four-bottle packs of Carlsberg Special Brew, a drink known for its potency. For good measure there were 431 litres of Grouse whisky, 400 bottles of Glenfiddich and Glenmorangie, 917 bottles of vodka and

165 bottles of white wine taken on board. In-flight records show that there were also 200 bottles of gin and 150 bottles of brandy drunk on the chartered flights to Gothenburg.

While most of the fifteen thousand Aberdeen fans who went to the final travelled by air 493 of them – including Gordon Strachan's sister Laura – packed into the *St Clair*, a ferry operated by P & O, for what would turn out to be a five-day trip that has lasted long in the memory. One of those on board as the Red Armada sailed was Kevin Stirling, who is now the respected historian of Aberdeen Football Club but at the time was simply an avid 21-year-old Dons fan, one who would have not missed the final for the world. The trip was not for the faint-hearted. It set sail at noon on the Monday, took twenty-seven hours to get to Gothenburg, left a few hours after the match finished and would not arrive back into Aberdeen until the Friday afternoon.

Like thousands of his fellow fans Stirling's trip to the final started long before he set foot on the ferry from Aberdeen harbour. He was travelling with his teammates from the Sunday-league football team that played out of the Castle Inn in Aberdeen. The Castle's proprietor decided to give his loyal customers a proper send-off, as Stirling explains.

> We turned up at the pub at eight o' clock on the Monday morning, gave him £5 each, and were told we could drink as much as we liked, and by god we did. We were pretty drunk when we rolled out of the pub and up to the ferry for the midday departure.
>
> I only got on the *St Clair* in the first place because of my dad as I had been to every Aberdeen game that season, apart from Albania because their government would not let any of us in, which meant by the time the final came around I was absolutely skint. I had to ask my dad Syd, who used to work as a seaman on the *St Clair*, to go down to the docks and pay the £35 deposit needed to secure me a £195 cabin for the five-day trip.
>
> There were cheaper options and for £50 I could have got a single seat on the boat but you couldn't sleep or dump your stuff anywhere. I went for the more expensive option because the boat was like a floating hotel, which meant I didn't have to book a hotel in Gothenburg when I got there as I could just go back to the boat to sleep.

The *St Clair* finally arrived in Gothenburg late on Tuesday afternoon, where the Aberdeen fans stumbled off to continue their party in the city. Some managed to make it back to the boat for a bit of a sleep but many others stayed out all night and didn't sleep again until after the final had been won, as Stirling vividly recalls.

> I remember it was pouring with rain from the minute we arrived in Gothenburg to the minute we left. Because it was so wet quite a few of us, just for a laugh, jumped in the fountain in the city square. It seemed a good idea at the time but when we got out we were freezing for the rest of our time there. That didn't bother us at all as we all knew it was a privilege to be in Gothenburg for the final. We were part of history.

While the fans had great fun in the centre of Gothenburg the team set up camp in the Fars Hatt hotel in the village of Kunglav, on the outskirts of the city. It was not a salubrious place by any means as it was so out of the way. The hotel name gave the players a bit of a laugh because in local Aberdeenshire dialect Fars Hatt can be translated to mean 'Where's that?' The Dons players wandered around the hotel when they first arrived saying 'Fars Hatt' to each other just to lessen the tension.

There was nothing to do in the hotel apart from playing on a solitary pinball machine in the lobby, which the players would gather round for hours. Not having much to do was fine for players like Willie Miller, who had turned sleeping into an art form and who saw relaxing as part of his pre-match build up. While the Aberdeen captain spent hours with his eyes shut his roommate Alex McLeish, by contrast, was going out of his mind with boredom. McLeish prowled the hotel trying to convince other players to play yet another game of pinball or go for their umpteenth walk along the river.

He never even slept in his bed but that wasn't because he was out and about all the time. The big centre half had hurt his back moving some paving stones at his home in Aberdeen and had been getting massages from team physiotherapist Roland Arnott. When he arrived in the hotel he couldn't get comfortable in bed because of his bad back and ended up sleeping on the floor, covered by a quilt. Miller had to tread carefully when he needed the loo in the middle of the night in case he fell over him.

Ferguson had made it clear that the team should be left alone to concentrate on the match and very few outsiders were allowed into the inner sanctum. One man who was allowed in was the legendary Jock Stein, whom Ferguson had asked to come along to give him advice. Stein sat in on the team meeting on the Monday evening when assistant manager Archie Knox went through the Real Madrid side player by player. He also told Ferguson he should try to lull Real Madrid manager Alfredo Di Stefano into a false sense of security. His plan was for Ferguson to go to the Real Madrid hotel on the day before the game to present Di Stefano with a bottle of whisky. It was a hard thing for Fergie to do, given that he was a man who kowtowed to no one, but Stein had suggested that it would do no harm for Di Stefano to think that the team from the north-east of Scotland was just there to make up the numbers. So, against his nature, Ferguson did his best to convince Di Stefano that his little team was thrilled just to be on the same pitch as the great Real Madrid. Whether Ferguson's mind games influenced the final outcome of the match is debatable but it certainly did no harm.

After the meeting with Di Stefano, Ferguson hosted a pre-match press conference for the Scottish journalists at the team hotel. Again he kept things relaxed to the extent that he poured them the tea and made sure there were enough biscuits to go round. At that conference he actually named the team, which was no real surprise, considering it picked itself. He then had to give another official UEFA press conference at the stadium for the Spanish press, at which he named his starting eleven yet again. Mike Aitken remembers the reaction of the Spanish journalists.

> The Spanish press thought it was a double bluff and simply did not belief a manager would name his team the day before the game, rather than just a few hours before kick-off. In saying that it was one of our own who was left a bit confused as the late, great Jimmy Sanderson had to ask who the new player William Ferguson Miller was, only to be told that was the full name of the Aberdeen captain!

The first the Aberdeen players saw of the Ullevi stadium was late on the Tuesday afternoon, just after Ferguson had completed his press conference. They were underwhelmed. The grass was on the long side, the stadium had seen better days and the rain was falling heavily. They were allowed out to train on it before the Real Madrid players, who arrived later for their warm-up. Then they went back to their hotel for an evening meal, before getting ready for what turned out to be a less-than-relaxing evening's entertainment. It was laid on by Allan 'Fingers' Ferguson – no relation to Fergie – who was the acting Aberdeen press officer for the trip, and who had build up a good reputation with everyone in the party. He was nicknamed Fingers because he had fingers in so many pies and had been brought along on the advice of Stein, who had advised Ferguson that dealing with the press in a game of that magnitude could be problematic, Someone of Ferguson's calibre, Stein counselled, would be invaluable. Fingers, who now runs a successful sports agency, explains his role.

> Nowadays every football club would have a press officer on hand for such a big game but back then having me there was the exception for Scottish clubs rather than the norm. I had been recommended to Alex by big Jock as I had done some work for Scotland at the 1982 World Cup. It was an honour to take up the post for those few days and there was huge interest from all over Europe in the match.

Along with Stein, Fingers Ferguson was one of the few people allowed to stay in the same hotel as the players, let alone be allowed to socialise with them. He was also appointed as the unofficial head of light entertainment, as he recalls.

> The hotel was a concrete monstrosity in the middle of nowhere and a place where there was nothing to do. Fergie liked it that way as he didn't want any distractions before such an important game. He wanted to be in control of how things went to the extent he even set up a quiz the night before the game to take his players' minds off what was ahead.
>
> I was drafted in as quizmaster and nicknamed Bamber by the players after the chap who used to present *University Challenge*. Now

if such a quiz was played in a light-hearted way then no problem. But you had professional sportsmen taking part, men who didn't like losing at anything. There were seven teams of three and the two front-runners by the end was one team captained by Gordon Strachan and the other by Willie Miller.

In the end the scores were tied, which meant I had to come up with a tiebreak question, which was: 'Which Scottish football team has the most letters in its name and how many are they?'

Miller's team got there first with their answer of Hamilton Academicals and nineteen letters, which was wrong. They were adamant they had guessed correctly and to make matters more confusing so did Gordon Strachan's team but because they had to come up with another answer they knocked off the letter s and made their answer Hamilton Academical and said it had eighteen letters, which was correct.

All hell broke loose. Willie Miller's team accused me of favouring Strachan's team, which had Archie Knox and Bryan Gunn in it, and claimed that I had been got at and had cheated. The more his players got heated up about things the more Fergie, who was sitting at the back, laughed.

It wasn't until long after midnight – this on the eve of the European Cup Winners' Cup final remember – that hands were shaken and every-body went to bed. As I brushed my teeth that night I had to yet again remind myself that this was the eve of the biggest match in the history of Aberdeen Football Club. Not one single person was on edge and as for me I had never felt so relaxed.

And I hadn't even been drinking!

Fingers was also involved in another surreal experience when, at break-fast, he was accosted by the Aberdeen manager and his assistant Archie Knox and challenged to a race round the lake.

I had run the London marathon a few weeks previously and was in good shape, which is probably why Fergie and Archie wanted to race me. We set off just after breakfast and it was a close run thing but near the end Archie and Fergie elbowed me out of the way and off the jogging track and sprinted to the finish. Both were so competitive, claiming they had won, and, knowing the pair of them, I declared it a draw to keep the peace. That run probably got rid of some of their adrenalin before the game and settled them down a bit, allowing them to think clearly during what was obviously an incredibly pressurised time.

It was clear the pressure was starting to build on the players as well, despite the manager's best efforts to keep them relaxed. Even the usually laid back Mark McGhee lost his temper when a member of the Aberdeen backroom staff joked after breakfast on the day of the game that McGhee had missed an easy shot on the pinball machine.

The players, as players always do, just wanted the game to start. They were ready for action but had long hours to kill before that happened. After a light meal around four they went for a walk, which was followed by time in their rooms before getting on the bus for the stadium. Being superstitious they all took their usual seats. John McMaster, Gordon Strachan, Stuart Kennedy (who had been given a place on the bench despite the fact he wasn't fit) Alex McLeish and Gordon Strachan all sat at the back.

The Aberdeen party finally set off for the Ullevi around six o'clock in the middle of yet another downpour, which was a problem for Gordon Strachan. The rain had straightened his hair to such an extent that when he was running he couldn't see through it, so the last thing the midfielder did before the biggest game of his life was to cut his fringe in the dressing room.

Just before kick-off, faced with a nervous group of players, Alex Ferguson delivered one of his greatest team talks, one that has stayed with Willie Miller to this day.

Fergie could rant and rave with the best of them but this time he started his team talk in a balanced manner, reminding us how hard we had worked to get to the final, and how our destiny was in our own hands. He spoke of the great teams we had beaten on the way to the final, teams like Bayern Munich, and how we could become overnight legends by beating Real Madrid.

He also got a bit emotional when he talked about how he wanted us to win the game for ourselves, our teammates, family and, very importantly, the fans. He mentioned the tens of thousands who had come across to support us and how we could not let them down. We were maybe a bit too fired up and nervous before kick-off but after the boss got a hold of us we were a bit more relaxed, and very focused on what lay ahead. I think the fact we were mentally sorted was part of the reason we started the match so well.

A bell rang in the dressing room. It was the signal for the Dons players to make their way to the tunnel for the biggest game of their lives.

Right from the off Aberdeen took the game to the Spanish giants and with the midfield functioning superbly controlled the early stages. Then, with just seven minutes on the clock, the Dons were in dreamland. Gordon Strachan, who had been darting all over the pitch, put over a corner that was met by Alex McLeish. McLeish didn't get enough power on the header, which got stuck in the mud inside the six-yard box. As the Real defenders desperately tried to clear their lines Eric Black showed his predatory skills by getting to the ball before them to score.

Ferguson was confident his side could hold onto the lead but never in his worst nightmares did he think that Real Madrid would have been allowed back into the game because of a mistake by one of his most experienced players. Ninety-nine times out of a hundred Alex McLeish would have not been short with his back pass to Jim Leighton but, seven minutes after Aberdeen had opened the scoring, he was guilty of a misjudgement. McLeish didn't take the heavy pitch into consideration and that allowed Carlos Santillana to get to the ball before Leighton. The keeper did his best to stop the Spanish striker legitimately, but he made contact inside the box, giving Real Madrid a penalty. When Juanito slotted the ball home there followed a twenty-minute period in which the wheels nearly came off Aberdeen's European campaign. Neale Cooper, playing in the Aberdeen midfield, knows it could have ended in tears.

> We had started superbly but we lost our shape a bit after their goal and for twenty minutes afterwards they were all over us. We had to dig deep during that period to keep ourselves in the match. Luckily, we had experienced guys in key positions all over the pitch and we steadied the ship and managed to get in at half-time level.

In the dressing room Ferguson sat his side down and urged them to be more positive in attack and to keep a hold of the ball in midfield as the muddy pitch would sap energy. He asked strikers Mark McGhee and Eric Black to work back more to take the pressure off the midfield and for everyone to get the ball out wide to Peter Weir, who was on fire that night. The plan worked a treat and Aberdeen started to dominate possession.

The unsung heroes were Cooper and Simpson in the middle of the park. All those tough training sessions on Aberdeen beach in the wind and rain now paid off for the young midfielders, who were by some distance fitter than their Real Madrid counterparts. Despite the heavy pitch they managed to get from box to box, breaking down Real's forays and then launching counter attacks. Cooper in particular was linking up well with the forwards and he was involved in the move that led to a Black volley cracking back off the bar with the goalkeeper well beaten. McGhee also went close with a shot and it was all Aberdeen as the clock moved closer to the ninety-minute mark. Black, who had worked himself into the ground and had picked up a leg injury in the process, was replaced three minutes before the end of normal time by John Hewitt, a clever player who could always find good positions in the box.

As the match went into extra-time it looked like the game could be decided on penalty kicks, a thought that horrified Neale Cooper.

> We watched them train a bit on the Tuesday night before we went back to our hotel and they were taking lots and lots of penalties. We might have taken a couple at training but we didn't practise them as a team. When the thought dawned on me that I might have to take a penalty I was cursing myself for not practising a few at training.

Cooper's fears of a penalty shootout never materialised. The introduction of Hewitt, who was Cooper's roommate in Gothenburg, had given Aberdeen fresh legs in the forward areas of the pitch and his clever runs in behind Real Madrid caused them many problems. But sometimes his enthusiasm got the better of him, much to the annoyance of the manager, as Hewitt remembers all too well.

> It was only later that I was told by the gaffer that I was in danger of being hauled off for not following his orders. Imagine that. I would

have been the cup-final sub who was subbed. How embarrassing would that have been?

The boss had wanted me to stay up the park all the time but I was running about daft, all over the place. Having just come on, I was full of nervous energy and wanted to get in the action and was following the ball a bit too much for him. He wasn't happy but at least he kept me on. Both of us were happy that he did.

Hewitt wasn't joking. Nine minutes from the end of extra-time, Peter Weir, for the umpteenth time that night, set off on a run down the left wing. After leaving two Real Madrid defenders in his wake, he passed to McGhee, who had drifted out wide. Although his left was McGhee's weaker foot, and he had run himself into the ground, the striker still had the energy to put over an accurate left-foot cross, which Real Madrid goalkeeper Augustin just missed. Lesser players may have been put off by the movement of the goalkeeper but John Hewitt never took his eye off the ball and headed decisively into the back of the net. It was a wonderful moment for the substitute.

I just had this instinct that the goalkeeper was going to miss the ball and kept my momentum going through the ball and got my head to it. The feeling when I saw the ball in the net was just incredible. I knew there wasn't long to go and it was up to us to keep things tight.

To be fair that wasn't that easy because there was absolute pandemonium after I scored. Fergie was out on the touchline shouting the odds and telling us to keep our shape and see the game out. The fans were going nuts and we knew we were nearly there. But we knew against a side like Real Madrid we could never relax until the final whistle.

That proved to be exactly the case with Real Madrid throwing everything at the Aberdeen defence. Willie Miller admits that the men from the Bernabeu came close to snatching an equaliser.

I thought I had blown it with two minutes left when I gave away a free kick on the edge of the box, although it was a bit of a harsh award. The Spaniards had people who were experts with the dead ball and I was worried I would be remembered as the guy who gave away the free kick that let Real Madrid back into the game.

I remember as if it was yesterday that we cleared their first effort but the ref demanded it be taken again for reasons I am still not sure about. Salguero run up to take the retaken kick. I was just off the wall and ran out to try and block but the ball whizzed past me towards the goal. Everything happened in slow motion and, as I turned round, for a split second I thought it was going in as Jim Leighton looked like he couldn't reach it. Thankfully, it went just past the post and I breathed a huge sigh of relief. That let off calmed my nerves and made me realise we were going to hold on and win the match.

At the final whistle the Aberdeen bench rose as one to celebrate victory. There was no standing on ceremony, with substitute goalkeeper Bryan Gunn and Archie Knox accidentally pushing over Ferguson as he ran onto the pitch. On any other occasion the Aberdeen manager may not have risen off the turf with a big smile on his face but under the circumstances a bit of dirt on his big coat wasn't going to bother him. He set off, first to embrace captain Willie Miller, followed swiftly by the rest of his players and backroom staff. The manager's namesake, Fingers Ferguson, paints a vivid picture of the celebrations.

I had bought this big, white, knee-length jacket to wear to the game and I remember Fergie hugging me and leaving most of the muck he had picked up on it when he fell leaving the dug-out. I was covered in dirt and looked pretty ridiculous and when I went back inside I had to take it off as it was in such a state. All over the pitch there were people jumping into each other's arms and I remember Gordon Strachan having a wee dance of his own in celebration and John McMaster running about with the cup on his head.

Well-known broadcaster and author Archie Macpherson was another on the pitch at the final whistle and was also on the end of a Fergie bear hug.

It was a live game on Independent Television rather than BBC Scotland. That meant I wasn't doing a live commentary but I still went as the sports reporter for BBC *Breakfast News*, which had a huge audience at the time and whose main presenters were Frank Bough and Selina Scott. I did watch most of the game from the television gantry but after Hewitt scored I went down trackside as I just knew Aberdeen were going to win.

I had been with Celtic when they won the European Cup and Rangers when they lifted the Cup Winners' Cup and to be there when a third Scottish club won a European trophy was a real privilege. And to think I nearly never made it to the game in the first place. I lost my passport a few days before I was due to fly out and had to get an emergency one sent up to me in Aberdeen which arrived just before I was due to fly out with the team. I still count my lucky stars it arrived so I could witness one of the greatest nights in Scottish football history.

Once the initial celebrations had died down UEFA officials quickly organised the presentation ceremony, which was by today's standards very low key. There was no proud walk up the steps of the stadium to pick up the trophy, no firework display, no celebratory music. Willie Miller was still elated, the lack of pomp notwithstanding.

There was a table with the cup and the winners' medals on it that looked like it had just been brought in from a canteen. The team was standing all around, not even in any order, and I was summoned across to pick up the trophy. There was some guy from the Italian FA who had been given the honour of presenting the trophy but he would not let the thing go.

He wanted to be in the pictures too but I managed to get it off him eventually and I stood, arms outstretched, with the cup in my right hand. It was the proudest moment of my football life.

It was an incredible feeling.

When Aberdeen returned to the dressing room SFA chief executive Ernie Walker and Jock Stein – who had been such a rock to Ferguson in the run-up to the final – were there to greet them. Media demands meant they didn't have long in the dressing room on their own, as Fingers Ferguson explains.

One of my remits was to make sure if they won they would be in front of the television cameras on *Sportsnight*, which was the midweek Britain-wide sports show of that era and presented by David Coleman.

The players were in such high spirits it was difficult to get them all out of the dressing room and along the corridor to go live in front of the television cameras.

Fergie was interviewed, as was Willie Miller, with the rest of the guys standing in the background with big smiles on their faces. At that moment, with them appearing live on BBC television with the trophy, maybe it sunk in to many of them just what an incredible thing they had achieved.

The players lingered a long time at the stadium. The fans too were reluctant to leave the scene of the success, Kevin Stirling among them.

> The stadium was just twenty minutes walk from the ferry terminal where the *St Clair* was due to leave at midnight. We stayed in the stadium until security kicked us out and carried on drinking in celebration in the local bars as close to midnight as possible.
>
> Not surprisingly a few guys were late getting on board but nobody noticed or really cared. We had our carry-outs open and were celebrating and I think we finally set sail after one o'clock, which wasn't too bad.

When the Aberdeen players got back to their hotel the champagne started to flow. Many of them didn't need much alcohol to get them high as the adrenalin was still coursing through their veins. Some of them did not sleep at all: Mark McGhee ending up sitting on a rock on the beach at five o'clock in the morning, shooting the breeze with Fingers Ferguson. Inside the hotel the party was still going on with Fergie and senior players like Miller, McLeish and Strachan revelling in the incredible victory.

Some of the young bucks, like Neale Cooper, got a bit bored with it all and set off into Gothenburg to meet friends and family.

> Some of the senior players took their wives and girlfriends to Gothenburg and stayed in the hotel after the game to celebrate. The younger guys, like me and Bryan Gunn, wanted to go into town so we jumped into the taxi to see what the atmosphere was like.
>
> I also wanted to see my mum and sister, who were over for the game, and I had arranged to meet them in the Europa hotel, which

was the central point for the Aberdeen fans. Well, when I walked in there was a huge roar and me and Bryan were put on everybody's shoulders and carried over their heads from the front door, past the bar, to where my mum and sister were. I think they call it crowd-surfing when it happens to lead singers at rock concerts and it was an amazing feeling. It was at that moment, seeing all the fans celebrate, that it really sunk in for me what we had achieved.

I thought about how far I had come to get to this point. I was only nineteen and my big mate John Hewitt, who I had played schools football with, had scored the winning goal in a European final. I had to pinch myself to make sure it was real and not just a dream.

There were a few sore heads on the Thursday morning when the Aberdeen players, complete with the European Cup Winners' Cup, boarded the plane back to the north-east. The cup was passed round everybody and picture after picture taken. Mike Aitken of *The Scotsman* says it was a special time for the hard-bitten gentlemen of the press.

Even the most cynical journalist wanted their picture taken with the trophy and I got one with me, John Mann of the *Daily Star* and Alex Cameron and Ian Broadley of the *Daily Record* all holding it. It was a very special picture taken at the end of an unforgettable European odyssey for Aberdeen and their fans.

When the team landed at Aberdeen airport there were incredible scenes. Even the men who guided in their aircraft had Aberdeen rosettes and scarves on. In the terminal building hundreds of fans had gathered to welcome their heroes. And that was just the start. All the way into the city centre and to Pittodrie the crowds were three or four deep as they cheered their heroes. It was a great experience for Neale Cooper.

Being on that open-top bus was incredible. There were so many fans either side of the road it took ages for us to get through. We could have taken all day for me because I was absolutely loving it. People were hanging out windows, up lampposts. Every vantage point was taken to see us coming home. When we got to Pittodrie the stadium was full and we did a lap of honour with the trophy. By that stage I was absolutely knackered and running on adrenalin.

While the fans back in Scotland were welcoming back the Aberdeen team on the Thursday the fans on the *St Clair* ferry were still at sea, Kevin Stirling among them.

> We had drunk the alcohol supply of the *St Clair* by the Thursday night and all of our carry-outs had been downed as well. Then we heard a helicopter hovering overhead and we were wondering what was going on. It turned out the helicopter was flying in more cans of beer for us all and souvenir copies of the *Aberdeen Evening Express*, which had been specially prepared for those of us on the ferry.
>
> Remember these were the days long before the internet and we had no idea what the reaction had been to Aberdeen's win. When we read our copies of the *Express* we were left in no doubt. Their special edition had pictures from the final, from the homecoming parade and it was fantastic to see before we arrived back in Aberdeen.
>
> When we did dock there was Alex Ferguson and Mark McGhee on the quayside to greet us, which was a fantastic surprise. It took us ages to get off the ferry and pick up our stuff but when we had finished we headed back to the Castle Inn pub, where we had started our journey at eight on the Monday morning. When we got back there we walked in at exactly one o'clock on Friday afternoon. It had been an incredible five days and we finished back where we started.

For the players, still high on European success, the season was far from over. They were back training on the Friday morning, two days after their famous European win. The next day they were applauded onto the pitch by the Hibernian players at Easter Road before thumping them 5–0 in their last league fixture. It was not enough to win the title as Dundee United, with fifty-six points, finished just one point ahead of them.

There was still no rest because the following Saturday the same Aberdeen team that beat Real Madrid took the field for the Scottish Cup final against Rangers at Hampden. Not surprisingly that team, playing its sixtieth competitive match of the campaign, looked physically and mentally exhausted and did not perform well. Despite that they managed to hold the Ibrox outfit to 0–0 at full time and, knowing they had been let off the hook, rallied in overtime.

With four minutes left in the second period of extra-time a low cross from Mark McGhee was deflected by Rangers central defender Craig Paterson into the path of Eric Black, who scored, winning the cup for Aberdeen. Alex Ferguson publicly lambasted his players – with the exception of McLeish and Miller – for their poor performances, although he later conceded he was wrong to take such a tough stance. But that, says Willie Miller, is the mark of the man.

> That was just the gaffer's way. He was incredibly driven and wanted us to be the same. He felt the team had let itself down against Rangers, despite the fact that we won. He didn't care that we might be tired after a long, successful season. He was always striving for perfection and that has made him the greatest manager who has ever lived.
>
> He never settled for second best. Remember in that calendar year Aberdeen won the European Cup Winners' Cup and also the European Super Cup when we beat Hamburg. No other Scottish team has won two European trophies apart from Aberdeen.
>
> That sets that team apart from every other in Scotland and it always will.

Alan Pattullo

10

Berti Vogts, Scotland Manager

Alan Pattullo

As the Scotland squad made a sharp descent into Vagar airport, situated on one of the group of islands that make up the Faroes, few could imagine that the dive in fortunes already being experienced by the country's football team would be preparing to take another drastic, sudden dip. On 6 September 2003, the day before Scotland began their Euro 2004 qualifying campaign, the Faroes Islands were known in the main for the 'Grind'. This is a bloody slaughter in which fishermen slay pilot whales in the shallows. But from the next day and for ever more, if you are Scottish, they are known for visiting a terrible humiliation upon your country's football team. Scotland shared the points in a 2–2 draw, but had to endure all of the opprobrium having trailed 2–0 early in the game.

It has become a classic 'where were you?' moment. Where were you when Scotland went up a hill to play a football match and came down to a mountain of trouble? The pitch, recalls Kenny MacDonald, had been 'scooped out of the hillside'. The chief sports writer for the Scottish *News of the World* was making his second trip to the islands. Just three years earlier Scotland had travelled to the Faroes for another European Championship qualifier and had again come away with a point. But this had been much less hysterically received; perhaps because Scotland centre-half Matt Elliott's red card – on the say-so of a female assistant referee – attracted much of the attention.

Although the Faroes had recently built a new stadium in Torshavn, Scotland were taken back to the Svangaskarð arena in Toftir where one of their hosts' few points in international football had been secured in that 1–1 draw in the summer of 1999. Davie Weir – who had a further reason to feel nauseous about the trip – vividly describes the difficulties experienced by the Scotland party en route to the stadium.

> It's a surreal place – even to get there. You land and it's the shortest runway in the world. The plane stops and you feel as though you are about to fall down a mountain. And then there's the terminal, which is just a hut. You get on to a bus, and the bus takes you to a ferry. Then you have to get on to a bus again, which takes you on winding roads to a hotel with grass on the roof. There were sheep on the roof! The new stadium was within walking distance of the hotel but we were playing at the old stadium, which felt like hours away in a bus.

Scotland landed on Vagar, the most westerly of the large islands which make up the Faroes, but were expected in Toftir, a small settlement on the most easterly tip of Eysturoy, another island in the archipelago. Although Toftir had no restaurant or bars, the area is a favoured haunt of the twitcher. As well as the slaughter of whales, the Faroes are also known for a rich diversity of birdlife, as MacDonald explains.

> The complex where Scotland played is used for bird-watching parties. There is a primitive hotel, which I would guess had between twenty and twenty-four rooms. These were used as a kind of auxiliary press box. The actual press box in the stand was like one you would find at a junior ground.
>
> In these bedrooms there was obviously electricity and a wee window ledge where you could rest your laptop. It was two journalists to a room – the beds were still there behind us. It was certainly one of the more peculiar vantage points from which to watch an international football match. But it was perfectly fine. We were out of the chilly weather, and we had power for our laptops. From that point of view I have been to a hell of a lot of worse places.
>
> It's just what transpired on the park that made it a lot less pleasant.
>
> I was 'twinning' with Mark Guidi [chief football writer for the *Sunday Mail*]. I'll always remember when it went to 2–0 – and we were playing so badly it looked like we might concede more goals – hearing Mark mutter: 'I just cannot believe what I am watching.'

Although the Berti Vogts era was well under way with friendly defeat after friendly defeat, the competitive action under the new, expensively acquired successor to Craig Brown had yet to begin. After thirteen minutes of their opening Euro 2004 qualifier, it still hadn't. Scotland were swept aside by the Faroes, many of whose players had turned up for the match in jeans and jackets. The visitors had hardly got a kick. Two goals were conceded in a grisly opening spell, the memory of which still chills the bone. John Petersen, a dark-haired schoolteacher, claimed them both. Scottish football fans have grown resistant to calamity over the years, but this was a fresh hell. It was, according to *The Scotsman* newspaper on the Monday morning, the worst perform-ance by a Scottish team since the invention of international football.

But as he eyed the cluster of eighteen islands below him – and though others could smell apprehension in the air – Berti Vogts must have felt fairly confident as the plane carrying the Scotland squad, along with journalists, prepared to land. He was, after all, a non-Scot. He was not conditioned by an accident of birth to get an attack of the vapours when contemplating a fixture against what had to be consid-ered minor opposition. Over his shoulder, in one of the seats behind, he had Paul Lambert back on board. The Celtic midfielder, still just thirty-one and operating at the heart of Martin O'Neill's midfield at Celtic, had been persuaded by Vogts to reverse his decision to retire from international football. It was a significant public-relations victory for the German, something on which he was required to trade as his first outings with Scotland in friendlies became more and more alarming. A 5–0 defeat to a France team at the peak of its powers was almost acceptable, particularly since it was Vogts's first match in charge. But an unsatisfying, weather-affected tour to the Far East saw results continue to be poor and revealed the first straining of relations between the manager and the Scottish press. By the time Denmark came to Hampden Park for a fifth friendly and skipped away with a 1–0 victory, some serious concerns had formed. Vogts was now a man operating under considerable pressure.

But he promised there would be no mistake against the Faroe Isles, a team then – as now – made up of schoolmasters, farmers and trawlermen. 'This is a game we have to win and we will,' he told reporters on the eve of the match. 'Don't worry.' But Berti clearly had not been in Scotland long enough to discern one of the main fault lines running through the Scottish psyche: an inability to do what is expected. This was exactly the type of game that made Scotland worry. Vogts could be excused intimate knowledge of the reasons why Scots shuddered at the mention of Iran, Peru and Costa Rica. But he now knows only too well why the Faroes provoke such an extreme reaction, and are added to this roll of dishonour. But at least those other debacles had arrived while dining at football's top table. Peru and Iran, a 3–1 loss and a 1–1 draw respectively, succeeded in extinguishing the insane optimism that had built up prior to the 1978 World Cup finals. A 3–2 win over Holland, the tournament's runners-up, in the final group game summed up everything about Scotland.

Vogts would come to be acquainted with this ability the Scots had to raise their game against the top sides in the world. Costa Rica were not one of those, however. Scotland, true to form, fell to a dismal 1–0 loss against the Central Americans in the first game of the 1990 World Cup. They staged a recovery of sorts with a 2–1 win over Sweden before finishing up with an agonising 1–0 loss to Brazil, a result that put them out.

So perhaps what occurred in the Faroes was not quite such a shock, although Scotland had never underperformed quite so badly against a team of such lowly status. Since celebrating their enrolment in UEFA with a remarkable win over Austria in their very first official international fixture, the Faroese had tasted competitive victories against only San Marino, Malta and Luxembourg. But here came Scotland, descending from the skies at an even sharper gradient than the one tracing the downward trend of their FIFA ranking. It had plummeted from a high of twenty-one under Craig Brown to fifty-five and would eventually hit as low as eighty-eight. The Faroes, when they hosted Scotland, were down at 113, bookended by Barbados and Tahiti.

There are not too many ways to look at a 2–2 draw with a rocky outcrop of Danish dependent islands in the North Atlantic, but *The Scotsman* believed the ultimate depth had been marked by an afternoon where

Scotland had somehow allowed themselves to trail by two goals, before making the situation slightly less worse courtesy of a stolidly unheroic comeback. 'The worst performance by a Scotland team since 1872.' That was the year, of course, when Scotland helped give birth to international football, with a match against England. The nadir had arrived 130 years later against part-time opposition assembled from a population that would not fill Hampden Park.

Almost more humiliatingly, the draw Scotland later scrambled had to be viewed as tough on the hosts, who might have scored a winner in the closing minutes but for a fine save from Hjalgrim Elltor by Robert Douglas. The goalkeeper was making his competitive debut that afternoon, and wondered into what he had stumbled. Ostensibly, this was international football but it had more in common with his days keeping goal for Meadowbank Thistle, as he recalls.

> Your only thought that day as a goalkeeper was just hoping it would not be too windy. Of course, it was blowing a hurricane. And before we knew it we were 2–0 down. I'd also had to make a sliding tackle about the penalty spot! But I think, by that point, it was just about doing anything possible to keep the ball out of the back of the net.

No-one could believe what they were watching. The colour on David Taylor's face had visibly drained away due to a combination of the cold and the realisation that he – as chief executive of the Scottish Football Association – would have to face the music. Taylor, too, had an unusual vantage point.

> You were not expecting luxury in Toftir, but I think I was sitting on an overturned fish crate which was being used as temporary seating. It was my worst experience in football. Normally you go in for a cup of tea at half-time. But we were 2–0 down and I could not face going in. I had to stand outside. It was a shocking experience. Shocking.

On reflection, it was a strange Scotland team that found itself desperately trying to stem the flow against the rampant amateurs. 'I don't mean to disrespect anyone, but you look at the players – they have not really stood the test of time,' says Weir, for whom the Faroes game marked the beginning of a near three-year long hiatus in his international career. He was one of the least eyebrow-raising inclusions. Paul Dickov had featured under Craig Brown but as a striker with a licence to pester; a role he had perfected in the Premiership with Manchester City and Leicester City. So Vogts positioned him on the wide right of midfield. The Scotland strike force of Kevin Kyle and Scott Dobie were hardly likely to strike fear into the hearts of anyone, not even the Faroese. The pair had mustered only two goals between them, and these were claimed by Kyle in a 4–0 win over even less stellar opposition: a Hong Kong select.

Perhaps surprisingly, only one member of the side did not feature again for Scotland. Allan Johnston, then of Middlesbrough, had scored the equaliser in the 1–1 draw on Scotland's last visit. This time around, however, he had managed only the impact of a rusty winger. Remarkably, Johnston was one of two members of the starting eleven who, despite the match being in September, had still to make a first competitive appearance of the season for his club. Indeed, he had yet to be included in a squad. Not being considered for a mid-ranking Premiership team need not necessarily preclude one's involvement with the Scotland team of the time, however.

'I actually didn't think I did too badly all things considered,' he told me, when asked to reflect on his call-up a few years later. 'It was just one of those days. I had been asked to play, and you don't turn that opportunity down.' Stephen Crainey, the Celtic left back, was another who had been parachuted into the team from nowhere. He, too, had not featured for his club so far that season, yet lined up against the Faroes. His lack of match practice was exposed in ruthless fashion. Both of the home side's goals stemmed from crosses from the right, although blame was apportioned elsewhere by Vogts, and with significant consequences for the manager.

According to Weir, the most depressing aspect of the afternoon was sitting in the dressing room at half-time with this oddly cast team and wondering whether they had it within them to do anything about a situation that threatened to define their career. Even Lambert, a European Cup winner with Borussia Dortmund five years earlier, might have struggled to see this distinction supersede helming a Scotland team thrashed in the Faroes. For a while, it looked as though this might be the case, with Petersen, a handsome geography teacher, looking as though he might score every time he took aim at the goalposts. His first goal, after just six minutes, came via a header after a cross had evaded Christian Dailly. His second, with a barely credible twelve minutes having elapsed, was clipped in with a degree of expertise by the same player, again from a cross from the Faroese right.

'A cross came over my head and it was great finish from the lad, to be fair,' recalls an honest Weir, whose recollections of the scene at half-time does not tally with the report, which did the rounds at the time, of Lambert taking centre stage in front of a shell-shocked dressing room. Weir recalls a lot of shouting and bawling from others, too. But most of all he remembers feeling a depressing sense of hopelessness as they contemplated the task that lay ahead.

> The story, which has grown arms and legs, is that Paul Lambert got up and had a real go at everyone during the interval. He and Berti were very, very close. He [Lambert] set himself apart a bit as the elder statesman, not that he was very old at the time. There were the players, then Paul, then the manager.
>
> There was obviously a realisation during half-time that it was not good enough. And it was a disaster, or at least a potential disaster. There was shock as well as a determination to get it right. But to be honest there was also a feeling of 'I don't know if we are capable of it'. That was probably the worst feeling of all.

The two centre-halves that afternoon later had the blame pinned on them by Vogts in an interview with the German sports agency SID. Although the manager protested that his words had not meant to sound as brutal as those published, they pushed Weir over the edge. Dailly, Weir's partner in the centre of defence, shared the blame. Notably, while Weir responded by retiring with immediate effect from Scotland, Dailly flourished in the months and years ahead under Vogts and became the unofficial mascot for the Tartan Army. But Weir, whose second son had just been born, wondered whether it was still worth it. He had, after all, been one of the few established players to make himself available for the tour to the Far East earlier that year and yet still found himself targeted by Vogts. Weir felt let down. His manager at Everton, David Moyes, was also furious, and pledged to come to Iceland for the next game, to stand up for his player. 'It's like a father looking after his son,' he told Weir. But there would be no next time. At least, Weir believes, not while Vogts remained in charge.

> You were happy to make sacrifices but I had begun to think to myself: 'This is not working. I am not getting any enjoyment out of it.' If you were being 100 per cent honest you were questioning yourself all the time, and the team. That result [against the Faroes] was an accumulation of all the doubts coming up to it. I came back and was on a big-time downer, then that [German newspaper] report happened. Berti never phoned me about it, although I did eventually speak to him. He told me he had not said it. But he had. The headline was that it was not the young boys' fault; it was down to Christian and me.

Weir phoned David Taylor, the SFA chief executive, and was told to write a letter confirming his intention to retire from international football. There was also eventually a phone call with Vogts. 'There was a conversation going on but not one where there was any feeling in it,' Weir recalls. He put this down to the language barrier that still existed between Vogts and the players, and also the press.

The poor communication had already caused problems, revealing itself as early as Vogts's first game. Gary Holt was sent on at half-time against France and then withdrawn again less than thirty minutes later. It was reported later that this unusual substitution of a substitute was due to a communication breakdown between pitch and touchline. Almost comically, Holt had been trying to explain that Dominic Matteo was injured, but was himself taken off instead. Prior to the game, Kevin McNaughton, the Aberdeen full-back, had been described as being 'nervous' in training by Vogts, and left out. The accusation would have stung any professional footballer. But again the suggestion was that Vogts, in seeking to relay the player's rawness, had injudiciously selected a word that inferred the player lacked bottle, something far more damaging for a footballer's reputation. On the same trip to Paris, Vogts had also encountered a situation that saw him risk falling out with a valued member of his squad. Again communication – or mis-communication – appeared to be at the root of the problem. The player in question was Rab Douglas.

Although he had featured in a number of squads under Craig Brown, Douglas had still to make his debut for Scotland. But he was under the impression that he would get his first cap against France, and so – despite the fact his wife Debbie was expecting their first child – he made the journey. In the event, Neil Sullivan played the whole match, while Douglas fumed on the bench. His daughter had been born on the eve of the game and the choice of her name now makes the big keeper smile.

> We were going to call the wee one Paris, instead of Brook. I had Sully awake half the night. I told him he might end up being the godfather! Berti and I had words at the airport. Looking back, it should maybe have been done privately. But he gave me my cap later on. Perhaps he was impressed by the fact I stood up for myself and had a belief in myself and what I thought I was entitled to.
>
> Obviously it was a dramatic misunderstanding, maybe between Berti and Hodgy [Alan Hodgkinson, the Scotland goalkeeper coach], or maybe even between me and Hodgy. Maybe even myself, maybe I misunderstood. But it was disappointing. I desperately wanted my first Scotland cap, but I would certainly have put it on the back burner to see the birth of the wee one. The problem was that I didn't get my cap and I didn't get back [for the birth] either.

A few months later, while the Scotland squad were on tour to the Far East, Vogts seemed to reach an early breaking point. Defeats were racking up by this time. According to Jonathan Coates, who covered the trip for *The Scotsman*, one of the manager's press briefings in Hong Kong became 'a bullet-point checklist of rebuttals and retaliation'. Among them, Vogts vented his anger at an apparent reference in one writer's report to the Second World War. 'What do I have to do with the Second World War? You can criticise me when I make mistakes, that's okay.

But without the war, without the German [link],' he fulminated. He had erroneously deduced that it was an attempt to mock him through mention of something that, given his nationality, was clearly a sensitive subject. It was pointed out to him that the article in question had referenced the war only while communicating a football statistic, where the Second World War is routinely employed as a date line.

Vogts was struggling with the subtleties of the English language, understandably so. This inability to grasp what people were saying only increased his paranoia and made him more suspicious. It certainly caused problems in the immediate aftermath of the match in Toftir, with Scotland having snatched what was generally considered to be an undeserved draw thanks to goals from Lambert – courtesy of a helpful deflection off Weir's boot – and Barry Ferguson.

'The press conference after the game had been so brief – and understandably so, he was obviously a bit shell-shocked by the performance and the result,' recalls Kenny MacDonald. But the *News of the World* reporter had managed to pose the question that really had to be asked, though it was misconstrued by Vogts. 'I said to him: "Do you think had we lost the game you would deserve to have kept your job?"' Vogts, it later transpired, treated the question as an overly aggressive one. He felt the press were trying to hound him out of his job. He thought MacDonald was saying he should resign now. In response, all he said to MacDonald was: 'Ask me at the end of the qualifiers.' It was his stock answer, repeated several times. To the question of how was it possible for Scotland to be so comprehensively outplayed, he replied: 'I don't know, you tell me the answer.' It was an unimpressive performance, one that matched his team's earlier that afternoon; as inadequate as it was brief.

The press wanted, needed and, finally, demanded more. Due to the absence of floodlights at a Toftir stadium that only just met the pitch dimensions required by UEFA, the game had had to kick-off on the Saturday afternoon, rather than in the evening. It meant the sports reporters, and sports editors at home in the newspaper offices, had more time to digest what had unfolded. More reaction was required, so those reporters present decided to approach Vogts again. Unfortunately for the manager, the complicated nature of the transport logistics meant this was possible. Press, players and manager were all thrown in together for the short ferry ride between the islands, on the way back to Vagar airport. Before that, though, the Scotland party were permitted some time in which to gather their thoughts away from prying eyes. On the bus, during the first stage of the journey from ground to airport, there was a stunned, uneasy silence. Jack McGinn, the SFA president, sensed the need for a statesmanlike contribution, and rose to his feet at the front of the vehicle.

David Taylor supports his colleague's noble intention to lift spirits:

> He said: 'Listen – do not let your heads go down too far. This is a difficult place. We are glad we came away with something.' They were good comments to make at that time. Because we all felt it was a disastrous result, although at the end of the day it did not end up being too disastrous. We ended up second in the group behind Germany, which had been the aim.

But most had gone down the line of writing Scotland off immediately following the dropping of two points in that first outing. Even Vogts had emphasised the need to take three points from the first game. Whatever happened in the future, the present had still fully to sink in. On the ferry, the second stage of the painfully long journey home, it was possible to cut the atmosphere with a knife. Players stood around in huddles, acutely aware that the reporters standing with them on the same deck had been busily trashing their efforts on the park that afternoon. David Weir recalls the atmosphere on that crossing.

> It was devastating. First of all it was the start of the campaign, and that was us on the back foot right away. We also knew we would get absolutely caned by the press. We were with the press on the way back, on the boat. And, of course, it was the last thing we wanted. There we were depressed about the result, on a boat we did not want to be on and surrounded by guys who we knew were going to hammer us or had already hammered us. And it wasn't as if it was just a two-minute crossing either.

There was plenty of time for the press to approach Vogts, and they did so via Andy Mitchell, the SFA's director of communications. Mitchell was initially reluctant to even ask Vogts. But pressure was applied. When he returned, there was a surprise for MacDonald. Berti would speak, but only if the *News of the World* reporter was not present. 'Apparently he didn't like the question I asked at the press conference,' recalls MacDonald. Vogts's reaction was a surprise; it revealed the thin skin of a man labelled *der terrier* when a player, while it also made observers wonder how he ever coped as manager of a team like Germany, where the pressure was far greater. As Glenn Gibbons argues in *The Scotsman*, the question – whether he would have resigned if the Faroes had held on to their two-goal lead, or, as was possible, had increased it – was, compared to the outright insults hurled at national team managers in places such as Brazil, Spain, Italy or even Germany, 'like asking the time'.

MacDonald, certainly, was taken aback by the manager's precondition ahead of returning to talk again to the press: his exclusion. He was also concerned, for Vogts's own sake.

> I said to Andy: 'Look, I don't blame you at all, but if I was you I would go and say to him this is not the way to handle this.' If he [Vogts] has a problem with me speak to us all first, then he can speak to me privately. But if he goes through with this it will be all over the paper tomorrow: not only has he had a horrendous result in his first competitive game but he has taken a petted lip because the *News of the World* has asked him a question. But Andy said Berti was adamant. I said: 'On his own head be it.' The boys went away to speak to him and naturally they gave me the quotes anyway. I remember going to see Andy Mitchell. I said: 'Look, I am duty bound to report what has happened. And it's his own fault.'

The second press conference of the day took place without MacDonald's presence, while seagulls squawked overhead. It helped keep things surreal. MacDonald, as tends to happen among colleagues eager to help each other out of difficult situations, was furnished with the quotes in any case. As expected, his paper made a further drama out of an afternoon that had been ripe enough for headlines. 'Berti tries to gag our reporter!'

it trilled. The game was over, although the baiting was most certainly not.

'I am surprised he didn't put a couple of them [reporters] over the edge of the boat,' reflects Rab Douglas, who had earlier felt the need to be restrained. The flak had flown during the game as well. What had unfolded was beyond the pale for even fans recognised as being among the most resilient. 'In senior football no one goes out *not* to play well,' reflects Douglas, as he sits in a Dundee hotel eight years on.

> We were being slaughtered by the boys behind the goal. Coming from a working background, that's what really got my goat. No-one went out there not to do well. Some of the boys were really out of order with their criticism of Berti and the players. I know they spend a lot of money to go and watch Scotland, but we got it back. We could quite easily have lost. Just because we are Scotland going to play a smaller nation did not mean we had a divine right to win.

But such circumspection was not shared by many. It was insane to expect it. Whatever the whys and wherefores, Scotland had just been held to a draw by the Faroes. A hostile undercurrent could also be detected upon the team's eventual arrival back in Scotland later that night, as Kenny MacDonald observes.

> I remember when we got back to Glasgow airport, Davie Provan was waiting. He hadn't been at the game but was working for Sky at the time. He was waiting for a sound bite and Berti blanked him. Davie walked along the front of Glasgow airport to try and get him to speak and David Taylor was running along after him, saying 'Leave the man alone, leave the man alone; let him get home.' It ended up as a really squalid scene: the chief executive of the SFA shouting at this reporter not to ask the manager any questions. It was low farce rather than high comedy, I suppose.

Taylor himself recalls being chased by a radio reporter all the way to his car. 'I remember he was hassling me,' he says. 'He was lucky I didn't take a swing at him!'

Later, after a 2–0 win in Iceland had provided some salvation for the beleaguered manager, MacDonald met Vogts to discuss what had happened in the Faroes. MacDonald's wife, Catherine, worked in the communications team at the SFA and facilitated the meeting at the Barbarossa restaurant, not far from Hampden, and MacDonald explains what was said as they broke bread together.

> I tried to explain to him that I was not in the business of getting managers the sack. I had merely asked him a question: Whether you would have expected to have kept your job had you lost in the Faroes? That's not the same as saying you should be sacked. I don't write opinion pieces. My job is to report. Whether or not he took it on board I really don't know. But I do remember he wolfed down his lunch.

Vogts got his appetite back, and, for a while, so did the Scottish supporters. 'One thing about Berti is that he helped bring the crowds back to Hampden,' claims Taylor. 'In a perverse way, while we were struggling a bit, he got the whole thing going again.' Indeed, nearly fifty thousand were at Hampden for Vogts's last home competitive match in charge, against Norway. It was the fourth highest attendance for an international game that day in Europe. In the friendly match prior to the farce in the Faroes, Scotland had hosted Denmark in a friendly at Hampden and attracted the biggest crowd for an international anywhere else in Europe on the same night. Vogts had noted this fact in a message written to those members of the Travel Club preparing to make their way to the Faroe Isles the following month. In it, the manager had employed the tone of someone aware that things were not going exactly to plan. 'Though results have not been good, your patience and understanding at the rebuilding of the team has been much appreciated,' he opines. 'This visit to the Faroe Islands will I hope be a turning point in the team's fortunes and a good victory is the only item on my agenda.'

In fact, Vogts had to wait until the 2–0 win in Reykjavik against Iceland, in Scotland's next competitive match after the Faroes, for some relief. It was a particularly welcome win for the manager, who had had to deal with the issue of Weir's withdrawal from the international scene as well as the fall-out from the Faroes. He employed three centre backs, with Steven Pressley and Lee Wilkie joining Dailly, who had been retained. Indeed, Dailly settled nerves with the opening goal.

It meant Scotland, in a group that also included Lithuania, were back in contention to finish behind Germany, who were all but ensured a place in the finals. Almost a year to the day of the 2–2 draw, Vogts's side managed to gain a smidgeon of self-respect with a 3–1 win over the Faroes in front of an impressive crowd of forty thousand at Hampden, though an equaliser scored by the visitors after thirty-five minutes had prompted distressing flashbacks. Iceland were also overcome in Glasgow, although a 1–0 away defeat to Lithuania in the following outing put the securing of a runners-up spot back into jeopardy.

But, in customary Scottish-style, the stand-out performance of the campaign came on a summer's day against Germany, when Vogts's reputation was very much on the line against a team featuring many of the side beaten in the World Cup final in Yokohama less than a year earlier. Hampden was alight as Scotland secured a draw following the early blow of the loss of a goal to Fredi Bobic's first-half header. Scotland equalised through Kenny Miller with twenty-one minutes left, following a quickly taken free-kick from Colin Cameron. It was a satisfying result for Vogts, whose time in charge of Germany had ended without much fanfare after the 1998 World Cup in France. It also gave Scotland renewed impetus. They secured second place in Group 5 with a 1–0 win over Lithuania at Hampden in the last game. Somehow, despite the horror start, Vogts had achieved what he had set out to do.

Indeed, on the afternoon of 15 November 2003, he perhaps exceeded the hopes and dreams of the Scottish people with a victory as famous as any seen in the country. The Netherlands, Scotland's opponents in the two-leg play-off, came to Hampden boasting a team of all-stars, but faced the kind of Scottish performance that contained the necessary ingredient for success: lung-bursting effort. Dailly shackled Patrick Kluivert, while Lee Wilkie, then just twenty-two, snuffed out Ruud Van Nistelrooy. It was a surreal afternoon all right, adorned by James McFadden's deflected winner.

So the Tartan Army marched onto Amsterdam in good heart, although Dailly – a stand-out at Hampden in a defensive midfield role – had collected a booking, and was suspended for the return. A draw or even another victory in the Dutch capital was all that was needed to see Scotland not only progress, but also, as Graham Spiers articulated in *The Herald* on the Monday before the midweek encounter, 'cap the quickest transformation from so-called incompetent curmudgeon to tactical maestro ever witnessed by Scottish football'.

But it wasn't to be. In the forbidding surroundings of the Amsterdam ArenA the goals cascaded into the Scottish net. Scotland, 4–0 down at half-time, eventually fell by six goals. It was a wearied, chastened retreat from Amsterdam. 'Such scorelines as 6–0 are rarities in international football these days but Scotland on Wednesday secured their own bleak entry in the annals of embarrassment,' wrote Spiers the following day. He concludes that responsibility for the margin of defeat lay with Vogts as much as it did the players. He seemed unable or incapable of reacting tactically to Holland's fluid 3-2-3-2 system, with Scotland picked apart time after time. It was a mess.

'You just wanted it to stop,' recalls David Taylor, who left the SFA in 2007 to become general secretary at UEFA. 'That might have been a harder one to take than the Faroes. We were having our noses rubbed in it. 2–0 you could just about accept, even 3–0. But 6–0 was hard.'

Robert Douglas was an inevitable target for criticism, and – along with Vogts – unfairly carried the brunt of it. He is still bitter about what happened.

> We got a tanking over there. I remember I was to blame for at least one or maybe two goals. But I was the only player absolutely slaughtered in the papers. I hold my hands up. I am too honest for my own good often. I take my criticism. But there were other guys that night who got away with murder – those with friends in the press. I will hold my hands up and say I was not good enough that night. But we were destroyed all over the pitch.
>
> It very quickly went from the sublime to the ridiculous.

Draws, as much as multi-goal losses, defined Berti Vogts's tenure as Scotland manager. His era ended not in defeat, but with another bitterly disappointing draw against another minor football nation, Moldova. Scotland's World Cup qualifying campaign, which Vogts had promised would see him 'with my team in Germany in 2006 on the pitch – not in the stands with a hot dog and Coca-Cola,' was all but over after three matches, the first of which had been a hugely deflating 0–0 draw at home to Slovenia. These results, combined with an alarming 4–0 friendly defeat to Wales and slightly more acceptable thrashings by such traditionally strong countries as France and the Netherlands, brought down the Vogts experiment, in which Scotland turned to a foreigner for the first time after fifteen successive appointments of native Scots.

It hadn't seemed an outlandish notion at the time, although some bridled at the thought that Scotland, the country of such managerial titans as Matt Busby, Jock Stein, Bill Shankly and Alex Ferguson, could not now find anyone they trusted enough to take the reins of the international team from within their own shores. England had, just a year previously, turned from Kevin Keegan to Sven Goran Eriksson and on September 2001 – the day Scotland had dropped two home points against Croatia, in Craig Brown's last qualifying campaign – had humbled Germany 5–1 in Munich.

It is understandable that, given the state of the Scottish game at international level, looking beyond these shores was attractive. Brown's days as manager were coming to an end after what must be considered – certainly with the advantage of hindsight – an undeniably successful spell. But Brown's last match in charge, against Latvia, had been a miserably downbeat affair. The team was on its last legs. No one could have denied that. Not then, not now. Scotland were ripe for change. Iconic skipper Colin Hendry had already departed the scene, sidelined by a six-match suspension for elbowing a San Marino opponent in the throat. Of those who started Brown's last meaningful game, against Belgium in Brussels in September 2001, only five would go on to feature in Vogts's plans.

David Taylor has had time to reflect on the appointment of a non-Scot.

It wasn't a case of we must appoint a foreign coach. I remember the first board discussion about whom we should appoint. I put forward various considerations: 'Do we want this kind of person, or do we

want that kind of person?' We just went through various characterist-
ics to build a profile of the kind of coach we might be interested in.
I remember the point was raised: must it be a Scottish person or
would we accept candidates from outside Scotland?

There was a feeling among the SFA board at the time that we
should seek the best candidate irrespective of nationality. He did not
necessarily have to be a Scotsman. There was no particular desire to
follow England. In Scotland, we normally want to do the opposite!
The last days of Craig – who was a great Scotland manager – kind of
fizzled out very poorly. I think we only had a crowd of about 20,000
for the last match against Latvia when we did not qualify for the
2002 World Cup. Things were at a low ebb and many of the team
were over thirty. It felt like the end of an era. There was a desire for
change. That was the prevalent mood of the time – change.

Taylor recalls an appetite to appoint someone from outwith the Scottish
football establishment. It was hoped someone might come in to 'stir up'
Scottish football. That certainly happened, for better and for worse. It
was accepted that Vogts had to make drastic changes, and for a while
he could rely on the forbearance of the Tartan Army. Brown's side had
served the country well, but had become slow and predictable. Vogts
– a World Cup winner with West Germany when a player – was the
man selected to wield the new broom.

It had always seemed odds-on that Scotland would look to abroad
for Craig Brown's replacement, and few could argue with Vogts's
credentials. But it represented a huge step. The last two appointments
had been from in-house, with Andy Roxburgh and then Brown pro-
moted from within the SFA. But now here was Scotland throwing
their arms open to a man whose knowledge of Scottish football did
not extend far beyond the four matches he played against Scotland for
West Germany, in an international career that spanned an impressive
ninety-six caps. Vogts was also in charge of Germany when they took
on Scotland in a friendly at Ibrox Park, in a game made memorable by
an overhead kick from Duncan Ferguson, which almost saw Scotland
take the lead. Instead, they fell to a 1–0 defeat following a mistake by
Craig Levein, one of Berti's successors as Scotland manager.

Vogts might also have caught a fleeting glimpse of Scotland at Euro 96. But while the Scots did their usual and clocked off at the end of the group stage, Germany had gone on to triumph in the final against Czech Republic, having beaten England on penalties in the semi-final once again. It's hard enough to credit Scotland going from this failure to qualify for the knockout stage of a major finals by a single goal, to their relief just six years later at salvaging a scrappy draw in the Faroes. But what about Vogts? His fall was even more marked, from Wembley glory with his own nation to a fiasco on a cliff-top in the north Atlantic, with a group of men he hadn't heard of twelve months previously.

As Taylor says when looking back at Vogts's appointment: 'What you have to remember about Berti is that he had won the tournament which we were just about to enter – which was the European Champion-ships.' Although in charge of Kuwait when Scotland came calling, the German was still permitted to regard himself as among the elite of European coaches. Even Sir Alex Ferguson had appeared to sanction his appointment. The Manchester United manager was among those notable figures contacted by the SFA to provide input. 'Sir Alex did not specifically endorse Berti,' points out Taylor. 'But he offered advice and his knowledge. There was nothing there to indicate that he thought there was a problem.'

*

Germany played 102 games with Vogts as coach and lost only 12. Yet he was still hounded out of office and labelled 'the symbol of the downfall of the national team' by a Frankfurt newspaper. But as far as Scottish footballers were concerned, Vogts's name still carried a reson-ance. He made a good impression, pleasantly surprising them with some practices brought from abroad.

In a bid to improve team spirit he gathered the players together the night before the game, when once they might have retired to their rooms, or hung around in smaller groups, or formed cliques. He encour-aged, indeed welcomed, a moderate amount of alcohol. It helped the players relax, he reasoned, and fostered team spirit. The players were not going to complain, even if it felt strange – particularly given the troubled relationship of the Scottish international player with alcohol – to be sitting on the eve of a game with a beer in their hand. Davie Weir was clearly taken aback by the new way of doing things.

> It was not a case if you wanted a beer or not. Everybody had to come down. And it wasn't seven at night. It was ten or eleven at night. Everyone had to come down. You didn't obviously have to have an alcoholic drink, but you had to participate, you had to be there. So if you wanted an early night you could not go to bed.

Douglas, who came to professional football relatively late and brought a refreshing sense of perspective with him, was all in favour, as he now confirms.

> I think it is meant to help you relax. At some clubs you get sleeping tablets – so I didn't have a problem with this. I am a beer man. I had a beer. It was not forced upon you, some of the boys had a glass of wine, others a beer. Others did not drink. Each to his own. In the mornings we would go for a walk and a stretch. That was maybe a bit strange. We might be in a car park in Loch Lomond, having a stretch in your Scotland tracksuit.

Vogts looked after the players. 'He would do anything for the players – anything,' reflects Douglas. 'He knew if the players were not happy there would be problems. I think he thought if he got the players on side then that would be half the battle.'

Perhaps the incident with Weir emphasised he had to work harder at building a relationship with them. He was particularly good with the younger ones, with James McFadden flourishing in his charge. Lee Wilkie was another who came into the fold, perhaps more hurriedly than would have been the case had it not been for Weir's retirement. The then Dundee centre-half came in for the next game against Iceland, when Scotland improved beyond measure to win 2–0. He then scored the vital winner at Hampden Park in the return fixture.

'If anyone asks me about my best moment in football, it is that goal,' he says. 'And Berti gave me that.' The memory is made more potent given the defender's history of knee problems. When we speak, in December 2009, Wilkie, then skipper of Dundee United, is fighting another battle to save his career. Sadly, he had to admit defeat. The defender announced his retirement from the game the following April.

Vogts certainly had his supporters amongst the players. Even Weir reflects on the German's manifest good nature. 'You could not dislike him,' he says. 'He was gregarious, and very pro the players. He wanted the best for the players: the best flights, the best hotels. That was what he was used to with Germany. His foot was very much in the players' camp.'

We are sitting in deli-cafe in the west end of Glasgow, and I ask Weir, whose career has extended into a glorious Indian summer with Rangers, what would happen if he saw Vogts walking down the street towards him? 'I would shake his hand,' he says. 'I don't have a problem with anyone I have met in a football sense though obviously you get on better with some rather than others. But I would shake his hand and have a smile. I think he would too.'

But Vogts would also have to reflect on his own failures, and acknowledge the part he played in his own downfall. He was forever promising wins from perilous assignments, while he made unwise decisions, both away from the pitch and on it. There was the decision to write a column for one tabloid newspaper. The contributions were hardly statesmanlike and simply served to alienate him from other newspapers at a time when he should have been seeking broad support. The columns soon stopped, but the pastiches did not, with *Scotsman* chief sports writer Stuart Bathgate creating a 'Berti McVogts' alter-ego that had the Scotland coach denying responsibility for a team in decline 'since 1314'.

While it was not the manager's fault that Scotland had stopped producing world-class footballers, there was a wild, somewhat-cobbled-together element to his squad selections. Between March 2002 and February 2004 he awarded twenty-nine debuts to Scotland players in twenty-three matches. His predecessor, Craig Brown, granted fifty-one first caps, but over a period of eight years and seventy-one matches. Jock Stein took seven years to decorate thirty-five players, and among them were the likes of Paul McStay, Steve Nicol and Maurice Malpas rather than Graeme Murty, Brian Kerr and Peter Canero.

As the stock of Scottish footballers fell, Vogts was forced to drift around a twilight zone consisting of the Walsalls, Readings and Prestons of the world, handing out caps like confetti. In truth, he was not much nearer to finding a settled team at the end than when he started. It was as frustrating for him as the fans, but he often did not help himself, as David Taylor reflects.

> It did not work out for Berti – that is the bottom line. In his favour, he introduced a lot of young players, which we had to do at the time – the likes of [Darren] Fletcher, McFadden and even Andy Webster. He made Darren Fletcher captain when he was just twenty years of age. I always thought he was quite an adventurous coach in his systems, which was odd, because he was a defender, and a rather dour one at that. I felt he was almost over-estimating Scotland's style and capabilities.
>
> But in a competitive sense he did what he was expected to do. He got us to the playoff. We were one game from qualifying. We have not been there since. There have been another three tournaments, and we have never even got to the playoffs. He did what he had to do. I think he is unfairly judged by the Scottish media, because his competitive record was not too bad.
>
> Friendlies were a disaster. But his competitive record shows that he only lost four of thirteen games. He won more than he lost.

Taylor admits that, with hindsight, all parties might have been better served by a parting of ways following the bloodless 4–0 friendly defeat in Wales in February 2004. It was a new low, but, alert to the issue of compensation and also the pledge to hand Vogts the chance to turn things round over two qualifying campaigns, Scotland retained his services, despite the clamour for his removal. 'It [the Wales defeat] really was the beginning of the end, I suppose,' says Taylor. 'If we had our time again then maybe we should have changed the manager then.'

Taylor also concedes that the 'biggest issue' with Vogts was communication, with both his players and the media 'It wasn't at the level that was necessary,' he admits now. 'That was a weakness, I suppose, with the appointment. It was something we underestimated at the time, to be honest.' One possible reason for this is that Vogts's grasp of English appeared fairly robust when compared to the Italian Nevio Scala, a fellow candidate for the post, as Taylor explains.

> He [Scala] was one where we did realise there was going to be a language problem. His English was more limited than Berti's. You see some of these other managers, such as Fabio Capello with England, who did not have English but seemed to manage. But the communication thing was perhaps underestimated by us. It was a problem, looking back.

The SFA attempted to improve Vogts's image by employing a public-relations agency, but this, too, was doomed to failure. Alex Barr, a leading light in the scene in Scotland, was hired and dealt personally with the issue of Vogts's media portrayal. David Taylor sums up an era that casts a shadow over his own period in office at the SFA.

> We went to Spain for a friendly, which was called off half way through because of heavy rain. What I remember about it is that the night before we tried to organise a special reception for all the press who had come over. But it did not make any difference. The press were happy to come along and drink the wine and then brand it as the latest public-relations stunt. There was no way back really.
>
> It was a period of change – it was not a period of success. I suppose it was an experiment which failed in its own way. There are no hard feelings towards Berti. He is still very welcome. He did his best. But it was the wrong time for him really, and his ideas.

Kenny MacDonald also attests to Vogts's good nature. There was an added complication of a marriage break-up to cope with as the German sought to make a success of what might be considered an impossible job in a foreign land. It was certainly not a post for someone struggling with issues that stretched beyond the already significant problem of Scottish football's decline.

> In fairness to Berti, he rode out the storm. When he left Scotland after the Moldova match I think there was a genuine feeling that we would never see him again. But there were sightings of him, because his son was still at university in Glasgow. People would see him shopping in

supermarkets in the city, and this was a year later. He was still coming back and forward. He had no shame in being there. And nor should he have. He had been brought in to do a job.

In the end, however, it just didn't work out for Vogts – or Scotland.

The Contributors

The Contributors

John Cairney has been an artist for more than fifty years. He has worked as an actor, recitalist, lecturer and theatre director. He is also a published author and an exhibited painter. Trained at the Royal Scottish Academy of Music and Drama, he was a notable Hamlet at the Citizens' Theatre, a popular Cyrano de Bergerac at Newcastle and Macbeth at the Edinburgh Festival. He was also the star of *This Man Craig* on television and has appeared in many films including *Jason and the Argonauts* and *Cleopatra*.

He is much in demand as a lecturer, writer and consultant on Robert Louis Stevenson, Charles Rennie Mackintosh and Robert Burns. Dr Cairney has written books on each of these famous Scots, as well as other books on theatre and his native Glasgow. In addition he has penned two books on football: *The Scottish Football Hall of Fame* and *Heroes Are Forever: the Life and Times of Jimmy McGrory*. He also contributed a chapter on John Thomson for *Ten Days that Shook Celtic*.

Recently John Cairney was made a Freeman Citizen of Glasgow.

Hugh MacDonald is one of Scotland's leading journalists. He has spent his entire working life in newspapers and among many other roles he has been a chief sub-editor and a literary editor. Currently, he is the chief sports writer for *The Herald*. Born in Glasgow and raised in Possil and Busby he has been a football obsessive since early childhood. His sporting interests are extensive, however, and he has written a book on the Williams sisters, Serena and Venus, charting their rise in the world of tennis. Hugh MacDonald's sports beat encompasses Scottish, European and world football and he also covers the golf and tennis majors. His professional ambitions include covering Scotland, once again, at World Cup or European finals and witnessing Andy Murray winning a major.

Frank Gilfeather is an experienced journalist, broadcaster, football historian, playwright and public-relation consultant. Born in Dundee he moved to Aberdeen in April 1969 as a news reporter on the *Press and Journal* and the *Evening Express*. He later became chief sportswriter and deputy sportswriter on the *Evening Express*. He has worked for many newspapers and broadcasting organisations including *The Herald*, *Sunday Herald*, *The Times*, ITN News, Sky Sports, Grampian Television, the BBC and Northsound Radio. In addition to his work as a journalist Gilfeather has penned two books: *Confessions of a Highland Hero* (with Steve Paterson) and *Ross County: from Highland League to Hampden*. He set up Frank Gilfeather Associates, a public-relations company, in 1989. In addition to his media work Frank is something of a sportsman himself; he is a former Scottish amateur boxing champion and internationalist.

Matt Vallance has been a sportswriter for more than forty years, covering more than fifty different sports, from archery to yachting. A former sports editor of the *Paisley Daily Express*, now semi-retired from journalism, he continues to cover football and rugby matches on a freelance basis and writes obituaries of sportsmen and women for both *The Herald* and *The Scotsman*. He lives in Ayrshire.

Terence Murray is a book editor and football writer. He wrote a long essay on the tragic life of Sam English for the book *Rangers, Triumphs, Troubles, Traditions* and more recently he assisted Rangers legend Tom Forsyth with his autobiography. An Ayr United supporter for more years than he cares to remember, Murray pines for a Somerset Park team that could emulate the exploits of such greats as Rikki Fleming, Dick Malone, John 'Spud' Murphy and Alex 'Dixie' Ingram. He lives in Ayrshire.

Ronnie Esplin is a sports reporter, football writer and author. His last book was *Totally Frank*, the story of former Celtic and St Mirren striker Frank McGarvey and prior to that he wrote *Down the Copland Road*, and co-authored *Barcelona Here We Come* and *The Advocaat Years* with Alex Anderson. He also edited *Ten Days That Shook Rangers* and co-edited *It's Rangers for Me?* with Graham Walker.

Graham McColl is a historian of some renown with more than ten football books to his name, many of them published by major houses such as Headline, Carlton, Virgin Books and Transworld. His titles include works on Scotland, England, Manchester United and Celtic. He is also an experienced journalist and has contributed to *The Times* since 2003. He lives in Glasgow with his wife, Jackie, and their young son, Joseph.

Rob Robertson, a former Scotland Campaigning Journalist of the Year, is a sports writer with the *Scottish Daily Mail*. He began his daily newspaper career with the *Aberdeen Evening Express* and has held staff positions at many other top Scottish newspapers. He collaborated with former Aberdeen captain Willie Miller on his column for *The Herald* newspaper for five years and went on to work with him on his best-selling biography, *The Don*.

Robertson has written books charting the rise of tennis star Andy Murray and another revealing the inside story of how Vladimir Romanov took control of Hearts.

In a varied career he has been on assignments in Bosnia during the Balkans crisis, Northern Ireland during the Troubles, and Russia, as Boris Yelstin came to power. In the sporting world he has covered the rugby World Cup, eleven Wimbledon finals and major football matches throughout Europe.

He lives with his partner Claire in Edinburgh and has three children, Kirsten, Clare and Bruce.

Stephen McGowan has been a sportswriter with the *Scottish Daily Mail* for ten years after spells working in the Middle East, Far East and at the *Scottish Daily Express*. He has had one book published, *Flawed Genius, Scottish Football's Self-Destructive Mavericks*. A father of twin girls he lives in Greenock.

Alan Pattullo was born in Dundee and joined *The Scotsman* as a sportswriter in 1998. He has worked at two World Cup finals as well at Wimbledon and Open golf championships. He regularly reports on Scotland matches at Hampden and elsewhere but is far from a lucky emblem: in his first seven away trips with Scotland he witnessed the team concede twenty-goals and score . . . none! These awful experiences included a 6–0 thrashing in the Netherlands, the pain of which was exacerbated by the breaking news that Dundee FC, the team he has supported all his life, were on the verge of administration. Pattullo lives in Edinburgh and is currently writing a book about the Scottish footballer, Duncan Ferguson.